THE
CONSERVATIVE
MOVEMENT

Revised Edition

SOCIAL MOVEMENTS PAST AND PRESENT

Irwin T. Sanders, Editor

THE
CONSERVATIVE
MOVEMENT

Revised Edition

Paul Gottfried

Twayne Publishers • New York
Maxwell Macmillan Canada • Toronto
Maxwell Macmillan International • New York Oxford Singapore Sydney

The Conservative Movement: Revised Edition
Paul Gottfried

Copyright © 1993 by Twayne Publishers

Twayne Publishers
Macmillan Publishing Company
866 Third Avenue
New York, New York 10022

Maxwell Macmillan Canada, Inc.
1200 Eglinton Avenue East
Suite 200
Don Mills, Ontario M3C 3N1

Library of Congress Cataloging-in-Publication Data

Gottfried, Paul.
    The conservative movement / Paul Gottfried. — Rev. ed.
      p.   cm.
    Includes bibliographical references and index.
    ISBN 0-8057-9749-1 (cloth : alk. paper). — ISBN 0-8057-3850-9 (pbk. : alk.
paper)
    1. Conservatism—United States.   2. United States—Politics and government—
1945–1989.   3. United States—Politics and government—1989–   I. Title.
JA84.U5G67   1993
320.5′2′0973—dc20   92-26659
                                                       CIP

10 9 8 7 6 5 4 3 2 1 (hc)
10 9 8 7 6 5 4 3 2 1 (pb)

Printed and bound in the United States of America.

Contents

Preface to the Second Edition

This second edition of *The Conservative Movement* seemed to me necessary for at least two compelling reasons. The first is the recognition of historical events: The postwar conservative movement analyzed in the first edition had largely disappeared by 1990. The earlier edition already dwells on the weakening of this movement, whose leaders tried to combine notions of limited constitutional government and a rearguard action against the welfare state with a militantly anticommunist foreign policy. That postwar conservatism, taking definitive form in the 1950s, was derailed, according to the first edition, by cold war liberals, federal bureaucrats, and Washington foundation builders who came to dominate a politically disheartened and morally confused American Right. This group is explicitly identified with the neoconservative and the New Right, who are depicted as turning conservatives into welfare state ideologues.

This view of a derailed postwar Right may, in retrospect, have been exaggerated. To some extent Thomas Fleming and I were still in agreement with the interpretation put forth by the New Right activist Paul Weyrich, who has recently argued that the old faith "had been rejected by a majority of the conservative movement." Like most conservative leaders, Weyrich denounced the first edition and accused me personally of inventing "a conspiracy theory" to explain the transformation of the Right. The particle of truth in Weyrich's assertion was our failure to look deeply enough into a movement that was never a model of principled opposition to an intrusive and leveling welfare state. The movement's driving force, it now appears, was an impassioned anticommunism, which could be and was paired with changing domestic agendas. Anti-Soviet New Deal Democrats, in fact, became the preferred allies of the American Right in what came to be viewed as "the protracted struggle." Moreover, international trade unionism and the free market were reduced to interchangeable antiphonies, to be played in unison with the invariable anticommunist chorus. In the first edition I thought we had documented the evolution of the archetypal postwar conservative William F. Buckley, Jr., from Old Right champion into a harmless representative of respectable opposition. In fact, Buckley has always been a flexible anticommunist, taking as allies monarchists, libertarians, or trade unionists as it suited his overriding concern, and he continues to move back and forth between expressions of admiration for Senator Joseph McCarthy and democratic socialist Sidney Hook. Since both actively opposed the same communist enemy, it is possible for Buckley to venerate them within a single cult.

Another continuing trait among prominent postwar conservatives, since the founding of *National Review,* has been the desperate quest for esteem from the opposition. This sense of obvious insecurity has expressed itself least ominously in the way that some conservatives have chased after celebrities on the other side, exemplified by Buckley's publicized friendships with Liberal Party activist Allard Lowenstein, economist John Kenneth Galbraith, and *New York Times* editor A. M. Rosenthal. But the same worry about respectability has resulted in less-tolerant behavior as well. Consider the periodic excommunication of political and intellectual dissenters who are perceived as out of step with the age. Most of these purge victims have not been anti-Semitic bigots but consistent critics of the New Deal and of a broadly interventionist foreign policy, some of them Jewish. Though the *National Review*'s circle should express useful disagreement with those representing prewar conservatism, the humiliations inflicted on "right-wing" dissenters over the years—to the thunderous applause of the official opposition—inevitably raise embarrassing questions about who is really in charge of the Conservative house. The standard argument put forward by the neoconservatives, that they place "democratic values" above the right to morally offensive speech, is only a variation on the argument of William F. Buckley's first and perhaps most famous book, *God and Man at Yale.* There Buckley insisted that universities should not remain aloof from the battle "between democracy and totalitarianism." Alumni and other university benefactors were urged to oversee the teaching of academic disciplines, making sure that salutary values were being taught, much as the victorious Allies were then restructuring the consciousness of the defeated Axis nations.

The second reason for revising the book stems from my growing awareness that postwar conservatism marked an end as well as the beginning of a movement. In the first edition we ignored, perhaps excessively, a persistent theme in George Nash's voluminous study of postwar conservatism: the ties between conservative trends of the fifties and the nascent neoconservatism of the seventies. In a telling if partisan review of our book, Nash criticized our overemphasis on the disjunctions in recent American conservatism. His point is well taken. Even so, there is a second subtext in Nash's work that we accepted all too uncritically: that American conservatism only became something deserving of serious national attention in the postwar period. Before that, or so one may come away from Nash believing, there existed only bridges to the postwar movement, many of them created by Central European émigrés, in an environment generally without conservative intellectuality.

There can be no doubt that European émigrés enriched American conservative thought. Even so, the preoccupation with their contribution has tended to obscure the actual history of conservative opposition and has permitted the neglect of rich, indigenous American conservative traditions—Southern Agrarian, Taft Republican, and Brahmin individualist—that did not fit into the procrustean synthesis created in the fifties. There was no dearth of conservative thinking before that time, and the postwar movement long remained parasitic on older American conservative traditions. Ironically, despite the iron discipline that Buckley and his circle tried to impose on their movement, the small band that later rose against the neoconservative ascendancy of the eighties appealed to allegedly postwar conservative ideals. The Old Right, which has produced the paleoconservative last stand against "social democratic interlopers," has misunderstood its own roots. Those roots should not be sought in a postwar conservative movement characterized by anticommunist activism, the search for liberal approval, and intermittent purges conducted by communist defectors and their disciples. The source of a defiant conservatism, one undaunted by any shifting majority, can only be found by examining older traditions and movements that did not always sail under a conservative flag. Neither anticommunist émigrés nor postwar New York intellectuals nor any combination thereof produced the seedbed of this older American conservatism.

Some explanation may be needed as to why the concluding chapter devotes at least as much attention to paleo- as to neoconservatives. Though both have struggled against each other, the neoconservatives, it may be argued, are by far the more powerful faction, having already swallowed up most of the New York–Washington conservative establishment. The paleoconservatives, nonetheless, have kept up their end of the struggle, despite the lack of media access and despite vilification in both the liberal and neoconservative press. Paleoconservatives have remained surprisingly resilient, to the consternation of their enemies. While their syndicated *Washington Post* critic Charles Krauthammer finds them to be "narrow, xenophobic, and ultranationalist," he also fears the possibility that their self-declared spokesman Patrick J. Buchanan may "liberate it [the Republican Party] from neoconservative deviationism." The overriding reason, it seems to me, that paleoconservatives have survived the ignominy and obscurity imposed by journalists is their studied irreverence, not their rootedness, as Krauthammer would have his readers believe, in some unenlightened past. Unlike the neoconservative Suzanne Garment, who in the *Wall Street Journal,* on 19 December 1986, described her friends as "people who have arrived," paleoconservatives hack away at the political and journalistic establishment as ostracized intellectual outsiders. As critics of the present age without any liberal flank to protect, they apply the kind of relentlessly harsh analysis to modern pluralistic democracy that only some disaligned Leftists, perhaps most successfully Christopher Lasch, have been able to match. It is precisely this willingness to criticize what Garment calls "the established order" in New York and Washington that is both the paleoconservatives' major attraction and key liability.

An expression of thanks is due for this second edition to Thomas Fleming, who was my coauthor in the first. Dr. Fleming worked diligently in the initial preparation of this edition but later withdrew from the project as an act of intellectual integrity; as an engaged participant in many of the events herein discussed, he felt he could not describe them with the critical detachment necessary for a scholarly work. Though I too have participated in what John Judis calls accurately "conservative wars," my own involvement has been less direct than that of my longtime collaborator. We therefore decided that I would finish the work on my own.

Among others who made contributions to this work are Donna Berry and Jean M. Avery, who typed and retyped hastily composed revisions; Professors Irwin Sanders, Claes G. Ryn, and W. Wesley McDonald; James B. Taylor; Carol Chin and Jacob Conrad of Twayne Publishers, who offered useful editorial suggestions; and my daughter Beth Anne Gottfried, who assisted in the arduous preparation of footnotes. Finally, I acknowledge the contributions of Drs. Gerhard Spiegler and Frederick Ritsch, president and provost of Elizabethtown College, who listened indulgently to the principal arguments of this second edition. Even more indulgently, they awarded me a stipend necessary to complete the text.

Paul Gottfried
1991

Preface to the First Edition

This book treats the American Right primarily as a political movement—or, more properly speaking, as a series of movements—since World War II. The preparation of this study required the making of far-reaching structural decisions. In order to focus on postwar conservative movements, we limited discussion of prewar American conservatism to a few scattered pages. Even less attention is given to the European and classical antecedents of modern conservatism. These thematic decisions, though necessary, were, for us, painful because of our scholarly interest in classical civilization and in European thought. Many of the ideas in this book came out of conversations we held in the course of translating Greek philosophy. The shades of Plato and Aristotle were present to inspire us, even where they are not acknowledged in the text.

Yet one conclusion that may be drawn from this book is the increasing irrelevance of prewar, especially non-American, traditionalist thinking for the postwar Right. A distinctive feature of the contemporary American Right is its emphasis on progress: moving beyond the past toward a future of unlimited material opportunity and social improvement.

One prominent conservative congressman, Newt Gingrich, added a revealing subtitle to his book *Window of Opportunity,* namely, "A Blueprint for the Future." He even went so far as to invite a leading science-fiction writer to compose a preface. While conservatives may well take a justifiable pride in their willingness to face the future, some of them, at least, may have less justification for describing themselves as conservative. Whereas the older traditional Right, particularly in Europe, looked backward for its ideals and values, the politics of nostalgia has been in decline on the American Right for at least the last two decades. The Moral Majority may deplore the breakdown of the family, but its leader, the Reverend Jerry Falwell, also praises the advances in civil rights and sexual equality that have taken place during the last generation. Moral Majoritarians are careful to invoke the spirit of social progress and to confine their attacks to "extremists" who carry change too far. Granted, a more thoroughgoing antimodernism can still be found on the American Right—for example, among disciples of Russell Kirk and among those of the Southern Agrarians—but its impact on American conservative politics at this time continues to be negligible.

In November 1985 the editors of *Commentary* magazine invited more than thirty recognizably conservative, neoconservative, and center-left intellectuals to respond to questions about American developments since 1945. The majority of the respondents lamented the continued power and oppressive policies of the Soviet Union, but they maintained that Americans had made social as well as economic progress since World War II. Most of the writers depicted the America of 1945 as a country tainted with racial and religious bigotry. Among the achievements since then, as one contributor put it, "[t]he Southern part of the U.S. has seen and shaken off its medieval torpor and, if you happen to have been black, cruelty."[1] Peter L. Berger, a leading sociologist of religion and a frequent contributor to conservative journals, was perhaps the most emphatic in celebrating the American success story since 1945. Berger extolled the "gigantic political efforts to ensure that no group within it [America] is excluded from the cornucopia of industrial capitalism" and marveled at how "racial discrimination was abolished in the span of a few years."[2] Looking toward a future of further improvements, he proposed "constructing a specifically American version of the welfare state" without the kind of officialdom that has accompanied similar projects in Europe. Less optimistic voices were raised in the symposium; a few contributors, most notably Robert Nisbet, were even vitriolic in decrying what they saw as social decay in America. There were also critical remarks about crime in the streets and eroded educational standards mixed in with the hymn to contemporary America. But something notably absent from most of the responses was that skepticism about progress that in earlier generations characterized the thought of intellectuals identified as conservatives.

This raises the question of an editorial decision that was willy-nilly thrust on us, deciding who is—or who is not—a conservative. There are sound philosophical criteria that might be used to exclude obvious non-conservatives. No one, except in an academic debate or as a member of the extreme Left, would call Gloria Steinem and George McGovern conservatives. Both favor extensive economic redistribution and speak more positively of socialist than capitalist or quasi-capitalist economies. But even more critical than their policy prescriptions is their theoretical point of departure. They favor a state-controlled economy, because they believe it can implement more easily than the free market the overriding good of a class- and gender-free society. True conservatives do not object to social and sexual distinctions, certainly not on principle. One is justified in making this assertion even though there are different types of conservatives, ranging from religious traditionalists to almost thoroughgoing skeptics.

Whatever the differences that characterize their various schools of thought, conservatives, as much as Leftists, are united by a distinctive approach to reality—particularly nature. For the Left, the concept "nature" suggests infinite plasticity; for the Right, by contrast, it is something fixed, and even normative. One sees nature as a material condition to be adapted to the "rational" goals of social planners; the other views it as a source of unchanging truth in a world otherwise in flux. This sense of human limitation is an important link between Old Right "reactionaries" and those neoconservatives who have effectively documented the "unintended consequences" of many social programs. In the end, it may also be a set of attitudes, not rigorously developed views, that define conservatives; adherence to these attitudes was once deemed essential to conservative self-identification.

One such attitude is a view of history as "the funded wisdom of the past," in the phrase of the postwar conservative Will Herberg. Conservatives view history not as a burdensome legacy but as a cumulative and morally binding set of guidelines for life in the present. Robert Nisbet, the conservative social theorist, makes this point with eloquent clarity: "Whereas the progressive rationalists see the present as the beginning of the future, the true way—the conservative way—is to see it as the latest point reached by the past in a continuous, seamless growth." Furthermore, "From the conservative point of view social reality was best understood through a historical approach. We cannot know where we are, much less where we are going, until we know where we have been."[3] For the authentic conservative, history must remain a constant point of orientation for the individual as well as the store of received assumptions needed to maintain a decent social existence.

Another conservative attitude is Aristotelian. In the *Politics,* Aristotle discusses the need for differentiated social roles and responsibilities. The philosopher stresses the differing ways in which the head of the household deals with his wife, children, and servants. The master and each member of the household must acquire his (or her) own form of excellence in order to advance the good of the whole, upon which the individual good remains dependent. Aristotle asserts that contrary to Socrates "there are not simply courage and justice, but two different types: the courage of commanders and the courage of subordinates, and the same applies to other things."[4] Aristotle goes on to chide those who deceive themselves by interpreting "excellence in general as a sound state of mind or a manner of acting well." Far better, it seems to him, "to enumerate forms of excellence as a means of defining it."

Our choice of authorities is certainly not arbitrary. Aristotle, who classified governments and social groupings as well as flora, fauna, and the rules of logical discourse, exemplified conservative attitudes. He considered monarchy, aristocracy, and limited democracies all to be forms of government that satisfied man's rational, material, and social needs, and he saw the weaknesses and strengths of each without being a political reductionist. He also emphasized the need for governments to be suitable to the specific historic conditions of peoples. Aristotle recognized that a well-ordered society protected an ascending order of good through the institutionalization of rank. One who commanded was expected to show greater excellence of mind than one who served. And though not all social and familial hierarchies corresponded to the differential capacities of their individual members, ascribed ranks were not purely capricious. There were differences between men and women, parents and children, and even masters and servants that make one group more suitable for rule than another.[5] Moreover, the operation of custom (to which Aristotle assigned greater social and moral significance than law) ensured the acceptance and exercise of responsibility by members of the political community as well as by those of the household. Not only Aristotle, but also Plato, Cicero, Montesquieu, Edmund Burke, and Alexis de Tocqueville exalted custom as the protector of social morality. All of them suggested what finally became a conservative truism: We learn to be good not so much through reasoning as through the learning of ancestral ways.

Related to the conservatives' sense of order is a high regard for civility. Edmund Burke (and his American disciples) lamented the death of chivalry, but in the 1960s the progressive incivility on college campuses forced many respectable liberals to acknowledge their conservative inclinations. In a time of crisis, people are forced to choose a position on one side or the other of the barricades. Those who became neoconservatives opted for civility.

Another conservative characteristic—even among statist counter-revolutionaries—is a high regard for personal autonomy, or, in a word, liberty. King Charles I of England went to his execution proclaiming himself the defender of liberty and "the martyr of the people." If there is a common thread that runs through the pages of *National Review* (Old Right), *Conservative Digest* (New Right), *Public Interest* (neoconservative), *Reason* (libertarian), and *New American* (John Birch Society), it is the idea of defending personal liberty against the growing power of an increasingly socialist state. Conservatives quarrel over which freedoms take precedence over others, but none would endorse the leftist exaltation of the state as the source of public virtue.

We are not seeking to justify conservative thinking against its critics. It may be true that conservatives have sometimes disregarded the costs of maintaining a traditional society; they may well be guilty of turning custom or liberty into idols to which greater goods have been sacrificed. Such recriminations are beside the point if the stated goal is to provide a workable description of an ideal conservative. The theoretical conservative welcomes human and social diversity. According to one French critic of the Left, he also rejects "abstract, universal egalitarianism" as incompatible with what he knows—or believes—about human nature.[6] This conservative distaste for abstract universalisms came out very clearly in the response that a founder of *National Review*, James Burnham, made in 1972 to Peter Berger's call for a "conservative humanism": "Conservatism can be considered humanist only if humanism is interpreted to mean a concern with the interests and well-being not of abstract Man or Mankind, but of existential Man, historical Man, or of actual men as they actually exist in space and time."[7]

Burnham was not inventing his own political doctrines but paraphrasing Edmund Burke, a recognized father of European conservatism who had defended the "liberties of an Englishman" against the French Revolution's Rights of Man. Like Burke and Burnham, theoretical conservatives believe in historic, not human, rights and view men in the context of established communities. Man's "natural" condition is not to be *apolis*, without communal identity; Aristotle taught that only gods or beasts could exist in such anarchy. This Aristotelian view of man's social and historic nature pervades the works of recognized European conservatives. It can also be discovered in the self-declared European liberal Friedrich Hayek, and in American conservative writings well into the 1960s. Significantly, what have been described as conservative attitudes may no longer be relevant to what are now the dominant tendencies in American conservatism.

This raises the methodological question: Should we abandon the theoretical definition in order to treat as conservatives those who are conventionally identified as such? Up to a point, we must work within a relative frame of reference. In a relative sense, for example, S. M. Lipset, Daniel Bell, and Sidney Hook, all strongly anticommunist and moderate social democrats, are politically more conservative than George McGovern and Gloria Steinem; the latter advocate radical social reforms and avoid at all costs making anticommunist remarks. This judgment can be made without assuming any kinship between Sidney Hook and Edmund Burke or between Daniel Bell and James Burnham, although such connections are not always hard to locate. Moreover, some of our subjects may be considered conservative in the purely descriptive sense of defending the political-economic status quo. Inasmuch as they criticize attempts to carry income redistribution or social engineering beyond points already reached, they become the party of resistance to further change. Presentism, as viewed by reformers, has conservative effects, even if it happens to support a society radically altered by earlier change.

It may be justified to exclude from our discussion elements of the lunatic Right, more specifically the American Nazi party, the Ku Klux Klan, the Liberty Lobby, and the most recent practitioners of white racist violence (mostly from the mountain states), the Posse Comitatus. The combined impact of these groups on postwar conservative politics and thinking has been at most negligible. Main-line conservative publications, starting with *National Review,* have spared no effort in condemning the politics of violence and racial hostility.

It may also be redundant to devote more than a few words to the John Birch Society and to Robert Welch, its founder. Although Birchers have not generally preached violence or racism (one of their early leaders was George Schuyler, a black journalist), the conspiratorial view of the spread of communism, which led some Birchers, including Welch, into accusing Dwight Eisenhower of being a conscious Communist agent, caused them to become marginalized within the postwar conservative movement. By the late sixties, William F. Buckley, Jr., Russell Kirk, and other conservative celebrities were openly contemptuous of both Welch and his followers. By the mid-seventies, John Birch membership rolls numbered no more than in the low thousands. The claim made by Welch at that time of having 80,000 members whose names he would not divulge met with understandable skepticism. It was perhaps Kirk who best expressed the mainstream conservative attitude of amused scorn for the John Birch Society when he responded to Welch's charge against the president: "Eisenhower isn't a Communist—he's a golfer!"[8]

We have chosen, in practice, to employ a relative and structural definition of conservatism, ascribing that designation to those who answer it and who are associated with it by others. But this choice may also lead to a misunderstanding, namely, taking a policy that is objectionable to the political Left for an expression of conservative belief. A specific illustration may help underline this problem. The American Right since the 1950s has steadily opposed Soviet expansion and the Soviet regime generally. This anti-Soviet stand is apparent whether one looks at the *National Review* of the late fifties or *Commentary* and the *New Republic* during the 1980s. Yet, as one proceeds from the anti-Soviet polemics of one generation on to those of another, a thematic change becomes obvious. The older conservative writings express hostility toward communism as the enemy of the Western religious heritage, of historic nationalities, and of metaphysical as well as political freedoms. The recent anticommunist writings rest on the stated or implicit assumption that American democracy with its mixed economy is the supreme human good. Articles in *Commentary* and other neoconservative publications, like Michael Ledeen's "How to Support the Democratic Revolution" (March 1985), call for redoubled American efforts on behalf of exporting our democratic way of life. Part of the change, we are told, is dictated by expediency. It is, at the very least, rhetorically necessary for conservatives to distance themselves from anticommunist military dictators. Apart from this political pragmatism, we are led to believe that spreading democratic values is at the heart of our national heritage. The National Endowment for Democracy, which has been set up and funded by the Reagan administration, promotes global democracy. The model that the advocates of the democratic revolution wish to advertise or, in some cases, impose is as far removed from a traditionalist worldview as from Marxist-Leninism: It is secularist, politically and sexually egalitarian, and opposed to pure capitalism as well as pure socialism.

Eric von Kuehnelt-Leddihn, an Austrian classical liberal and a cofounder of *National Review,* seemed utterly mystified when he recently discovered how closely American conservatism had become identified with democratic equality. "Do not forget," he warned an interviewer from the *Washington Times,* "that democracy, *in itself,* by its very principle, is totalitarian. It is the politicization of the whole nation."[9]

One explanation for this crusade may lie in the desperate response of anticommunist conservatives faced by the growing unpopularity of the Cold War and the identification, particularly in the media, of Marxist revolution with social justice. But this approach scarcely applies to every case. Among the advocates of the democratic revolution are those who still associate themselves with the anticommunist democratic Left; indeed, some representatives of this position, notably Jeane Kirkpatrick, are today admired everywhere on the political Right. Besides, the democratic globalism that members of the current Right preach against the Communists creates geopolitical imperatives different from those advocated by the older postwar Right. The older conservatives sought to contain and, where possible, push back the Soviets and their clients; the democratic globalists hope to impose their own vision of progress on both allies and enemies.

The current anticommunists may also have gained control over the issue of anticommunism at the expense of the older Right. Critics of democratic globalism have come from the ranks of theoretical conservatives as well as from elsewhere. In 1972 James Burnham noted that there were those still in transition from liberal beliefs who rejected part of their old doctrines but clung to "the emotional gestalt of liberalism, the liberal sensitivity, and temperament." Such people typically insisted on applying universal yardsticks to foreign policy and sought to substitute their own conception of "compassion, kindliness, love and brotherhood" for "those virtues indispensable to organized human society." Against what he considered doctrinaire universalist politics, Burnham appealed to the ancient values of the city: "Courage, duty, discipline, and especially self-discipline, loyalty, endurance, yes patriotism."[10]

The historian and historical conservative John Lukacs has ridiculed postwar American conservatives for believing that America's destiny is to "make the world safe for democracy." Lukacs sees the American Right as the victim of its own *American* "ideas of progress and modernism and American exceptionalism at the expense of the kind of historical understanding that had been enunciated by Burke."[11] Lukacs identifies the Right's global anticommunism with Woodrow Wilson's vision of a world transformed by American democracy. This identification may be far more accurately applied to the democratic globalism of the 1980s than to the Cold War anticommunism of the 1950s. Lukacs himself, in *Outgrowing Democracy,* gives at least two views (neither of them flattering) of the postwar conservative movement: one of primarily Midwestern, Anglophobe politicians and their intellectual spokesmen who glorified power politics; and the other of democratic globalists seeking to convert the world to "the American way of life," but ignoring the threat posed by unprotected borders being overrun by Third World flotsam.[12]

Although both pictures contain caricatures, they do represent phases in the evolving postwar Right. The democratic globalists of the eighties have little in common with the more traditional anticommunists of the fifties and sixties, save for the "anticommunist" label. James Burnham's *Suicide of the West* was a work that American conservative journals and the Conservative Book Club lavishly praised in the mid-sixties. In it Burnham attacked the universalist, egalitarian premises of the intellectual-journalistic community. He failed to see that the "liberal" premises he despised would eventually provide the substance of a transformed American Right. Like other traditional conservatives, Burnham underestimated the anticommunism of those he considered democratic ideologues. Nor did he and his colleagues 25 years ago foresee a fateful irony, that those whom they blamed for the self-destruction of the West would soon, in some cases, be rallying anticommunists in the name of democratic universalism.

If, as some would have it, the essence of conservatism is the preservation of a status quo, then it is perfectly natural that its principles should always be in flux; it is far more changeable than liberalism or Marxism, both of which possess something like an agenda. In this sense, it is possible to regard conservatism as a series of trenches dug in defense of last year's revolution. While we believe there is more than stupid tenacity to conservative politics, it is, nonetheless, an important element. The 40 years of postwar conservative thought might well be summed up by inverting a common French proverb: The more things stay the same, the more they change.

Many people have lent their assistance to the authors in preparing this work. Special thanks go to Robert Nisbet, John Howard, Michael Warder, and Allan Carlson for reading parts of the manuscript and offering detailed suggestions and critical comments, to Cynthia Calvert for painstakingly correcting the text, to Anita Fedora for typing it under pressure, to Jean Avery for helping to prepare an early version, to LeAnn Manning for handling a thousand vexing details, and to our wives, who endured the disruptions of everyday life and the extended political monologues that inevitably accompany a work of this type.

Paul Gottfried   Thomas Fleming
                                                            1988

Chronology

1943   Publication of Alfred Jay Nock's *Memoirs of a Super-fluous Man.*

1943   Publication of Ayn Rand's *The Fountainhead,* a widely sold novel and a statement of objectivist libertarian thought.

1944   Publication of Friedrich von Hayek's indictment of socialism, *The Road to Serfdom.*

1947   Irving Kristol becomes editor of *Commentary,* later the leading magazine of neoconservatism; Norman Podhoretz assumes the post in 1960.

1949   Publication of Ludwig von Mises's monumental economic treatise, *Human Action.*

1949–1950   Trials of Alger Hiss, former U.S. State Department official found guilty of perjuring himself on his past communist affiliation; his chief accuser, Whittaker Chambers, publishes his account of the trials in the autobiographical *Witness* in 1952.

1950   Senator Joseph R. McCarthy launches his career as an anticommunist with a speech delivered in Wheeling, West Virginia; a rebuttal of McCarthy's critics, *McCarthy and His Enemies,* published in 1954 by William F. Buckley, Jr., and Buckley's brother-in-law L. Brent Bozell.

1951   Publication of William F. Buckley's *God and Man at Yale* by conservative publisher Henry Regnery.

1953   Establishment of the John M. Olin Foundation.

1953 Publication of Russell Kirk's classical exposition of postwar traditionalism, *The Conservative Mind, from Burke to Santayana.*

1953 The Intercollegiate Studies Institute founded by Frank Chodorov, originally as the libertarian Intercollegiate Society of Individualists.

1955 Establishment of *National Review,* the premier magazine of the postwar conservative movement.

1957 Founding of Old Right scholarly journal *Modern Age.*

1960 Formation of Young Americans for Freedom.

1962 Organization of the New York Conservative party. Publication of Milton Friedman's *Capitalism and Freedom.* Publication of Murray N. Rothbard's *Man, Economy and State.* Publication of Robert A. Nisbet's *Quest for Community.*

1964 Nomination of conservative Senator Barry Goldwater as Republican presidential candidate.

1965 Formation of American Conservative Union as national action organization.

1968 Presidential candidate George C. Wallace, running as right-wing populist, picks up five Southern states and almost 10 million votes.

1969 Publication by conservative political researcher Kevin P. Phillips of *The Emerging Republican Majority.*
Founding of Young America's Foundation.

1972 Neoconservatives cross party lines to support reelection of Richard Nixon.

1973 Establishment of Heritage Foundation.

1972–1974 Watergate affair unfolds culminating in President Nixon's resignation.

1974 Reorganization of Sarah Scaife Foundation.

1974 Paul Weyrich forms Committee for the Survival of a Free Congress.

1974 Formation of National Conservative Action Committee.

1976 Ronald Reagan challenges incumbent Gerald Ford for Republican presidential nomination.
Founding of the Rockford Institute by John Howard and of *Chronicles* by Leopold Tyrmand.

1977 Founding of Cato Institute.

1978 Californians pass antitax referendum Proposition 13.

1979 Jerry Falwell launches Moral Majority.

1980 and 1984 The presidential victories of Ronald Reagan.

1981 Appointment of neoconservative Jeane Kirkpatrick as permanent U.S. representative to the United Nations.

1981–1983 Neoconservative ascendency in the Reagan administration; appointment of William Bennett as Director of National Endowment for the Humanities and Secretary of Education.

1982 Establishment of Ludwig von Mises Institute.

1985 Formation of Lynde and Harry Bradley Foundation.

1985–1986 Beginning of so-called conservative wars.

1987 Publication of Allan Bloom's *The Closing of the American Mind.* Philanthropic Roundtable organized by Leslie Lenkowsky and Michael Joyce.

1989 Rockford Institute dismisses its New York director R. J. Neuhaus, precipitating further splits on the Right.

1990–1991 Collapse of the Communist bloc.

1991 The Gulf War precipitates the acceleration of division on the American Right.

1991 Patrick J. Buchanan challenges President George Bush from the Right as paleoconservative candidate for the 1992 Republican presidential nomination.

Chapter One

Forming a Worldview: Conservatism in the Fifties

Origins of American Conservatism

The categories liberal and conservative are of limited use in understanding the history of American political ideology. While it is possible to find a vein of aristocracy in the Adamses or to point to an occasional spirited reactionary such as Orestes Brownson or T. S. Eliot, American elections have rarely represented a contest between Left and Right. From decade to decade, our political struggles have been defined more in terms of section, class, and occupation. Freight rates, tariffs, slavery, monetary and banking policies, internal improvements have all had their day, and many of them have passed away only to return and haunt a later generation.

If there is a consistent political and cultural divide, it is probably the fault-line that split open during the constitutional debates between the Federalists, who were really nationalists, and the anti-Federalists, who favored state above national power. The split ran right through Washington's cabinet, between his treasury secretary Alexander Hamilton and his secretary of state Thomas Jefferson. Jefferson thought of himself as a progressive proponent of the European Enlightenment, and he was both a deist in religion and a philosophic rationalist. His defense of local government was predicated on his faith in the yeoman farmer as the bearer of democratic sentiment. Then, too, Jefferson saw in rural society his natural ally in a struggle against the commercial aristocracy of the

cities. Led by Hamilton, Jefferson's adversaries admired the British Constitution and railed against the French Revolution. So the Virginia planter
became a localist, for a number of reasons, in opposing what he considered the privileged class of the urban North. The increasingly conservative faction that rose up around Jefferson, the onetime devotee of
revolutionary France, engaged in an arduous struggle against government centralizers and, eventually, international commerce. Transforming
itself from generation to generation, the party of Hamilton found new life
among Henry Clay's National Republicans and Whigs, in Abraham Lincoln, and in the Republican party from the administrations of Grant down
to the presidency of Herbert Hoover. The most prominent Jeffersonians,
by contrast, were sectionalists and included the great Southern spokesmen John Randolph and the Tertium Quids, John C. Calhoun, and Jefferson Davis. The populists, most prominently William Jennings Bryan, also
proclaimed Jefferson their hero, even though they advocated policies
(such as public ownership of utilities) that would have horrified the aristocratic Virginian.

The politics of the twentieth century, although too complicated to lay
out on one or two axes, nonetheless reveals the old contest in changing
forms. The Progressive movement, for example, has a distinctively
populist-Jeffersonian color in the Midwest and South, where suspicion of banks and railroads ran deep. Even the probusiness Republican,
Robert LaFollete, Sr., believed that state ownership of railroads and
utilities would not only help the farmers but also serve to break up the
cartels and monopolies that stifled competition and destroyed smaller
businesses.

The Midwestern populists and progressives tended toward isolationism and opposed imperialism on moral as well as practical grounds.[1] But
there was also another form of progressivism, one associated with the
nationalism and imperialism advocated by Theodore Roosevelt and eventually by Woodrow Wilson. (LaFollete, while initially a supporter of TR,
eventually denounced him both as false to Progressive principles and a
tool of big business. Both Bryan and LaFollete opposed American en-
trance into the First World War, while Wilson and his advisers saw it as
an opportunity to institute the centralized economic controls that had
been part of the Progressive and even populist platforms.)

Many Progressives followed Wilson in supporting American involvement in World War I, and they continued to regard themselves as Wil-
sonians throughout the 1920s and 1930s and welcomed the election of
Franklin D. Roosevelt as a man who would curb the arrogance of Wall

Street and the technocratic model of government introduced (or rather reintroduced, since economic planning had been experimented with during the war) by Hoover. Many of them were quickly disillusioned by the establishment of the National Recovery Administration, an experiment in economic corporatism that would institutionalize the role of big business in government planning. Senator William Borah, a Progressive Republican from Idaho and a longtime economic reformer who saw the NRA as the death knell for small business, summed up the opposition case in a letter to William Hammam (7 October 1934):

I look upon the fight for the preservation of the "little man," for the small, independent producer and manufacturer, as a fight for a sound, wholesome, economic national life. . . . It is a fight for clean politics and for free government. When you have destroyed small business, you have destroyed our towns and our country life, and you have guaranteed and made permanent the concentration of economic power. . . . The concentration of wealth always leads, and has always led, to the concentration of political power. Monopoly and bureaucracy are twin whelps from the same kennel.

As a Republican, Borah described himself as Hamiltonian, but Walter Lipmann was closer to the mark in tracing his ancestry to Bryan and Jefferson. Lipmann (whose words were reprinted in *Congressional Record* of 18 April 1936) called Borah "a lineal descendant from the earliest American liberals, an individualist who opposes all concentration of political power, political or economic, who is against private privilege and private monopoly, against political bureaucracy and centralized government." Senator Borah was hardly alone in these opinions of the 1930s; he was only the most impressive member of a coalition that opposed the New Deal's domestic policies as well as FDR's foreign policy, which it regarded as warmongering imperialism. In the 1930s and 1940s this coalition, to name only members of the Senate, included Hiram Johnson of California, Gerald Nye of North Dakota, Bennett "Champ" Clark of Missouri, Robert LaFollette, Jr., of Wisconsin, Arthur Vandenberg of Michigan, George Norris of Nebraska, Burton Wheeler of Montana, and eventually Robert Taft and John Bricker of Ohio.

None of these men was known as a conservative, since that label was most often applied to the unqualified defenders of business interests, especially big business interests. But common cause was eventually made between anti–New Deal "conservatives" and old-time Progressives, most importantly on the question of war. The America First movement was a coalition that brought together such "conservatives" as Douglas Stuart, the founder of the movement, isolationist businessmen William Regnery and H. Smith Richardson, and aviation pioneer Charles A. Lindbergh, together with the arch–New Dealer General Hugh Johnson (head of the NRA), journalist John T. Flynn, a Wilsonian Progressive, and the committee's Progressive supporters in the Senate. The first chairman was a liberal-minded corporate leader, General Robert Wood, Chairman of the Board of Sears Roebuck.

The Roosevelt administration opposed the isolationists with all the rigor that the combined forces of the FBI and the New Deal–press could muster. They were excoriated as German sympathizers, "Copperheads," and demagogues who used fear of communism as a pretext for introducing fascism. Pearl Harbor settled more than the question of America's entry into the war; it also destroyed the America First Committee and the coalition that it represented. Borah had died in 1940, and both Champ Clark and Gerald Nye failed to win reelection in 1944, and Wheeler was soon to follow them into retirement after the election of 1946. Vandenberg remained, but only as a major architect of a postwar anticommunist coalition that repudiated isolationism.

The careers of the most prominent isolationist journalists also went into decline. John T. Flynn had lost his column in the *New Republic* in 1940 and soon found that no other major magazine would take his work. In the same year World War I revisionist Harry Elmer Barnes was cut from the New York *World-Telegram* and Oswald Garrison Villard saw his column dropped from *The Nation,* the very magazine he used to edit. H. L. Mencken and Albert Jay Nock, libertarian isolationists, were no longer welcome in the *American Mercury* after the editorship changed hands in 1939. There was a positive aspect to the wartime censorship: shut out of national outlets for their political views, both Nock and Mencken began to devote more time to writing their memoirs.

Many isolationists, in opposing the New Deal, had become more "conservative" in the sense that they became as suspicious of government as they were of big business, and one important strain of postwar conservatism is a continuation of this development, which found its best expression in two Ohio Senators, Taft and Bricker. Taft was no ideologue and played the politics of compromise during the Korean War. He also lacked the suspicion of business interests that had marked so many other Midwestern isolationists. Nonetheless, his family connections, combined with his obvious talents and courage, made him the natural political leader of what came to be known as the Old Right.

The Taft Republicans were anti-Communist without being ardent cold warriors, favored free enterprise, and opposed most New Deal social legislation without repudiating all government responsibility for social welfare (Taft himself advocated federally subsidized housing). They were generally suspicious of foreign entanglements represented by the United Nations, and many supported John W. Bricker's proposed amendment guaranteeing the precedence of the American Constitution over any foreign treaties.

Beginnings of the Postwar Right

Although the conservative movement that took shape at *National Review* was to go in different directions, it is important to recall that there had been a postwar Old Right, even before William Buckley graduated from Yale. This Right, however, was neither organized nor coherent in any real sense. It included big business Republicans and other heirs of Hamilton, but the dominant concerns were a commitment to local liberties and limited government. What it lacked in coherence, the Old Right made up for in its freedom from the changing ideological orthodoxies that have come to characterize the contemporary American Conservative movement.

In 1966 Murray N. Rothbard, a prominent libertarian-individualist, celebrated the tenth anniversary of *National Review* (founded in 1955), by recollecting what the Right had been like 10 years earlier. In 1955, he pointed out, the American Right was still under libertarian influence; in that year a major right-wing group called for the abolition of conscription and a prohibition on foreign wars that were not a response to a direct threat. A year earlier, the celebrated novelist Louis Bromfield had published *A New Pattern for a Tired World,* in which he praised individualism and denounced statism, war, conscription, and imperialism. Though Bromfield was more of a radical individualist than a conservative, he nonetheless expressed what was also an American conservative dislike for the collectivist modern state.

In finding a genealogy for his own kind of American conservatism, Rothbard might also have pointed to three women and certain individualists of large reputation: Rose Wilder Lane, Isabel Paterson, and Ayn Rand, and in addition to Louis Bromfield he could have named Robert Frost and Robinson Jeffers, two poets bitterly opposed to FDR's foreign and domestic policies, and Frost's Southern Agrarian friend, the essayist and poet Donald Davidson, whose *Attack on Leviathan* was an eloquent diatribe against the New Deal.

The strangest omission was Rothbard's Old Right hero John T. Flynn, who in 1955 had published *The Decline of the American Republic and How to Rebuild It.* Flynn's polemic concluded with a program that sums up the views of the anti–New Deal Right. First, it seeks to restore the Constitution by annulling all Supreme Court decisions since 1937. It also advises that the United States should withdraw from the United Nations, repeal the Sixteenth Amendment (income tax), and adopt the Bridges-Byrd amendment prohibiting the federal government from spending more than it takes in. Last and perhaps most important on Flynn's wish list was passage of the Bricker amendment annulling the provisions of any treaty or agreement that conflict with the Constitution. This amendment received surprisingly broad support from veterans' organizations, the Chamber of Commerce and other business organizations, and from such staunchly conservative groups as Pro America. In 1954 the proposal was soundly defeated by a coalition of internationalists with the support of the Eisenhower administration.

After World War II, libertarians were reacting to events in the English-speaking world abroad as well as to developments within the United States. At home there was deep-seated fatalism in their ranks as they looked at the administrative consolidation that had taken place since the early decades of the century. Government regulation of wages, the growth of a national civil service as an instrument of "democratic reform," the empowerment of labor unions by executive and congressional authority, and the steady increase of taxation at federal and state levels were all developments that American libertarians by 1945 could trace at least as far back as the energetic presidency of Woodrow Wilson. In February 1945, the historian Mortimer Smith, writing in *Christian Century,* lamented that "old-fashioned liberalism . . . is all but dead in our century," a casualty of government social planning accelerated by war.[2] In England, however, an even more ominous turn of events could be seen by American libertarians or, as some preferred to be called, "old-fashioned liberals," when the Socialists swept to power in the summer elections of 1945. On 2 August the *New York Times* reported the manner in which the newly elected Labour government had entered Parliament on the preceding day, noting that the exultant Labourites had sung the "Red Flag" and other songs that the revolutionary Left had popularized in the 1930s.[3]

Together with fatalism, American libertarians of the forties and fifties displayed an exuberant enthusiasm for organization: an incongruous combination of reactions to their time noticeable in their letters and memoirs. A persistent characteristic of postwar libertarians, however, has been a lack of clarity about what "state" they wish to oppose. For traditional Taft Republicans, who argued for divided and distributed powers among levels of government, this problem did not exist. What they resisted was the concentration of power in the modern welfare state and its administration. But more thoroughgoing libertarians have gone beyond Jeffersonian Democrats and Taft Republicans in positing an ideal society without political authority. This is particularly true of many present-day libertarians descended from the objectivists of the fifties and sixties, a group which will be discussed later. For these libertarians, getting rid of the welfare state has been less important than liberating self-proclaimed individuals from political enforcement of moral restraints, except in cases including the perpetration of physical harm. Faced by the virtual impossibility of abolishing or even significantly limiting the democratic welfare state, such libertarians have turned their efforts all the more vigorously to the task of liberation from state-enforced morality.

This problem should be broached at the outset of this study, for it explains at least some of the tensions between traditionalists who have opposed the expanding welfare state and various libertarian groups. In the present circumstances of shifting alignments on the Right, only a minority of libertarians have joined the remnants of the Old Right against the neoconservative defenders of the welfare state and of a global democratic foreign policy. Prominent self-described libertarians do not seem particularly bothered by either statist position. Though financial considerations are undoubtedly a factor in explaining the taking of sides in current conservative wars, it is also clear that many of today's libertarians are no longer as much put off by big government as by religious and social authorities. Legalization of drugs, an immigration policy approaching the creation of open borders, the outlawing of sexist discrimination, and the gaining of social approval for homosexual lifestyles have become bigger issues for most if not all libertarian foundations than the abolition of the American welfare state.

Some contemporary analysts make the useful distinction between right- and left-wing libertarians: between those who identify liberty primarily with the struggle against leveling social democratic government and those who wish to have people everywhere invested equally with the same rights to self-expression. While both may talk about the free market and free trade, they would not likely agree on too much else, such as the family, political equality, or the place of religion in society. It is obvious that most of the famous libertarians active around 1945 were certainly by our standards social traditionalists; those most often featured in leading newspapers today tend to be the opposite. Put a bit differently, democratic equality and moral iconoclasm are far higher values for contemporary libertarians than for those bearing the same label in 1945. Their shared characteristic has been a negative attitude toward the "state," though here too it is plain that libertarians have disliked government for largely different reasons in different ages. For example, some libertarians criticized the federal government in the fifties for imposing the civil rights revolution on the states; today libertarians assault government as a source of racial, sexist, and homophobic oppression. In the forties and fifties libertarians objected to the state for upsetting natural social hierarchies; today the complaint of others answering to the same name is that the state really cannot be trusted as a loyal ally in the war against discrimination.

In the immediate postwar period, however, libertarians were still united by their shared dislike for the American government in its New Deal phase. A number of free-market organizations were founded in the forties that served as rallying points for older individualists and younger libertarians. John T. Flynn was rescued by a veteran rightist group, the Committee for Constitutional Government. Albert Jay Nock was taken in by the National Economic Council, which published a monthly *Review of Books* under Nock's editorship. Nock's disciple, Frank Chodorov, after his dismissal from the Henry George School, founded the newsletter *Analysis* in 1944. It was also in 1944 that the weekly *Human Events* was launched by three isolationists: Frank Hanighen (coauthor of *The Merchants of Death,* an influential attack on the arms industry), former Haverford College president Felix Morley, and Henry Regnery, son of William Regnery of the America First Committee.

Perhaps the most significant free-market organization of the postwar years was the Foundation for Economic Education, founded in 1946 by Leonard Read, which, in the opinion of Murray Rothbard, has employed "virtually every prominent libertarian in the country of middle age or older." For most of its history FEE concentrated on its main purpose of education, sponsoring meetings and seminars, and providing a forum for discussing classical liberal economics.

One of the scholars attracted to FEE was Floyd Arthur "Baldy" Harper, who left Cornell at the invitation of Leonard Read. (Reportedly, Cornell's desire for federal funds had made Harper's free-market views unwelcome.) Frustrated in his desire to establish a more academic arm of FEE, Harper went to work for the William Volker Fund and eventually succeeded in establishing the Institute for Humane Studies, which has become an important academic center (at George Mason University) imbued with the principles of Austrian economics.

Postwar libertarians benefited from their contact with members of the Austrian School of Economics, which had been criticizing socialist programs and Marxian views of capitalism since the 1870s. One influential member was Ludwig von Mises, who had secured an international reputation during the twenties and thirties for his analysis of the business cycle. Mises had emigrated to New York in 1940; however, because of the unfashionable anti-Marxist tenor of his thought, his two wartime books, *Bureaucracy* (Yale 1944) and *Omnipotent Government* (Yale 1944), attracted little attention. Significantly, however, Murray Rothbard had gravitated to the Austrian school by 1949 and attended Mises's ongoing seminar at New York University. Then, in the early fifties several participants in the seminar, after taking part in the Youth for Taft campaign in 1952, formed the Circle Bastiat, named in honor of the French laissez-faire economist. In addition to Rothbard and his wife, the Circle consisted of Leonard Liggio (later the president of the Institute for Humane Studies), Robert Hessen (later a Randian), historian Ralph Raico, and Ronald Hamowy. The group's orientation was individualist, free-market, and passionately antistatist.

If Mises's influence was primarily upon a select group of students, his colleague Friedrich A. Hayek, attracted more general attention. Hayek provided his American admirers with an extraordinary polemical weapon in his *The Road to Serfdom,* published in 1944. An ethical defense of free enterprise, Hayek's work noted both the socialist impulse of fascism and the antiliberal character of the modern planned economy. To the chagrin of English Labourites (he wrote his book as an exile from the Nazis in England) and of American New Dealers (whom he came to know at the University of Chicago after the war), Hayek interpreted economic planning and material redistribution as a retreat from the age of individual liberty. This age had dawned upon the West with the passing of medieval authority. The socialists, under the guise of guaranteeing equality, were setting mankind back on the road to serfdom.

The Road to Serfdom brought fame to Hayek. *Reader's Digest* serialized his work, which was also selected as a Book-of-the-Month Club offering. In 1954, the Harvard historian H. Stuart Hughes, a man of the socialist Left, observed in retrospect, "The publication ten years ago of Friedrich Hayek's *The Road to Serfdom* was a major event in the intellectual history of the United States."[4] Hughes attributed the restored prestige of free market thought in the fifties largely to Hayek's moral defense of capitalism. Indeed, *The Road to Serfdom* was instrumental in the conversion of more than a few leftists. For instance, John Chamberlain, a leftist in the thirties, had come far enough to write the introduction to the book, and Frank Meyer, still a communist, gave the work a favorable review in the *New Masses*.

The attempt to revitalize the ideal of a free society, which Hayek so ardently encouraged, found expression on the international level with the creation of the Mt. Pelerin Society in 1947. A yearly gathering of classical liberal economists and social philosophers, it eventually numbered princes and statesmen among its guests and members. Ludwig Erhard, chancellor of the Federal Republic of Germany, for example, was long associated with this partial brainchild of Hayek's.[5]

Libertarian critics of the welfare state were conspicuous in laying the intellectual foundations of a postwar conservative movement. Among these critics were Frank Chodorov, who founded Intercollegiate Society of Individualists, a group that from 1953 on published and funded libertarian and other conservative scholarship; Albert Jay Nock, original editor of the individualist periodical the *Freeman*; Milton Friedman and Frank H. Knight, both professors of economics at the University of Chicago; and those members of the Austrian School who had emigrated to America, most notably Hayek and Mises. William A. Rusher, publisher of *National Review* and cofounder of the Draft Goldwater Campaign, recalls his own excited reaction when he encountered Hayek's writings as a Wall Street attorney in the early 1950s. Like other groping conservatives of the time, Rusher found his opposition to social planning strengthened even more when he turned to the *Freeman*, which three of Hayek's disciples, John Chamberlain, Henry Hazlitt, and Suzanne LaFollette, had reestablished in 1950. Rusher believed that the *Freeman* was "a sort of journalistic John the Baptist" for *National Review*, which first appeared in November 1955.[6] Between the two publications there were obvious lines of continuity. The Nockean editors of the *Freeman* eventually joined the staff of what became the more widely circulated, anticollectivist periodical. Their antistatist, individualist creed remained essential to the moral teachings of *National Review*—and was then imperfectly transferred to the conservative politics of the 1960s.

Two other libertarian journals furnished the staff and many of the early contributors to Buckley's enterprise. One was the *American Mercury,* which H. L. Mencken founded, primarily as a literary and cultural journal, in January 1924. In the early fifties, under the editorship of William Bradford Huie, the *American Mercury* entered its last phase as an intellectually serious publication, presenting feisty criticism of the welfare state in lively prose. Max Eastman, John Dos Passos, James Burnham, Frank S. Meyer, and the young Buckley all wrote frequently for the *American Mercury* before the birth of *National Review. Human Events,* organized in 1944, was another libertarian periodical that channeled talent into the incipient *National Review.* Although originally designed to report and interpret foreign policy from Washington, D.C., *Human Events* also came to focus on economic and cultural issues. Among its editors and regular contributors were Felix Morley, an educator who wrote on educational issues, and John Chamberlain, who was also associated with the *Wall Street Journal* and the *Freeman.* In February 1955 Buckley observed in a letter to Eastman that there were only three journals of value on the Right: the *Freeman,* the *American Mercury,* and *Human Events.*[7] While the *National Review* was going to dominate the world of conservative letters, absorbing the editorial staffs of other publications and going between 1955 and 1965 from 30,000 to well over 100,000 subscribers, it also eclipsed its predecessors. *Human Events* continued to publish, but only as a weekly news report for conservatives. The *Freeman* also survived but with fewer readers than before; *American Mercury* went under—after lurching briefly to the far Right.[8]

Red Scare

Anticommunism, together with opposition to Soviet imperialism, was a critical shaping force for postwar conservative thinking. The first attempt at making conservatism a political movement came during the early phases of the cold war. Thinkers who had once been on the far Left, like James Burnham, Frank S. Meyer, and Whittaker Chambers, tried to make the American people aware of the danger of Soviet subversion. Whittaker Chambers's *Witness,* the graphic account of its author's transformation from a communist agent into a self-declared counterrevolutionary, both inspired and galvanized American anticommunists. Chambers's understanding of his role in exposing Alger Hiss, a former State Department official, as a Soviet spy in 1948, was presented in stark, apocalyptic terms. Chambers saw himself participating in a struggle between "the two irreconcilable faiths of our time—Freedom and Communism." The cause of freedom, he thought, was doomed without "faith in God."[9] Such faith distinguished the traditional Western conception of freedom from the Promethean view, "the vision of man's mind displacing God as the creative intelligence of the world," that underlay the Communist system of servitude.

The anticommunism expressed by young conservative intellectuals in the 1950s had a metaphysical dimension already present in Chambers's writings. This metaphysical anticommunism was evident in the way that conservative intellectuals rose to the defense of Senator Joseph McCarthy between 1950 and 1954. McCarthy gained national attention after making charges against alleged Communists in the State Department and elsewhere in the government. His sweeping accusations and his often abrasive exchanges with the press made him rapidly into a controversial figure. By 1954 he fell out with members of his own party and with the military, which he accused of harboring communist sympathizers.

There were compelling historical reasons for the widespread support McCarthy commanded as a Senate investigator up to (and even after) the time the Senate censured him on 30 July 1954. Most attempts by his liberal critics to identify his following largely or exclusively with "reactionary" minorities—such as anti-Eastern populists, Irish and German Americans who had been sympathetic to fascism, or anti–New Deal Republicans—overlook the true extent of McCarthy's support. A Gallup poll in March 1954 showed that 46 percent of the American population had "a favorable opinion" of the junior senator from Wisconsin.[10] According to his most recent scholarly biographer, Thomas C. Reeves, McCarthy remained popular among newspaper editors and radio commentators even after he had fallen from honor in the Senate and within his own party. Reeves also notes the events that overlapped McCarthy's senatorial career and help explain his political ascendancy. The Korean War between the Soviet-backed North Koreans and the American-backed South Koreans coincided with his investigation. Information had been surfacing since the late forties about Communists who had obtained sensitive government positions during the war. In 1950 the British discovered that Klaus Fuchs, an atomic physicist who had formerly worked at Los Alamos, had given atomic secrets to the Soviets. Equally important for understanding the bitter anticommunism of the early fifties were the forced Sovietization of Eastern Europe and the fall of mainland China to Communist forces in 1949.[11]

In 1954 two conservatives in their twenties, William F. Buckley, Jr., and his brother-in-law Brent Bozell, wrote a defense of McCarthy's career as a Senate investigator. Their work, *McCarthy and His Enemies,* was concerned not only with substantiating McCarthy's charges but also with discussing the moral question that they believed he had raised at least by indirection. William S. Schlamm, an Austrian émigré, asserted in the prologue that political commitments mattered for McCarthyites. Those who had served, or had apologized for, Stalin bore a continuing responsibility for once aiding the communist enemy. Buckley and Bozell viewed the struggle bewteen McCarthy and his liberal enemies as one between the defenders of American society and the advocates of moral anarchy: "Not only is it characteristic of society to create institutions and to defend them with sanctions. Societies must do so . . . or else they cease to exist."[12] Conservatives believed that McCarthy's enemies were their own: the moral relativists who absolutized the open society. In a postscript on the McCarthy era in 1957, the usually skeptical James Burnham observed that the "issue was philosophical, metaphysical." Burnham thought liberals were correct, from their point of view, in discrediting McCarthy, because he had challenged their "secularist, egalitarian, relativist" understanding of the world.[13]

Libertarians who helped launch the postwar conservative movement embraced the interpretation of McCarthyism implicit in Burnham's comments. A striking case in point was Frank Chodorov. The son of Russian Jewish immigrants, he had become a libertarian as a young man, under the influence of Thoreau and the late-nineteenth-century social reformer Henry George. While Chodorov campaigned for George's plan for a single tax on unproductive land, he came into contact with Albert Jay Nock, another advocate of the single tax. With Nock's support, Chodorov was made a staff member of the *Freeman,* and after 30 years of involvement with that twice-refounded periodical, became, like other disciples of Nock, part of the founding generation of postwar conservatism.

Chodorov's thinking underwent definite changes, particularly from the end of the war until his death in 1966. He himself was affected by the broad conservative movement that he had worked to create—and that ultimately carried him beyond his early individualistic creed. Despite his religious skepticism and passionate belief in individual liberty, Chodorov sought the collaboration of religious conservatives, Southern regionalists, and others of a traditionalist persuasion when he organized the Intercollegiate Society of Individualists. His earliest collaborator in this enterprise, William Buckley, held theological views radically different from his. Yet Buckley, in a particularly moving obituary, notes that Chodorov grew increasingly concerned toward the end of his life with the moral preconditions for liberty. Chodorov was among the earliest to praise *McCarthy and His Enemies* and recommended it to readers of the *Freeman* as soon as it appeared.[14]

During the McCarthy era, prominent libertarians of the Right, notably Chodorov and John Chamberlain, asked the same critical questions about civil liberties as did other conservatives. By contrast, anticommunists who were social democrats, like Sidney Hook and Melvin Lasky, reacted less dramatically to what they perceived as the evils of communism. They did protest the absence of intellectual freedom in the Soviet bloc and organized the American Committee for Cultural Freedom in 1949.[15] The committee was to publicize the attack on free inquiry that took place under dictatorial regimes. But the libertarians of the Right considered such steps to be inadequate in a struggle between the principle of individuality and the total state. They also viewed the noncommunist intellectual Left as a soft ally with the same collectivist values as those the Communists claimed to honor. James Burnham often made this observation to his readers.

Some maverick libertarians, for example, Max Eastman, who remained a crusading atheist until the end of his life, unexpectedly became McCarthyites. But other libertarians turned zealously anticommunist as part of a deeper philosophical conversion. They were responding to the kinds of arguments that Buckley and Bozell made about the limits of the open society. Libertarians were also taking another look at the American experience. Yale professor of political theory Willmoore Kendall emphasized that the postwar notions of civil liberties were thoroughly modern. In interpreting the Bill of Rights in his essays, Kendall focused on the dispute between federalists and states rightists at the time of America's founding. The Tenth Amendment, which recognized state authority under the new federal system, he held to be basic to understanding the entire Bill of Rights.[16] Kendall warned against wrenching the First Amendment's guarantee of freedom of expression from its historical context. States rightists at the constitutional convention, said Kendall, favored a Bill of Rights in order to prevent the new federal government from exercising power which they wished to have reserved to the states. Kendall found ample precedents, going back to the early republic, for laws against sedition. He also quoted the Founding Fathers to underline their differences from modern interpreters of the First Amendment.[17]

Kendall and Buckley both insisted that the exercise of liberty was predicated on historical precedents and moral restraints without which all liberty degenerated into anarchy. They justified the suspension of ordinary First Amendment rights to known Communists by going beyond the appeal to pressing circumstances. Nor did they dwell on liberal hypocrisy in their discussion of civil liberties. For example, neither Buckley nor Kendall made much of the fact that the American Civil Liberties Union had repeatedly defended the wartime expropriation and resettlement of Japanese Americans. Postwar conservatives, and even those libertarians among them, were less concerned about liberal hypocrisy than about the proper limits of intellectual freedom. Although Buckley does observe that the American intellectual Left supported the House Committee on Un-American Activities while it was being used (up to 1945) to investigate suspected Fascists, his quarrel with liberals in *McCarthy and His Enemies* was mostly unrelated to this problem of inconsistency. He criticized liberals for denying, or pretending to deny, that American society should protect its values "against competing values."[18] Kendall let it be known that he opposed Communists as a "majoritarian democrat." Because their views and practices were inimical to the American political and moral sense, as he understood it, Communists were not entitled to consideration as legitimate members of the political community.

Despite the journalistic assistance that Republican politicians received from postwar conservatives during and after the McCarthy era, their agendas did not coincide. Midwestern Senators, most notably Robert A. Taft, John W. Bricker, and William E. Jenner, were quick to exploit popular indignation against the Roosevelt-Truman administration that had allowed Communists and fellow travelers to work for it, but Republican isolationism remained strong into the 1950s.

Early in the decade both Murray Rothbard and Frank Chodorov had debated Willi Schlamm on whether communism should be the central issue for American conservatives. Then in the November 1954 *Freeman* Schlamm and Chodorov squared off, with Schlamm emphasizing the menace of international communism and Chodorov warning—even in his title—against "A War to Communize America." (As a result of the debate Chodorov was dismissed from his position as editor.)

Throughout the Korean War John T. Flynn had portrayed the conflict as the waste of American life on a military adventure dictated by "the military industry." Flynn was an ardent anti-Communist, who had condemned the Yalta agreement and supported McCarthy; nonetheless, he consistently opposed the aggressive policy expressions of the cold war and described Eisenhower's domino theory as silly, an excuse for a military buildup to boost the economy. When Flynn attempted to make this case in an article submitted to *National Review,* William Buckley turned him down.

One of the Old Right's fundamental disagreements with *National Review* was over the assumption, stated as early as 25 January 1952 by William Buckley (in *Commonweal*) that to fight communism abroad it was necessary to institute *temporary* measures promoting internal security. Buckley endorsed the antistatist views of Herbert Spencer, Mencken, and Nock, but insisted that the "thus far invincible aggressiveness of the Soviet Union" required Americans "to accept Big Government for the duration." An anticommunist war could only be waged "through the instrument of a totalitarian bureaucracy within our shores." This meant, in practice, high taxes, a large military establishment, "atomic energy, central intelligence, war production boards and the attendant centralization of power in Washington." Once the communist threat had been disposed of, so the argument ran, America could move toward restoring its original republican government.

The founders of *National Review* firmly believed that only Western assertiveness, promoted by a powerful America, would keep the Soviets from expanding their control. Burnham and other postwar conservatives like Stefan Possony and Robert Strausz-Hupé were convinced that the war against the Soviets and their clients would continue until one side or the other had won.[19] They stressed the centrality of communist ideology in explaining the relentlessly expansionist nature of the Soviet state. Communist states did not operate in accordance with the kind of political principles that had informed traditional (including czarist) statecraft. They strove by every means to bring noncommunist societies under their control, practicing political coexistence only as a temporary expedient.

In the ideological struggle that the American intellectual Right waged against communism, it drew heavily upon former communists and Central European émigrés. Both were disproportionately present in the conservative intellectual movement of the 1950s. Although studies have already appeared on the specifically Marxist background of some postwar conservatives, the European roots of these and other conservatives deserve further attention. Almost all the repentant Communists who became conservatives were either originally from Central Europe—like Willi Schlamm, and the cultural anthropologist Karl Wittfogel—or had come out of Central European home environments—like Will Herberg and Frank Meyer—or in the cases of Burnham and Chambers had been strongly affected by European culture and ideas. The writing and thinking of these émigrés inevitably reflected a European point of reference: for example, when they described the struggle between Marxism and Western civilization as a dialectic of historical forces; or when they treated the American experience within the broader framework of Western civilization. Like the German philosopher Hegel, these modern conservatives interpreted history as a process that revealed the interaction of competing spiritual principles.[20]

Modern Democracy and Its Critics

Another aspect of postwar conservatism was the influence of European thought: the traditionalist critique of American mass culture. Herbert J. Gans traces this critique in the postwar years to those who were descended "from the European elite or who modeled themselves on it."[21] Russell Kirk is a case in point: although descended from New England Puritans and the author of a monograph on the Southern political thinker John Randolph, Kirk drew inspiration from Edmund Burke and Sir Walter Scott for his portrait of the "conservative mind." Kirk justified these transatlantic influences by describing the object of his study as a hyphenated entity, an "Anglo-American" mind that he first undertook to analyze as a student at St. Andrew's in Scotland. Other examples include the conservative sociologist Robert Nisbet, who has tried to revive the study of French and German counterrevolutionaries for the light they shed on the dissolution of social bonds in the modern world, and the two German émigrés—scholars who enjoyed the respect of postwar conservatives— Leo Strauss and Eric Voegelin, who both exalted the ideals of classical antiquity, although the rationalist Strauss and the mystic Voegelin differed over the ideals they wished to return to. While Hayek, a Central European, considers himself an "old-fashioned liberal," he too betrays a European traditionalist pedigree. Although a defender of democratic institutions, Hayek laments the vulgarization of political and social life under the welfare state. He admires nineteenth-century middle-class society and holds up the model of the traditional Swiss confederation as an example of a soundly functioning republic. Though many standard interpretations of postwar conservatism exaggerate its derivation from European ideals, clearly Europeans and European thinking left their mark on this American movement. This influence may be most evident in the antipopulist strains in some American conservative thought, which has a European as well as native point of origin.

What should be stressed, however, is that the postwar conservative movement, as it took shape around the issue of anticommunism, treated European intellectual legacies as selectively as American ones. European thinkers were invoked for their warnings against modern messianic ideologies culminating in expansionist communism. Old World critics of democracy became relevant as prophets of totalitarianism, particularly if they were willing to associate themselves with anticommunist publications and organizations. As in the thirties and forties when political progressives rushed to enlist figures from the Western past for the struggle against fascism (and Count Carlo Sforza discovered that Machiavelli had been a liberal anti-Fascist ahead of his time), in the fifties American conservatives turned to antitotalitarian Europeans who had warned against the revolt of the masses. Not surprisingly, William F. Buckley solicited essays for *National Review* from Spanish author José Ortega y Gasset who in 1929 had published his most famous tract, *Revolt of the Masses*.

The Protracted Struggle of *National Review*

The "protracted struggle" against the Soviets, and the appeal to moral norms in the context of this civilizational struggle, were recurrent themes in the early issues of *National Review*. In an editorial for *National Review* on 16 January 1962, William F. Buckley, Jr., defended the House Committee on Un-American Activities in America. Stating ideas that he and other *National Review* editors presented in greater detail in a book published in 1962, Buckley pilloried absolutist civil libertarians. Resuming themes already developed in *McCarthy and His Enemies,* Buckley professed to be amazed at how far liberals carried the principles of freedom of expression and association in dealing with Marxist revolutionaries: "The superstition that the hands of truth will rout the vermin of error seems, like a fragment of Victorian lace, quaint, but too brittle to be lifted out of the showcase. . . . We need to make definite strides forward in a political theory of freedom suitable to a world in which things like Communists and atom bombs exist."[22] On 10 April 1962, Jewish theologian and *National Review* writer Will Herberg offered similar observations in reviewing his colleagues' work, *The Committee and Its Critics*. Although Herberg, too, stated his belief in freedom as a political and spiritual value, like Buckley he stressed the struggle for civilization as the necessary context for understanding constitutional rights: "It is only when 'un-American' propaganda becomes a part of a conspiratorial movement allied with a foreign enemy bent on the destruction of our nation, of freedom, and of Western civilization that it becomes a proper subject for congressional inquiry, disclosure, and legislation."[23] It should be noted that Herberg justified the congressional investigation by appealing to a clear and present danger. Unlike Buckley and Kendall, he did not insist on making the concept of civil liberties fit a traditionalist social philosophy.

In the fifties and sixties, the editors of *National Review* saw themselves more as the custodians of the cultural past (epitomized in the phrase "Western civilization") than as the promoters of civil liberty or of democratic equality. This preference was evident in their response to the drive to create a black electorate in the South. Although Frank Meyer often invoked states' rights doctrine during the early phase of the civil-rights movement, the essential principle for him and other *National Review* conservatives was to maintain traditional Western values against an easily radicalized black voting bloc. The editors of *National Review* took this stand emphatically in a controversial statement of belief on 24 August 1957: "Should the White South be allowed to take such measures as are necessary to prevail politically and culturally, in areas where it does not predominate numerically? The shocking answer is Yes—the white community is so entitled because, for the time being, it is the advanced race. *National Review* believes that the South's premises are correct. If the majority wills what is socially atavistic, then to thwart the majority may be, though undemocratic, enlightened."[24]

National Review published articles in defense of this position by the Southern regionalist Virginius Dabney and James Jackson Kilpatrick, but by the mid-sixties some writers began to find other grounds for opposing the mounting demands of the civil-rights movement. Civil-rights activists and their supporters in Congress and among the judiciary were calling for far-reaching government efforts, such as the busing of students and the surveillance of the private sector, in order to achieve full racial integration. Dartmouth literary critic Jeffrey Hart, a later editor of *National Review*, ridiculed the attempt to "effect total Negro integration" as a "novel abstract pattern" that went counter to the process of social integration undergone by other ethnic groups in America.[25] The utopian aims of the civil-rights movement, were they to be realized, required the transformation of established cultural and social patterns. In a similar vein, Frank Meyer noted the shift from a "civil rights agitation toward confiscatory socialism."[26] Hart, Meyer, and Will Herberg all identified the civil-rights agitation of the sixties with social-engineering plans that would destroy communities that had been independent of bureaucratic control. In *Suicide of the West*, James Burnham supplemented these attacks on the revolutionary impulse of American liberals with critical observations on their "relentlessly driven" character. The liberal tries to overthrow the past because of his emotional makeup: "Even when there is no objective reason to believe that what he does can solve the problem," he presses on remorselessly "to appease the guilt in his own breast."[27]

Faith of Our Fathers

A traditionalism that invoked a vanished past was another part of postwar conservatism. Two seminal thinkers of this traditionalist revival were Richard M. Weaver (1910–63) and his more prolific admirer Russell Kirk (1918–). In his cultural criticism and essays on political rhetoric, Weaver identified himself as a Southern regionalist and an ethical Platonist.

A militant critic of moral relativism and mass culture, Weaver defended agrarian hierarchical values that he saw honored in the antebellum South and, in varying degrees, throughout Western civilization before World War I. Weaver was critical of the material and psychological reductionism that he associated with the social sciences and other characteristically modern disciplines. He believed that the failure of intellectuals to take the force of ideas seriously was one more symptom of "the dissolution of the West."[28]

As a Southern man of letters, the conservative Weaver was hardly an isolated phenomenon. A student and disciple of such prominent Southern writers as Donald Davidson and Andrew Lytle, Weaver was heir to an agrarian tradition of thought that crystallized around the 1930 manifesto *I'll Take My Stand,* a work that included contributions by John Crowe Ransom, Allen Tate, Andrew Lytle, Robert Penn Warren, and Donald Davidson. Despite differences in their opinions, the agrarians shared a conviction, transmitted to Weaver, that a strictly commercial civilization, divorced from the land and from tradition, lacked moral and spiritual roots. Because of their literary fame, agrarian writers were able to secure a hearing for their reactionary views out of all proportion with their numbers. They also succeeded in attracting disciples. In addition to Weaver and literary critic Cleanth Brooks, writers influenced by the agrarians include literary critics M. E. Bradford, and Marion Montgomery, poets Wendell Berry, Fred Chappell, and George Garrett, and the historian essayist Clyde N. Wilson.

Russell Kirk—a "Northern agrarian" and an admirer of Weaver— exerted perhaps a more profound influence on postwar thought, largely through his book *The Conservative Mind* (1953). William Rusher considers Kirk's study together with *The Road to Serfdom* and Whittaker Chambers's *Witness* the "three most powerful contributions to the conservative movement that was stirring intellectually in the early 1950s."[29]

In *The Conservative Mind* Kirk sets out to achieve two objects, both related to the task of creating a self-confident American conservative movement. First, he attempts to prove that, contrary to those who consider progressive thinking the American mainstream, "liberal" ideas have not generally defined the American experience. Kirk traces a continuing traditionalist strain among Anglo-American authors and statesmen, from the eloquent critic of the French Revolution, Edmund Burke, to the poet and literary critic, T. S. Eliot. Although he concedes that the present age of commercial greed and innovating zeal is hostile to the conservative impulse, Kirk finds congenial thoughts in the writings of such diverse minds as Nathaniel Hawthorne, James Fenimore Cooper, John C. Calhoun, John Adams, and Henry Adams.[30]

Second, Kirk undertakes to define conservatism as a body of belief. This body of belief, he argues, has been present and sometimes dominant in the Anglo-American culture since the late eighteenth century. He sums up the cardinal tenets of true conservatives in an introductory chapter that leans heavily toward nineteenth-century British conservatism. Kirk proclaims that social hierarchy is necessary to the proper order of the world, and he affirms both historical Providence and the divine source of traditional morality. He expresses his "affection for the proliferating variety and mystery of traditional life," his "faith in prescription" and in the role of imagination as a source of morals. He defends "the persuasion that property and freedom are inseparably connected." Kirk ends his statement of conservative belief with the observation "that change and reform are not identical and that innovation is a devouring conflagration more often than it is a torch of progress."[31]

Although Kirk later denied the dogmatic intent of his "canons of conservative thought," his rigorous formulation may have given many conservatives a coherent philosophy for the first time. Unlike Weaver, Kirk and his followers had not given up on the present age. They sought to restore America and the Western world to what they thought were its first principles. The postwar traditionalists found these postulates, not in the Age of Reason that Thomas Paine celebrated, but in a civilization extending back through the medieval schoolmen to classical and biblical antiquity. Rusher (among others) enthusiastically praises Kirk's "traditionalist heritage of Burkean conservatism."[32] But Kirk in fact expounded more than one "Burkean conservatism." The Burke of *The Conservative*

Mind was a critic of political rationalism, a traditionalist who appealed to "prejudice and prescription," inbred sentiments, and inherited rights, as the basis of political order. Kirk repeated Burke's warnings about viewing civil society as something artificial, a dissoluble agreement made to further individual self-interest. He was especially fond of Burke's description of the true social contract that bound together all generations—and the higher and lower natures of man.

In the late fifties, Kirk also found in Burke's writings a natural law doctrine that the Catholic Scholars Peter Stanlis and Francis Canavan had first discovered there.[33] Catholic conservative interest in Burke (who came from an Irish Catholic family and was a lifelong supporter of Catholic emancipation in England) went back in America to the forties. On 12 April 1945, the Burke Society was founded at Fordham University to foster a return to "the principles, values, and truths which are the heritage of the political and international society of Christendom." Kirk's later interpretation of Burke echo these sentiments, stressing Burke's ties to medieval and classical conceptions of the "higher law." According to this second view, Burke criticized revolution and abstract schemes being applied to political life, above all, as a member of Christendom, of a civilization that contained moral norms within its evolving historical institutions.[34]

Kirk found other sources for his conservative philosophy, both more recent and closer to home, in the writings of two Harvard alumni, Irving Babbitt and Paul Elmer More. As a scholar, Babbitt was well-known for his studies of Sanskrit literature and for his interpretations of nineteenth-century French literature. More was a Neoplatonist who became famous as a result of his literary and philosophical essays. Between Babbitt's secularized Buddhism, with its ethic of moral restraint and hard work, and More's attachment to Platonic ethics, a school of thought emerged that came to be known as the New Humanism. Despite the tirades of H. L. Mencken and Sinclair Lewis (in his 1930 Nobel Prize acceptance speech, Lewis referred to "a doctrine of the blackest reaction introduced into a stirringly revolutionary world"), the New Humanism won many learned adherents in the late twenties and early thirties; and well into the postwar years, young professors of literature were deriving inspiration from the ethical insights of Babbitt and More. Among the better-known literary and cultural critics influenced by the New Humanism have been T. S. Eliot, Peter Viereck, Austin Warren, George Panichas, the neo-Hegelian Claes Ryn, and—of course—Kirk himself.

The traditionalist ideas of the postwar conservative movement were essential to the process of conservative self-definition. The traditionalists gave to the American Right a set of interlocking beliefs that addressed religious and moral concerns. They appealed to the historical consciousness of a civilization that went back beyond the American past, into the medieval and ancient worlds. And though not reducible to any particular economic system, traditionalist beliefs were seen as compatible with a capitalist economy. Outside the South (where conservative intellectuals were often hostile to commerce), traditionalists made common cause with libertarians, while professing, like William Buckley, a higher allegiance to theological than economic matters. A distaste for social engineering united the two sides. In his six "canons of conservative thought," Kirk affirms that private property is a moral and social good. "Radical systems," says Kirk, attack established property relations in order to destroy family and communal ties. Precisely for that reason, Kirk and other traditionalists supported private enterprise against what they believed was an egalitarian welfare state.

Traditionalists and libertarians could also agree on common heroes. The libertarian idol Jefferson (whom Albert Jay Nock celebrated in a popular biography) was also the figure whom Southern conservatives exalted as an agrarian and states rightist. Albert Jay Nock, a cultural elitist, had fans among traditionalists and libertarians; both groups mourned his passing in 1945. Through the autobiographical *Memoirs of a Superfluous Man*, Nock left his mark on two later traditionalist thinkers, Russell Kirk and Robert Nisbet, both American soldiers when they first read his book. Each claimed that his life was profoundly changed by this man who condemned the modern state as "our enemy."[35] Both brought forth their most powerful indictments of modern social fragmentation in the same year, 1953, when Kirk published *The Conservative Mind* and Nisbet *The Quest for Community*.

Traditionalists and libertarians felt equally comfortable with certain economists whom both chose to honor. One was Wilhelm Roepke, an émigré from Nazi Germany who had gone to teach in Geneva and who vigorously defended both free enterprise and social custom. Roepke attacked socialist economies as much for their radicalizing effect on society as their incompatibility with individual freedom and initiative. Hayek also appealed to conservative as well as libertarian readers. In his postwar writings, the famous Austrian economist showed increasing appreciation for the evolutionary and organic view of society that he discovered in the writing of Burke. Hayek's concern with individual self-development in *The Road to Serfdom* was balanced in his later work by an increasing emphasis on the cultural and moral foundations of a free society. The widespread conservative interest in Burke went still further in bridging the distance between traditionalists and libertarians. Burke had claimed to despise revolutions but had supported American colonial grievances in the 1770s. Though a social traditionalist, he had praised the free market and had frequently cited Adam Smith's critique of mercantilism from *Wealth of Nations.*[36]

Buckley, Kendall, Chodorov, and others on the Right appealed to moral and metaphysical values as the necessary foundation of a free society. By the mid-fifties libertarians and traditionalists were embracing a synthesis of ideas that included absolute truths and personal liberty. The figure who tried hardest to build a theoretical bridge between the two was the Christian libertarian Frank Meyer. Meyer believed that his two overriding principles, freedom and moral-social authority, had already been synthesized in the founding documents of the American regime. The Founding Fathers had brought together traditions that had remained "bifurcated" in European politics: "The emphasis of virtue and value and order and the emphasis on freedom and the integrity of the individual."[37] Meyer himself justified liberty as an instrumental good and insisted that his position was in line with the authentic American political tradition of "fusionism." America's founders knew that political and personal freedoms were only beneficial for those who lived as loyal members of a community. By the same token, they recognized that only a free society allowed men to *choose* virtue, to will what is moral instead of having it imposed.

Meyer found the welfare state incompatible with both freedom and virtue. The modern "leviathan" state that Meyer despised was a product of the French Revolution's attempt to reconstruct human nature. Since the end of the eighteenth century, starting with the Age of Reason (from which Meyer always dissociated the shaping principles of the American regime), rationalists had been devising utopian schemes. In Europe these rash innovators had worked through revolution, but in America, bureaucrats and social engineers had managed to produce far-reaching social changes without political violence. The results, Meyer maintained, were similar in both cases: established patterns of community and long-accepted moral authority were sacrificed to the god of progress. Meyer believed that the activist Supreme Court under Earl Warren exemplified this tendency. An unelected body vastly exceeding the authority that the

Founding Fathers had assigned to it, the Supreme Court, as viewed by Meyer, was enacting its own vision of an integrated, secularized humanity without being accountable to any power beyond itself. The Court had no more regard for the Constitution than for the American public. It gave that document increasingly broad meanings, selectively looking for constitutional phrases that could be adapted to its reforming mission.[38]

Although Meyer thought that his historical theory would produce agreement on policy as well as principle, events proved him wrong. Some of his disciples, for example, went beyond him as advocates of individual liberty. Some emphatically rejected his views on Negro civil rights, maintaining that he had allowed his cultural prejudices to warp his judgment of the racial situation. David Brudnoy, one of his longtime disciples, expressed support for feminism and for movements aiming at black cultural self-expression. Meyer's more traditionalist admirers found him indecisive when it came to strong laws against pornography. Critics on the Right tried to elicit his libertarian opinions on censorship in the presence of young conservatives. Such a tactic, it was hoped, would lead more traditionally minded students into second thoughts about the "free-thinking Meyer"—or, better still, force Meyer into rethinking his own views.

Despite these battles, Meyer's fusionist view fitted the developing conservative vision of his time. It bestowed on that vision theoretical unity and the benefits of an extensive reading of the American and more general Western past. Although Meyer picked quarrels with traditionalists (particularly Russell Kirk) and with extreme libertarians (such as Max Eastman) and with the usually impassive James Burnham (whom he found insufficiently patriotic), he did so from the vital center of the conservative culture of the 1950s. More than anyone else, he constructed the edifice of ideas that would accommodate various conservative positions. And he achieved this not through a jerry-built structure of thought, but by carefully studying the past—albeit from his own perspective. He focused on the moral intention of America's founders and the cultural-religious traditions that had nurtured the American people. Meyer believed that most Americans inwardly accepted the fusion of positions that defined conservatism as a political force: economic libertarianism, cultural traditionalism, local government, and militant anticommunism. He insisted, until his death in 1972, that a conservative political majority would rear itself up as soon as Americans discovered what had happened to their constitutional and moral legacy.

Other conservatives accepted his fusionist view at least operationally. This is dramatically apparent from a debate that took place in *National Review* on 30 January 1962 between several members of its staff and M. Morton Auerbach, a prominent critic of postwar conservatism. Auerbach mocked the conservative worldview of the journal as a "fallacious attempt to link medievalism with classical liberalism," an error that Auerbach stated was already present in Edmund Burke.[39] The staff responded with a defense of the conservative case for ordered liberty. M. Stanton Evans, the future founder of the American Conservative Union, observed that what Auerbach called "inconsistency" was "in fact the vital equilibrium centered in the wisdom of conservatism, of the free society." Kirk, the traditionalist, maintained that the opposition to "the contemporary aggrandizement of the state" was founded on respect for "the freedom of the person." Such respect was quintessentially medieval and Christian since it presupposed human spirituality and denied power to a totalist, secular state. Meyer affirmed also that American conservatism was being consistent in fighting simultaneously for personal-material freedoms and traditional religious values: "American conservatives do not want to return to medieval conditions. They do wish, in modern conditions, to preserve and develop the tension between the transcendent ends of man and the freedom through which he can attain those ends, the tension which Western civilization has always expressed."

A fusionist view of the conservative tradition that incorporated freedom and moral-religious authority provided a common ground for Auerbach's respondents. *National Review* and *Modern Age* (a traditionalist journal founded by Kirk in 1957) may have gone too far in treating the pieces of what became the dominant conservative view as a seamless and self-evident whole. Yet, the pieces did fit together well enough to allow self-labeled conservatives who read conservative journals to agree on a common identity.

Auerbach, however, may have scored one point against his opponents on the Right. Fusionism, once triumphant among conservatives (even implicitly among Meyer's traditionalist critics), engendered political and intellectual problems that were not yet fully apparent in 1962. The mechanical yoking of religious and cultural traditionalism, free market teachings, and an activist foreign policy would result in making conservative principles appear politically partisan and inescapably modernist. T. S. Eliot foresaw this development in his correspondence with Russell Kirk. On 13 January 1956, the poet—a defender of royalism and Anglo-Catholicism—wrote in response to Kirk's request for his opinion about

National Review: "It seems to me too consciously the vehicle of a defiant minority."[40] A true conservative journal, said Eliot, would "put a good deal of emphasis on ideas and principles." In a subsequent letter to Kirk, Eliot objected to the editorial decision by *National Review* to have Joseph McCarthy (more likely a ghost writer) review the memoirs of Dean Acheson, whom McCarthy had repeatedly ridiculed in his speeches: "Such an article would carry more weight with a reader like myself if written by almost anyone else."[41]

Meyer epitomized the activist spirit on the postwar Right. Comparing conservatives to the church militant (and calling his column in *National Review* "Doctrines and Heresies"), he exhorted his readers to bring America back from the edge of catastrophe. In one particularly spirited column for *National Review,* he aimed his shafts at those who taught that the welfare state would grow smaller without the capital to pay for its programs. Such a view, Meyer, stated, made no allowance for the habits of servility that socialism instilled. The American people would rid themselves of "welfarism" only by recognizing its inhumanity: "the levelling that by reducing man to a statistical number degrades all men. . . ." Conservatives were urged to go before the public and to rally "men of spirit."[42]

The problem with such rhetoric is that it tied together all policy decisions with the overriding moral goals of "saving the Republic" and Western civilization. Proceeding from his fusionist understanding of politics, Meyer attached cosmic implications to every issue that he wrote on. Fiscal questions were raised to philosophic-existential issues as part of a struggle for the soul of mankind. The good side, as much as the bad, in this struggle held views that were seen as being of a piece. Meyer viewed his own fusionism as a true wedding of liberty and moral order. Any calm reflection on "politics' principles, or lack of principles" of the kind that Eliot recommended, went against Meyer's very nature.

In the late 1960s Meyer wrote against George Wallace's attempt to run a presidential campaign based on economic programs and opposition to liberal social policies. Although Meyer favored a populist revolt against social engineering, he considered Wallace an inappropriate leader for such a movement. He denounced Wallace, together with main-line Democrats, as unsuited to govern America and as "alien to the American conservative conception of constitutional republican government."[43] In 1968 Meyer took the view that all philosophically and politically sound conservatives were, like him, supporting the presidential bid of Richard M. Nixon. Noting the "civilizational crisis of 1968" unleashed by urban riot, he maintained that "Nixon's administration will turn the tide of the anarchy that threatens to engulf us."[44] The expressions "civilizational content" and "civilizational consensus" invariably accompanied Meyer's statements of political preference.

The appeal to activism became an integral part of postwar conservatism. Almost all of *National Review*'s staff participated in political campaigns: for example, Frank Meyer as vice-chairman of the New York Conservative party; William Rusher as an advisor to Barry Goldwater; and William Buckley as a candidate for mayor of New York City in 1965. This activist enthusiasm even spread into the ranks of traditionalists. A repugnance for modern political life had been characteristic of the early Richard Weaver. Although Weaver did write for *National Review, Modern Age,* and the publications of the Intercollegiate Society of Individualists, he felt little hope for the modern world of mass democracy and the cult of technology. In one (now famous) elegiac passage from the foreword to his book *Ideas Have Consequences,* Weaver offers this lament: "It seems to me that the world is now more than ever dominated by the gods of mass and speed and that the worship of these can lead only to the lowering of standards, the adulteration of quality, and, in general, to the loss of these things which are essential to the life of civility and culture."[45] The author of these lines (written in 1947) would ten years later be participating in citizens' councils in order to resist the forced introduction of racial integration into Southern schools. Another Southern conservative and antimodernist, Donald Davidson, the scholar and poet, took a similar position in the fifties. Like Weaver, his old student, Davidson opposed what he considered the equalizing, bureaucratic state through a gesture that he believed would have no real political significance. Davidson poignantly described his own plight, as a poet and "outright traditionalist," predicting "the ruin of modern, secularized society," while being "unheard or unheeded." All that he had was "the poet's curse," which he invoked "upon the deaf ears and faceless bodies" around him.[46]

Although expressions of futility can also be found in *The Conservative Mind,* Kirk became more involved in politics than either Weaver or Davidson, whether as a delegate to Republican state conventions in Michigan or as a supporter of Barry Goldwater. Others on Kirk's side went well beyond him in pursuing political agendas. In 1962 traditionalist intellectuals set up the New York Conservative party, a group founded in accordance with their ideology. By the 1960s postwar conservatism had become a political movement that tried to appeal to members of both national parties, by defending economic liberty and traditional social values and by opposing the expansion of Soviet communism. The activist phase that conservatism entered by the 1960s changed it significantly—and sometimes in ways that offended the theorists of the forties and fifties. This activism, however, was already implicit in the worldview of the *Freeman* and in articles printed in *National Review* and *Modern Age*. Although the first generation of postwar conservatives found much to deplore about the present time, they believed things could be set right. They themselves took the initiative when they moved from theory into practice.

Chapter Two

Before and after Goldwater: Conservatism in the Sixties

The conservative movement of the 1960s was held together more by ideological concerns than by economic interests. It is true that conservatives did appeal to opponents of an expanding welfare system by demanding harder eligibility tests for welfare recipients; they also advocated economic deregulation and spoke nostalgically of an older capitalist America. Despite such rhetoric, bankers and industrialists, outside of areas in the South and Southwest, withheld their support from candidates with "conservative party" labels.[1] In 1964 their preferred Republican presidential candidate was not the conservative Barry Goldwater but the more liberal Nelson Rockefeller.[2] Big business feared the election of visionary conservatives who might have threatened its working relations with government agencies. Though conservatives called for lightening the tax burden related to welfare, their programs, as many discovered, had another side. Their political candidates made no secret of their commitment to a strong military and to a more vigorous struggle against Soviet power.

Like the Socialists and Catholics in the German Empire between 1871 and 1918 whose party affiliations signified the acceptance of a worldview, the American conservatives of the 1960s based politics on a shared moral universe. They thought that elected office was a means for attaining ideological goals, not one for furthering material interests. In this respect, conservatives foreshadowed their leftist counterparts of the late sixties, who also came largely from the professional and leisure classes. Both groups disavowed the interest politics James Madison had once viewed as natural, and even beneficent, for the American regime; each preferred to offer the American people a politics of ideas. Moreover, Right and Left in the 1960s turned for principles and programs to engaged intellectuals grouped around journals and universities.

The Campus Right

Seymour Martin Lipset helped to formulate the standard opinion in a study of student politics in the 1960s, when he associated right-wing student activism predominantly with small church-affiliated colleges. This assumption was based on reliable data found in an investigation by Richard G. Braungart of student activism in the sixties. The largest conservative campus organization (founded in 1961), Young Americans for Freedom, drew fewer members from state universities and prestige institutions of higher learning than did its far-Left counterpart, Students for a Democratic Society. Unlike SDS, YAF was heavily represented in sectarian colleges and among students who professed religious allegiances. Lipset and Braungart also point out that YAF members generally were poorer and more vocationally oriented than student activists on the Left.[3]

Whatever its other merits, such information does not explain the origins of a conservative political movement on American campuses. Such a development began in large, widely respected universities, among faculty and students with a deeply theoretical bent. For example, the University of Chicago played a formative role in creating a conservative movement as well as a conservative worldview. The economics department contained outstanding defenders of capitalism such as Friedman, Knight, and George Stigler. Richard Weaver taught English and rhetoric in the University College; Friedrich von Hayek lectured on social philosophy to both undergraduates and graduate students; and another Central European émigré at Chicago, who occupied an endowed chair in political thought, Leo Strauss, attacked "value-relativity" as the mortal sin of the American intelligentsia. Friedman, Hayek, and Strauss all underlined the importance of putting sound teachings into political practice, and their students went into government as well as academic careers.

By the late fifties, Yale University was becoming another training ground for conservative activists. In the late forties, Willmoore Kendall had taught political philosophy there to the young William Buckley, just returned from military service. Though Buckley, in his first published book, *God and Man at Yale* (1952), protested the pervasive liberalism of the Yale professoriate, he nonetheless had kind words for Kendall. At Yale Buckley and his future brother-in-law Brent Bozell set about organizing the Conservative party in the Political Union. What began primarily as a discussion group of politically like-minded students that debated other such groups became a vehicle for preparing future conservative activists.[4] The same was even more true for the Party of the Right, an offshoot of Yale's Conservative party. Out of the Party of the Right came new contributors to *National Review* and eventually New Right activists of the seventies and eighties such as Anthony Dolan, Ron Docksai, and Larry Uzzell.[5]

In the 1960s Catholic universities, such as Fordham and St. John's in New York and Notre Dame, were especially important as centers of conservative activity. Fordham and St. John's provided support for both the postwar Burke revival and the organization of the New York Conservative party. Notre Dame was the focal point of a Catholic-conservative synthesis of thought to which publications such as the *Natural Law Forum,* the *Review of Politics,* and later, the *New Scholasticism* were intended to contribute. Behind these journals stood committed Catholics or Anglo-Catholics who complained of the moral decline of the West. They saw communist expansion as the nemesis of the West's spiritual decreptitude and of the lack of political will among its leaders. Waldemar Gurian, Stephen Kertesz, the Reverend Stanley Parry, and Gerhard Niemeyer, all political science professors, and Clarence Manion and Charles Rice of the law school represented these conservative tendencies among the Notre Dame faculty. The same tendencies could be found at the University of Dallas, which in the 1970s became a self-declared citadel of Catholic and traditional values. There Willmoore Kendall went to teach (and was converted to Catholicism) after years of social isolation at Yale. Disciples of Leo Strauss and of Richard Weaver graced the faculty at Dallas; the political science department boasted not only Kendall but Frederick Wilhelmsen, a conservative Catholic critic of secular democracy and one of the more provocative contributors to *National Review.* The University of Dallas also had one of the largest and most influential chapters of Young Americans for Freedom.

This brings us to a critical link between the early history of the conservative political movement, including its student phase, and the Catholic affiliation of many of its members. Of YAFers polled in the mid-sixties, 69 percent turned out to be Protestant, 26 percent Catholic, and only 5 percent Jewish. Among Leftist student activists whom the sociologist Richard Flacks interviewed in 1967, 60 percent had Jewish fathers, 36 percent were Protestant, and only 4 percent were Catholic.[6] Although social position may be one possible key to grasping the correlation between religious background and political affiliation (most Jewish left-wing activists came from wealthier, better educated families than their Christian conservative counterparts), one should not exaggerate the role of this particular variable. The members of the Harvard Conservative Club and of the Yale Party of the Right were by no means socially inferior to the SDSers at Wisconsin or Michigan. Moreover, one-sixth of the Jewish student activists whom the sociologist Samuel Lubell studied came from recognizable Old Left families, mostly of Eastern European origin.[7] The conservative students polled in another extensive study were mostly self-identifying members of churches, and, unlike SDS members, "felt a close relationship with one or both of their parents." The attitudes of these students cannot be entirely explained by looking to the professional or material standing of their parents.[8]

The Catholic Right

The Catholic presence in the conservative student movement was not only proportionately larger than the Protestant one but also more vital for that movement's growth. The association of conservative students with small, mostly Protestant colleges may come from identifying too closely right-wing campus activism with a predominant type of rank-and-file member. In the early sixties, the Intercollegiate Society of Individualists introduced conservative clubs on college campuses across the country. M. Stanton Evans has described the efforts of regional directors of ISI, most conspicuously Don Lipsett in Indianapolis, to carry its literature and ideas across the American heartland.[9] Small, sectarian colleges responded favorably to this attention. Conservative clubs were formed there that placed themselves on ISI mailing lists and often voted to join YAF. But these hastily won recruits were mostly passive and typified what S. M. Lipset thought was characteristic of conservative student organizations generally: "They have not been notably successful in building a movement which has much commitment from its membership, nor have they made any real impact on the campus."[10]

In fact, the most significant form of conservative student activism did not aim at converting large state universities. Conservative students went into government and journalism and campaigned for conservative political candidates. In all these activities, Catholic students, many from

Catholic colleges, made disproportionately large contributions. The post-war Right awaited them with open arms. *National Review* was accused by its critics of being militantly Catholic, a charge bitterly raised by Max Eastman before he resigned from its board. Even the Jewish editors, Meyer and Schlamm, were sympathetic to Catholic doctrine: Meyer became a Catholic on his deathbed; and Schlamm requested that a priest officiate at his funeral. The journal published the Catholic monarchists Otto von Habsburg and Erik von Kuehnelt-Leddihn; it also featured both Catholic traditionalists who were critical of the American democratic experiment, such as Wilhelmsen, Bozell, and Thomas Molnar, and such Catholic defenders of the American regime as Clare Booth Luce and members of the Buckley family.

Unlike the vestigial secularist connection of Jewish Leftists to things Jewish, Catholic conservatives wore their religious identity as a badge of honor. Non-Catholic conservatives praised the church as an upholder of moral absolutes and, more generally, of Western civilization. The Jewish religious commentator for *National Review,* Will Herberg, even attacked the efforts at "modernizing" church rituals under Pope John XXIII. According to Herberg, Catholics who welcomed change in their ancient ceremonies were like Esau, selling their spiritual birthright for a pot of lentils.

The philo-Catholic attributes of the intellectual Right were related to the largely justified image of the postwar church as anticommunist and antisecularist. Catholicism may also have seemed more congruent with the emerging conservative movement than were most Protestant denominations. Throughout the twentieth century, the leadership of main-line Protestant churches had drifted to the Left, theologically and politically. The more traditional American Protestants—such as Southern Baptists and Missouri Synod Lutherans—were widely perceived as rigidly biblicist and culturally narrow. Such groups often held isolationist views of foreign policy that jarred with the anticommunist activism of the postwar Right.

Conservative political strategists became convinced that Catholics were especially receptive to their positions. Several factors contributed to that perception. The Catholic hierarchy in America and in Europe were generally outspoken anticommunists; this situation was related to, among other things, the persecution of Catholics, particularly Catholic clergymen, under the Soviet-controlled states of Eastern Europe. American Catholics were also more outwardly religious than their fellow citizens.[11] According to Gallup polls in the fifties and sixties, the percentage of Catholics who regularly attended religious services was over twice as high as the percentage for Protestants and over three times as high as the one for Jews. [12] Polling on the abortion question started in 1963 (during the furor over deformed babies whose mothers had taken thalidomide drugs); it revealed far greater Catholic than Protestant opposition to the use of abortion, even in extreme circumstances. [13]

More importantly, the backlash against liberal social policies erupted first, outside the South, in Catholic ethnic neighborhoods. In 1961 Irish Americans supported Louise Day Hicks, a Democrat opposed to forced busing, as chairman of the Boston School Board. In 1964 Irish and other Catholic voters in Massachusetts enthusiastically backed George Wallace, the former segregationist governor of Alabama, during his first foray into the North in the Democratic presidential primaries. Racial tensions, court-ordered busing, and a dramatic leap in the number of violent crimes in the 1960s made the traditionally Democratic Catholic communities in Northern Cities appear to be at the point of moving permanently to the Right.

New York Conservative Party

The first group that tried to arrange a match between the postwar conservative worldview and a preponderantly Catholic constituency was the New York Conservative party. The Party's "Declaration of Principles," in February 1962, opened with a statement that combined libertarian and anticommunist themes: "Our country is strong, and everywhere it is in retreat before Soviet Communism. It was founded and grew great on the free energy of free men and everywhere encroaching bureaucracy overpowers and strangles the free energy of free men." The declaration also deplored "so-called liberalism" that rendered national leaders less able "to resist the onrush of Communist conquest or to stem the subtle tide of bureaucratic socialism." To resist the foreign enemy and domestic evils, the declaration called for the reestablishment of the conservative principles of liberty, justice, and national vigilance and the vigorous pursuit of a program consonant with these principles. [14]

The Conservative party featured among its founders prominent Catholic traditionalists such as Daniel Mahoney, Henry Paolucci, and Thomas Molnar. Another cofounder, Frank Meyer, was sympathetic to the Catholic Right. Essential to the declaration is its appeal to voters as churched members of family units. The Conservative party's founders were appealing to social and moral concerns as well as pocketbook issues. Not individuals but "the fabric of society was threatened by the mounting wave of crime." The Conservative party of New York was not simply a taxpayers' league that used anticommunist rhetoric to widen its appeal. It opposed the welfare system for, among other things, the same reason it protested crime on the streets: as a symptom and cause of social degeneracy. In attacking Aid to Families with Dependent Children, for example, the declaration criticized not the awarding of the grant but the fact that it entailed no social responsibility on the part of its recipient. The welfare mother was free to spend the money as she pleased, without being forced to use the grant on the child rather than herself. The declaration urged not that the granting of such aid be stopped but that it take place in the form of food and other necessities given directly to the child. Moreover, the same document states that if the welfare mother lives in "blatant immorality," then the state should remove the child from her care and place it (if possible) with more suitable parents.

Such proposals indicate that the New York Conservative party never viewed itself as being strictly libertarian in dealing with domestic matters. A sense of man's corporate nature—and of the power of original sin—informed the Declaration of Principles. The declaration took stands on First Amendment issues that had particularly strong appeal among Catholic voters: in favor of aid to parochial schools and in opposition to pornography. Its support of "religious observance in our public life" may also have been intended to attract the same voters; Catholics in the fifties and sixties, in responding to surveys, were far more supportive than Protestants of a religious influence being brought to bear on society. Although most of the votes involved were middle-class Republican rather than blue-collar Democratic, 25 to 30 percent of the ballots in Catholic Assembly districts in New York City went to William F. Buckley, the Conservative party's candidate for mayor, in 1965. In 1967 the Party received 71,477 votes statewide, of which 33,747 came from New York City. These votes were predominantly from non-Hispanic Catholics in Brooklyn and Queens registering concern over welfare programs and crime in their neighborhoods.[15]

Republican Majority

Despite this attempt to build an urban conservative constituency upon a Catholic ethnic base, such a strategy played no appreciable role in the conservatives' quest for the presidency in the early sixties. In 1961 conservative Republican activists, led by F. Clifton White and William

Rusher, formed a committee to work for the election of a conservative president. From the start, their choices were exceedingly limited. White, Rusher, and their group—who by the end of 1961 were head-quartered in the Clarion Building, suite 3505, in midtown Manhattan—sought an electable candidate who was both an uncompromising critic of the welfare state and an anticommunist interventionist. Senator William Knowland of California was a prominent conservative who fit this de-scription. But in 1958 Knowland abandoned his Senate seat (for nonpo-litical reasons) to seek the governorship of California—which he failed to gain. In 1960 a conservative academician, John Tower, won a Senate seat from Texas. Although conservatives considered Tower insufficiently prominent to be a plausible presidential candidate, they book his election as a sign of their growing strength in the Southwest.[16]

An essay by William Rusher published in *National Review* on 12 Feb-ruary 1963 lent credibility to such thinking. Rusher maintained that con-servative Republicans could capture the presidency by winning the demographically expanding South and West, even without the Northeast and Upper Midwest.[17] Rusher, and others who were swayed by him, stressed two factors: a growing Republican vote in the once Democratic South as the national Democratic party moved to the Left and embraced unreservedly the civil rights movement; and the shift of population from the more liberal North and East into the more conservative South and West. Rusher's arguments, in some ways, anticipated those of Kevin Phillips, who in *The Emerging Republican Majority* (1969) plotted a Re-publican strategy centered on the Sunbelt and the West.

But the difference between Phillips's views and Rusher's apparent an-ticipation of them may be as significant as their oft-noted similarity. Un-like Rusher, Phillips urged Republicans and conservatives to campaign vigorously in Northern cities as well as in the South and West. A North-ern Irish Catholic and a former conservative student activist, Phillips viewed the ethnic Catholics in Northern cities and suburbs as prospective converts to the political Right. He proposed a new political coalition that would include both Sunbelt Republican and Democratic ethnics. The ar-chitects of this coalition would appeal to traditional family values and hos-tility to the counterculture and its allies in government. Phillips's model politicians would abandon anti–New Deal rhetoric and uphold the welfare state, as the price of maintaining close ties with blue-collar workers. Phillips addressed his prescription to the Republican party, which he urged to move economically to the Left and socially to the Right. He offered such advice with the benefit of hindsight, when the miscalculations of the conservative politics of the mid-sixties could already be assessed.[18]

Goldwater and After

In April 1963, White, Rusher, and their financial backers, who came predominantly from the Sunbelt, chose a Senator from Arizona, Barry Goldwater, as their presidential candidate. The group thereupon transformed itself into the Draft Goldwater Committee. According to White, Rusher, and William F. Buckley (then a nonaffiliated member of the committee), Goldwater tried long and vehemently to dissociate himself from his backers. He never believed that he could win the presidency, especially after John F. Kennedy's assassination in November 1963. Later, his presidential campaign became mired in divisive quarrels with the liberal wing of his party led by Governor Nelson Rockefeller of New York. Having emerged from party primaries with an extremist label, Goldwater spent the fall of 1964 desperately responding to the same charges from his Democratic opponent that the Rockefeller forces had leveled against him during the spring. His dissent from the 1964 Civil Rights Act—on the ground that its public-accommodations provision infringed on property rights—was construed as crass support for racism, although Goldwater had long attacked antiblack discrimination. His critical remarks during a campaign speech about public ownership of the Tennessee Valley Authority allowed him to be depicted as a reckless, indiscriminate opponent of New Deal programs. His insistence that the American government prosecute the war in Vietnam more vigorously (or leave) became for his political and journalistic adversaries proof of his belligerence.[19]

Surveying Goldwater's presidential bid, which culminated in his losing to Johnson by a margin of nearly 16 million votes and being beaten in all but six states (five in the Deep South), White observes: "It was not Republicanism that was beaten so badly in 1964, nor even the real Barry Goldwater. It was radicalism; or rather the illusion of radicalism as represented by a cruel caricature of the candidate."[20] Although White blames the Goldwater defeat partly on the effectively vicious tactics of the Johnson campaign, he also recognizes the role of historical forces. Republican opponents of the welfare state were too open in their contempt for Great Society programs: "What many of them failed to take into account was that in the latter half of the twentieth century practically everyone wanted, indeed *expected,* something from the government and large numbers of them were perfectly willing to trade their votes in order to get what they wanted."[21] Seen from this perspective, "Lyndon Johnson was a conservative defending the established order, while Barry Goldwater, the true conservative, became a 'radical' bent on upsetting the applecart of peace and plenty." Apart from using the phrase "true conservative" to apply to Goldwater, White's analysis foreshadows the view held by neoconservatives of the seventies and eighties looking back at the contest of 1964.

William Rusher may have been right in calling 1964 the "watershed year" in postwar conservatism. Goldwater was personally unable to represent the full range of postwar conservative thinking; nor was the historical moment propitious for anyone to do so. His campaign was narrowly focused on a few economic and foreign-policy issues and on invidious questions that journalists and politicians raised about his moral and intellectual competence. Even if one allows for the vulgarizing process that turns philosophic principles into electoral issues, the intellectual richness of the postwar Right, typified by James Burnham, Frank S. Meyer, Friedrich Hayek, and Russell Kirk, was notably missing from the Goldwater campaign. As one traditionalist critic, Craig Schiller, observed, Goldwater went down to defeat as the brutally wronged but inept candidate of the "Hoover-Taft" wing of his party. The charge is just, even if Schiller is inaccurate about Hoover and Taft.[22] Although Goldwater characterized Russell Kirk as his favorite philosopher and was in turn praised by Kirk for his anticommunist foreign policy, Goldwater could never shake his image as a brash defender of unqualified capitalism. Kevin Phillips criticized Goldwater and his campaign managers for paying insufficient attention to the Northern cities, particularly their (non-Hispanic) Catholic voters. Despite the rightward lurch of Northern ethnics in the Democratic primaries of 1964, according to Phillips, "when November's votes were counted, the backlash was exceedingly weak. Boston and Baltimore wards that had gone heavily for Louise Day Hicks and George Wallace went six- and eight-to-one against Barry Goldwater."[23] Phillips correctly inferred that "[w]hatever the appeal of the 1964 GOP nominee's civil rights stance, it was outweighed by the unpopularity of his position on labor legislation, aspects of the Social Security system and economic issues in general (none of which handicapped free-spending populist Democrats like Mrs. Hicks and Governor Wallace)."

After 1964 no "conservative" politician would speak as explicitly as Goldwater had about rescinding the New Deal. Republicans would denounce further deficit spending, extol individual self-reliance, and call for trimming budgets. "Conservative" politicians would repeatedly seek votes by deploring the growth of bureaucracy. Yet, the obvious lesson of 1964 would not be forgotten. The majority of the American electorate voted for the welfare state and against its unabashed critic. This electoral fact according with the findings of Gallup and other polls in 1964, that most Americans favored the continuation of existing federal social programs and supporting the Civil Rights Act of that year. A Gallup poll of rank-and-file Republicans on 13 January 1965 revealed that their top priorities were to replace Goldwaterites, such as Dean Burch and Richard Kleindienst, in positions of party leadership and to adopt a "more moderate" platform.[24] These opinions are noteworthy even if one takes into account the bitter aftertaste of the 1964 election.

Conservative writers, particularly William Rusher and Jeffrey Hart, have tried to show the Goldwater campaign was subsequently vindicated. It produced an expanding core of Rightist activists whose principles triumphed in Ronald Reagan's election in 1980.[25] This interpretation is only half true. The 1964 presidential race created a wave of conservative political activism that continued to grow and shows no signs of receding. Coextensively with this, conservative foundations that dealt with policy questions and electoral strategies were launched. Yet, two characteristics of what has been termed "second-generation, postwar conservatism" were its lack of a philosophic (and certainly traditionalist) focus and its willingness to compromise (without admitting it) with a leftward-drifting public opinion. The traditionalist aspect of the conservative movement— represented by Kirk's Burkean defense of organic authority or Weaver's agrarian anticommercial values—had become politically irrelevant by 1964. In the 1970s even Goldwaterism became politically passé. Goldwater's *The Conscience of a Conservative* (1960), which was avidly distributed by his backers in 1964, was mostly a statement of its author's positions on leading political issues: states' rights, welfare, closed shops imposed by organized labor, and the "Soviet menace." Though Goldwater properly accused the Left of being fixated "on the material side of man's nature," it is unclear whether his own declaration of belief differed in this respect. For example, he insisted that the American educational system be limited to the "training of the mind," through the transmission of factual knowledge without moral or philosophical values.[26] His stated conviction that the formation of values takes place exclusively in the family and in churches was not the purely defensive reaction to growing liberal control of education that many of Goldwater's traditionalist supporters imagined it to be. It betokened the secularist, technocratic cast of his thinking that became more pronounced in the seventies and eighties, particularly in his bitter comments against the advocates of school prayers. Goldwater by the seventies also came to advocate environmentalist restrictions. He shocked his old backers even more by defending the Supreme Court's imposition of judicial remedies to fight the effects of antiblack discrimination.[27]

Goldwaterism in its pristine form may have vanished with the challenge that Congressman John Ashbrook of Ohio mounted in 1972 against President Nixon. Dissatisfied with Nixon's policy of detente and support of a national family-assistance plan, the American Conservative Union and several veterans of the Draft Goldwater Committee induced Ashbrook to oppose Nixon in the Republican primaries. Ashbrook, an unreconstructed Goldwaterite, never gained more than 10 percent of the vote in any primary; he withdrew from the race in June 1972. Although the weakness of his presidential campaign has often been attributed to the fact that Ashbrook challenged an incumbent of his own party, this explanation is too pat. Eugene McCarthy jolted an incumbent president in the Democratic primaries of 1968 because he found a liberal, antiwar constituency. Ashbrook found no corresponding constituency on the Right: most conservatives could live with Nixon, albeit with a certain amount of grumbling. Indeed, some of them—such as Jeffrey Hart, a senior editor of *National Review,* and Patrick Buchanan—wrote speeches for him. The support was not entirely one-sided: establishment Republicans, particularly Nixon, went out of their way to hire conservative journalists. Such people served as liaisons to the embattled Republican Right and helped justify the shifting administration policies to conservative purists.

If postwar conservatism has been a series of movements rather than the orderly unfolding of a single force, the Goldwater campaign is the most crucial turning point in its history. Goldwater's acquisition of the Republican presidential nomination dramatized the political power of the postwar Right. It also mobilized masses of supporters. Before Goldwater's appearance on the national scene, observed William Rusher and James Burnham, there were no more than about a hundred conservative activists, mostly centered on *National Review.*[28] After 1964 there were tens of thousands ready to mobilize behind other conservative candidates for high office. Although this analysis may not take account of the right-wing campus activism of the late fifties and early sixties, it is correct about the catalytic effect of 1964 in engendering a conservative mass movement.

The Goldwater campaign, however, hurt the older conservatism in two ways: by equating its social philosophy almost entirely with free enterprise; and contributing to a conservative movement more concerned with electoral victories than unifying principles.[29] The multitude of activists, once assembled, became the major force among conservatives. A movement that Kirk, citing T. S. Eliot, hoped would fight for the "permanent things" became increasingly concerned with opinion polls and electoral majorities. And since both the welfare state and coexistence with Soviet tyranny were perceived to be the will of the American people—including a majority of Republicans—conservative activists were forced to seek victory by being discreetly critical of the status quo.[30]

Even before the Goldwater Republicans were leading conservatives into political activism, the fusionism of the late fifties began to disintegrate. In 1961 two alumni of the Circle Bastiat, Ralph Raico and Ronald Hamowy, joined fellow students at the University of Chicago in forming the *New Individualist Review* under the auspices of the Chicago chapter of the ISI. Raico was made editor, Hamowy the book review editor, and the three advisors were Milton Friedman, Friedrich Hayek, and Richard Weaver. Over the next few years the individualist students would put out the most consistently, interesting conservative publication of the sixties. The journal published articles by Friedman and Hayek as well as by such younger libertarians as Leonard Liggio, Murray Rothbard, and the editors themselves. Contributions were also made by the antiwar historian Harry Elmer Barnes and the isolationist congressman Howard Buffett.

Seeking to bridge the widening gap between libertarians and conservatives, the editors also solicited pieces from Russell Kirk, Richard Weaver, and economist Wilhelm Roepke. Even so, it was not long before the strain became apparent. In the third issue, Hamowy squared off with the editor of *National Review* over the journal's claim to the conservative label. Hamowy accused Buckley and his associates of perpetrating a "revolution within the form," contending that while the older right had been antigovernment and isolationist, this new right was willing to sacrifice all the old principles for the anticommunist crusade. Hamowy observed that, despite invocations of Christian natural law, Buckley and his friends were willing to support brutal socialist dictators for reasons of state. Moreover, they had come to favor conscription and had blunted their criticisms of state intervention in the economy.

Buckley made a typically witty reply in the form of "Three Drafts of an Answer to Mr. Hamowy," in which he denied (without entirely rebutting) the charges. He was able to point to the individualists still writing for his magazine and accused Hamowy of being a member of SANE. In answering the more general accusation that his magazine had gone statist, Buckley repeated his 1952 argument that "it becomes necessary to forfeit a part of the freedom one might ideally exercise, in order to secure the greater part of our freedom."

Hamowy was unimpressed by both the wit and the argument. In a response published in *New Individualist Review,* he denied being a member of SANE, politely declined to be grateful to Buckley for protecting less-expansive freedoms, and added that the individualists at *National Review* were not "consistent conservatives in the Buckley tradition."

Hamowy, it seems, had made his case all too well. *New Individualist Review* subsequently decided to ban discussions of foreign policy from its pages, and some years later the sponsoring organization, the Intercollegiate Society of Individualists, changed its name to the Intercollegiate Studies Institute, thereby severing itself from its founders' libertarian ideals.

What particularly irritated Hamowy and other individualists was the growing shadow cast on American conservatism by the European Catholic Right. In the genial liberal monarchist Erik von Kuehnelt-Leddihn they could see only the dark forces of medievalism and were unable to distinguish between the relatively benign statism of the Old Order and the newer and more rigorous statisms of the twentieth century. The young libertarians preferred to see themselves as rebels against an oppressive regime, rather than as defenders of an historic civilization. More to the point was their suspicion that *National Review* was gradually moving away from its commitment to limited government and moving in the direction of the probusiness, anticommunist, Republican party moderates who had learned to profit from the New Deal.

More radical libertarians, Leonard Liggio in particular, had never signed on to *National Review*'s fusionism, and by the mid-sixties Liggio and Rothbard were attempting to find common ground with antiwar Democrats and Leftists. Rothbard, who had backed Adlai Stevenson in 1960, became a leading member of the League of Stevensonian Democrats, and in 1965 he and Liggio created (along with George Resch) *Left and Right: A Journal of Libertarian Thought.* The purpose, as Rothbard recalled later, was "to influence libertarians throughout the country to break with the Right-wing and to ally themselves with the emerging New Left . . . and secondly, to 'find' the New Left ourselves as a group to ally with and possibly influence." In a series of articles for the new journal, Liggio constructed a revisionist account of recent history that not only restored the isolationism of the Old Right to center stage but also put it into the left-wing framework set up by William Appleman Williams in his critiques of American imperialism.

Throughout the sixties and early seventies the editors of *Left and Right* moved steadily leftward, championing black militancy, condemning conservative traditionalists for their fealty to European aristocracy and Southern slavocracy, and lamenting the death of Che Guevara. The journal's impact was considerable. Many young conservatives all over the country were radicalized, and one entire YAF chapter (University of Kansas) went over to SDS. Ronald Hamowy was able to tout the left-right coalition's positions in a *New Republic* article, and in 1967 former SDS President Carl Oglesby adopted the Rothbard-Liggio line on the Old Right in an attack on the Vietnam War co-authored with Richard Shaull, *Containment and Change.*[31] The libertarians and the New Left needed each other, warned Oglesby, if the one was to escape the imperialism of the right and if the other was not to revert to Stalinism.

Karl Hess, a Goldwater speechwriter, gravitated toward the left-right alliance before going all the way into radical anarchism. In 1969 Rothbard and Hess were instrumental in forming the Radical Libertarian Alliance, which participated in a series of meetings and exchanges—not always fruitful—with the student Left.

As many young libertarians made common cause with the Left, they also ran the risk of becoming Leftists, pure and simple. Yet, the New Left never fulfilled its early promise as an individualist movement, and its more radical factions went well beyond Oglesby's warning against Stalinism. The libertarians, however, were not reabsorbed into the mainstream Right, and their alienation led some into the third-party politicking that resulted in the formation of the Libertarian party in the seventies. Others had already been drawn into the overheated little world of the "Ayn Rand cult."[32]

Ayn Rand was, herself, a strange figure. Along with her Russian Jewish family, she had survived the revolution but became dissatisfied with life in the USSR. Inspired by the hope of prospering in the west as an author of fiction, she decided to emigrate to America. There she took the name Rand, which she had found on a Remington Rand typewriter. A moderately talented writer, this Russian émigré soon enjoyed some success as a playwright and Hollywood scriptwriter, but with the publication of *The Fountainhead* and *Atlas Shrugged,* she gained acclaim as a voice for individualism and the virtue of selfishness. Never a serious intellectual, Rand was profoundly influenced by two older women writers,

Isabel Paterson and Rose Wilder Lane, whose ideas she borrowed without acknowledgment.[33] She also borrowed the conception of her bloated
novel *Atlas Shrugged* from Garet Garrett, down to such details as the
name of her hero and the opening sentence, "Who is Henry Galt?" asks
the narrator in Garrett's *The Driver.*[34] (She later accused her mentors of
stealing from *her.*)[35]

Rand's message was simple and appealing: All virtues stem from individual creativity, and it is the egotistical pursuit of self-interest that is
responsible for all the greatest achievements; however, in the twentieth
century mass democracy, egalitarianism, and the altruistic ideals of
Christianity have all conspired against the individual genius. There was
enough truth in the message to make *The Fountainhead* a best-selling
novel and a profitable movie (starring Gary Cooper), but there would
have been no movement (much less a cult) without the contributions
made by Rand's chief disciple and lover, Nathaniel Branden and his wife
Barbara.

Under the Brandens' influence Rand moved to New York, where she
attracted a following, whose inner circle was dominated by the Canadian
Jewish relatives of the Brandens. The most successful member of the
Randian inner circle, Alan Greenspan (eventually head of the Federal
Reserve), was related by marriage to Joan Mitchell, who later married
Barbara Branden's cousin, Allan Blumenthal.

The Ayn Rand circle soon developed all the apparatus of a political cult.
Through lectures and her newsletter *The Objectivist* Rand was able to
lay down a party line on everything from economics to music and literature. Her own strange tastes—she loved Rachmaninoff and Mickey Spil-
lane—became law, and every minor decision made by group members
had to be justified by the strange rationality of objectivism. Branden, by
now a practicing psychotherapist, was empowered to practice his skills
on the members to liberate them from residual subjectivities. These individual and group therapy sessions became an important part of the
movement and gave Rand and the Brandens effective control over the
personal lives of their followers.

On objectivist grounds, Rothbard (only a fellow-traveler in the group)
was told to divorce his Christian wife, and it was on objectivist grounds
that Greenspan was able to fire his Randian secretary, who had asked
for a raise. On appeal to the inner circle, the secretary not only lost but
was expelled from the movement. When Edith Efron was expelled from
the movement, her Randian assistant at *TV Guide* was instructed not to
speak to Efron except on business.

The bizarre sex lives of the movement leaders, documented in a series of self-service books by both Brandens, were the immediate cause of the movement's breakup. The married Rand, shocked to discover that Branden had betrayed her as well as his wife, read Nathaniel and then Barbara out of the movement, and denounced her former chief disciple for laziness, dishonesty, and deviation from the true principles of objectivism. Many Randians were alienated by the sudden change and the nastiness with which Rand conducted her purges, but even without this soap-opera episode the movement was doomed. Rand had expelled or alienated all the first-rate members (with the exception of Greenspan, who did not discuss economics with Rand), and the movement's cohesiveness can only be explained on psychological, not philosophical, grounds. Nonetheless, Rand's novels remain the most popular conservative books published in America, and her former friends, disciples, groupies, and fellow travelers went on to hold positions of influence.[36]

In the 1970s many Randians became active in the Libertarian party, which for several years gave the appearance of being an effective third-party challenge. The party was founded in Denver in 1971 by David and Susan Nolan and a number of friends, all of them alarmed by President Nixon's imposition of wage and price controls. Among the earliest libertarians attracted to the party were philosophy professor John Hospers, investment adviser Edward Crane, and New York corporate attorney Edward Clark. Hospers, as the first Libertarian party presidential candidate, received fewer than 4,000 votes, but the party received national attention when Roger MacBride, a Republican elector from Virginia, cast his vote for Hospers.

From the beginnings the movement was plagued with dissensions. Many Southern libertarians were something akin to classical Republicans and defenders of the Second Amendment, but the party mainstream was divided between anarchocapitalists, who were opposed to all forms of the state, and the Randian "monarchists," who thought some state functions were essential. This disagreement was papered over by the Dallas Accord of 1974, at which the party's platform committee agreed to refrain from endorsing either state action or anarchism. The Dallas Accord remained an operating principle of the party, but it could not heal the deeper fissures that were social rather than psychological.

Libertarianism (like anarchism) has always attracted a significant number of misfits, but it was not long before a conflict surfaced between the underemployed countercultural element and the "conservatives" in business suits who contributed most of the money, ideas, and organization.

In the convention for the election of 1976, Roger MacBride was selected as the presidential nominee over the objection of the more freewheeling element who objected to his conventional clothes and patrician demeanor. The real fight, however, was over his running mate. Bypassing McBride's selection, the rebels put forward first an unemployed tax rebel and second the proprietor of a gay bar. According to Murray Rothbard, philosopher Robert Nozick had put forward the argument that while the party was not morally obliged to pick a homosexual, it could not refuse to support a gay candidate once his name was put forward. In the late eighties Rothbard and many of his allies left the party, which by then had become a negligible force even in the eccentric politics of the Right.

The Nixon Dilemma

In 1968 Governor George Wallace of Alabama, running as a third-party candidate in the presidential race, captured 13.5 percent of the vote. Although *National Review, Human Events,* and other main-line conservative publications interpreted Wallace's support as evidence of popular dissatisfaction with government programs of social engineering, the conservative establishment swung behind Nixon. Wallace's background as both a strident segregationist and a New Deal Democrat who remained a liberal on many issues made many conservatives distrust him. Another factor that contributed to Nixon's conservative support was the established relationship of conservatives to the Republican party. For better or worse, conservative activists and spokesmen were wedded to that party that they had partly taken over in 1964. This marriage continued in 1968, though it required conservatives to affect enthusiasm for a protean politician who in his second term disgraced them and his party. The endorsements of Nixon, which came from Goldwater, from Strom Thurmond (the former Dixiecrat who turned Republican), and from Ronald Reagan, undoubtedly helped make Nixon more palatable to the political Right.[37] Perhaps the same effect was achieved when *National Review,* once openly contemptuous of Nixon, reminded its readers that Wallace was (unlike Nixon) a "big-spending" Democrat.

Despite these assurances, conservative activists by the late sixties had reached an impasse. They had become mere foot soldiers in a party that they had once hoped to control. Even the Nixon loyalist Pat Buchanan complained that under the current administration liberals received the substantive rewards and conservatives only the symbolic.[38] The Wallace constituency of 1968 and 1972 (before the shooting of Wallace during the Democratic primaries) offered a tempting target for conservative re-cruitment. Yet Wallace voters were, for the most part, socially conser-vative New Deal Democrats who were not ready to join the majority of conservative activists as members of the Republican party. Indeed, some of these activists themselves came to doubt what advantage *they* derived from being Republicans. In the 1970s, M. Stanton Evans, William Rusher, and Kevin Phillips explored the possibility of creating a third party that would bring together economically conservative Republicans and socially conservative Democrats.[39] The fusion of Goldwaterites and Wallaceites within a single national party never came to pass, although Republican, and even some Democratic, politicians exploited blue-collar grievances against busing and other judicial remedies intended to end racial inequalities.

Part of the reluctance of conservatives to step unambiguously outside the two-party system came from their conviction that it provided political stability. Even the creation of state conservative parties was justified as a temporary tool, a means of nudging the Republican party toward the Right on social-economic matters. This point was made explicit when the New York Conservative party came into existence. Frank Meyer, upon returning from the party's first meeting, declared that "conservatives neither desire nor demand clearly wrought ideological parties and are firm, principled supporters of the two-party system." What galvanized the temporary breakaway was opposition to the attempt of the Republi-can leadership "to make their party as close a carbon copy of the recon-structed Democratic Party of Franklin Roosevelt as it can force upon its Republican constituency."[40] Daniel Mahoney had made the same argu-ment in 1962, in his defense of the New York Conservative party. The new party (really pressure group), by allowing Republicans to vote for conservatives in gubernatorial and Senate contests, would discredit the state Republican leadership. It would restore the state party to older Republican principles. Moreover, the Conservative party, said Mahoney, would be able to appeal to socially conservative (mostly ethnic Catholic) Democrats who could never bring themselves to pull a Republican lever. Once these voters became used to supporting a Democratic party that reflected their real views, they would join traditional Republicans in an expanded Republican party without its Left wing.[41]

Unfortunately, this analysis rested upon the neglect of one overshad-owing fact: continued blue-collar, ethnic support for New Deal economic programs, except for those that went almost exclusively to the urban underclass. Kevin Phillips tried to get around this divorce between blue-collar and moneyed conservatives, but his political strategy was based on a highly problematic trade-off. Hoover-type Republicans and Sunbelt Goldwaterites were to abandon anti–New Deal economics in order to build a winning coalition with Catholic Democrats. Yet it remained unclear in Phillips's scheme what free-enterprise Republicans would obtain—beyond a compromised victory—if they renounced their economic principles. Nor was it a sure thing in 1968 that non-Hispanic ethnic Catholics would leave the Democratic party, even in pursuit of pro–New Deal, socially conservative Republicans. Catholic identification with the Democratic party remained high throughout the 1960s—even after factoring out the Hispanic vote. Significantly, Phillips himself was a Republican party strategist. His projected realignment was intended to serve the cause of Republican electoral victory; he dedicated *The Emerging Republican Majority* to the Machiavellian prince whose favor he was seeking, Richard M. Nixon.[42]

The first wave of post-Goldwaterite conservative activism ended as an exercise in futility. Unable to push the Republican party in a conservative direction, it failed equally to obtain leverage among blue-collar, antiliberal Democrats. But the radicalization of liberal politics in America—what appeared to many its assault on patriotism, educational standards, and family values—was already by the early 1970s generating a new wave of antiliberal activism. The new activists were not all Republicans or even defenders of private enterprise. Some were intellectuals with leftist backgrounds, and others were religionists becoming politically involved for the first time, in response to the abortion issue or the possibility that Gay Bills of Rights might be enacted in their states. Moreover, some of those who had become activists in the sixties began to adopt more sophisticated approaches to political conversion. They set up think tanks, hired statisticians, and produced and distributed position papers. They also attempted to draw scholars long identified, but increasingly disenchanted, with the Left into anticommunist or pro-capitalist foundations.

Delusions of Grandeur

By the seventies, however, many conservative activists had lost their own philosophic bearings. Entering conservative politics after college, they had once dreamed of translating their historical vision into political practice. They had seen that vision vulgarized by the attempt to make it salable to voters. Conservative activists spent years in the antechambers of power, as the valets and messengers of the "country-club Republicans" whom they professed to despise. They became trimmers, because they were powerless and because they had no hope of putting their principles (which they sometimes forgot) into practice. The conservative students and professors who abandoned the universities for the "real world" of politics may well have deluded themselves. In largely turning their backs on the institutions where ideas were transmitted, and by failing to devote themselves more energetically to what M. Stanton Evans prematurely called in 1961 a "conservative revolt on the campus," the American Right withdrew from the battle over principles. The supposedly conservative foundation of the seventies and eighties would generate alternatives to liberal policies, without directly challenging liberal principles and values. In 1985 the favorite presidential candidate of the Republican Right, Representative Jack Kemp of New York, proclaimed equality to be the key conservative principle; he defended democratic capitalism (actually a welfare state economy with capitalist incentives) as the best means for reducing social inequalities. Kemp's political doctrines have much in common with those of the intellectual Left; indeed, political differences between Right and Left have by now been largely reduced to disagreements over policies designed to achieve comparable moral goals.[43]

The Polish émigré novelist Leopold Tyrmand observed that the American Right offered political solutions to cultural problems. He was undoubtedly correct. Unlike the Left in the sixties that entered politics enjoying academic strength and highbrow respectability, conservative activists formed a movement without either. They may have hoped that electoral success would bring intellectual respectability to both them and their worldview. For a time, electoral success eluded them; when it found them at last, as we shall argue, they were no longer able to establish the ideological basis of what, by the eighties, was the conservative counterestablishment.

Chapter Three

Ivory Tower/Ivory Gate:
The Conservative Mind on Campus

The sixties and seventies were a period of creative ferment for the conservative movement. Issues crystallized, ideas took shape, lines were drawn. These were, to some extent, the issues and ideas that propelled a popular speaker at the 1964 Republican Convention first into the governor's mansion in California, and ultimately into the White House. Despite the brilliance of such political successes, intellectual conservatism suffered massive defeats on the most significant battlegrounds: the institutions and organs of cultural life in the United States, particularly the universities.

It was no secret that liberalism predominated in the postwar academic community. What Lionel Trilling described as the "adversary culture" had been on the increase throughout the century. In 1959 a *Harvard Crimson* poll of undergraduates revealed that two-thirds of the students supported the welfare state status quo, while up to a third supported the socialization of basic industries and the unilateral suspension of atomic bomb testing.[1] Of course, the indications were not entirely unambiguous. The late fifties also saw an increase of conservative student organizations. In 1961 the conservative columnist M. Stanton Evans was so encouraged by the signs of discontent that he titled his book *Revolt on Campus*. In a chapter ominously named "Chicago 1960," he gave a glowing report on the Youth for Goldwater and predicted, quite correctly, Goldwater's successful bid for the nomination in 1964. Still, as Evans admitted, there was not yet a "massive shift" to the right, and he conceded that his own interpretation of the students' political mood was at variance with the conventional wisdom.[2]

Campus Revolt

It would be tedious (and unnecessary) to rehearse all the events that disturbed the serenity of college life in the sixties and early seventies. A number of generalizations, however, may be in order. First and foremost, it is important to recall the circumstances. Campus unrest was not, by and large, a response to conservative principles, because such principles were in short supply in academic circles. On this point, Evans was absolutely correct. The faculty and administrators of the sixties ranged, on a political spectrum, from liberal supporters of the New Deal to radicals of every description. Nathan Pusey, who was later forced to resign as Harvard president after using the police to dislodge student protestors, had earlier professed enthusiasm for campus radicalism as a sign of intellectual ferment. Academic supporters of Lyndon Johnson were typically derided as reactionaries. Republicans were beyond the pale.

Even the Eisenhower years may not have been quite the return to "normalcy" that was advertised. The restoration of American ideals, which characterizes the postwar years, was to some extent constructed by popular writers like Walter Lippman and the Catholic theologian John Courtney Murray, and by image-makers like Henry Luce, the publisher of *Time* and *Life*. As Allan C. Carlson, one of Luce's admirers, expresses the mission of *Life* magazine: "*Life* would not merely reflect and defend values; it would create values for the new social, political, and cultural environment that appeared to be emerging in America. Luce determined to shape a spirit for his age, one that would be compatible with a new era and still be in service of the good in America's past." In this, the American century, the United States found itself in danger of losing its soul because of the new responsibilities and temptations that presented themselves. In his view, Americans had to resist godless communism while at the same time celebrating its past and looking toward a bright new future. For the stability it needed, the country would have to depend on the family-centered culture of the suburbs and the moral teachings of generic religion.[3]

In one sense, the 1950s were nothing more than a temporary sigh of relief after the troubled decades of depression and war. The adversarial radicalism of the thirties was still deeply entrenched in academic soil. In their study of the 1972 election, Ladd and Lipset sum up the results of a series of academic surveys, all of which show that throughout the twentieth century, "the political weight" of academics has been to the Left.[4]

Second, the campus revolution was largely an upper-class affair. Students were sensitive only to fashionable segments of the underclass but openly hostile to blue-collar workers. Michael Lerner, a former student radical, complained of the double standard by which the "respectable bigotry" of "an upper-middle-class peace matron toward a lower-middle-class mayor" is not scrutinized with the same care as a policeman's bigotry toward blacks.[5] The most prominent radical group, Students for a Democratic Society, was a predominantly upper-middle-class organization. At a time when family income in the United States averaged $8,000 a year, and the Harvard family average was $17,000, Harvard SDSers came from families averaging $23,000 a year. Stanton Evans's informal survey of conservative students (taken about 1960) pointed to family income of only about $5,000.[6]

Finally, many students who took part in demonstrations were motivated as much by high spirits, the onset of spring, and the feeling of student solidarity as much as by any political principles, even as low a principle as fear of the draft. If the "movement" was not especially threatening to the peace of the commonwealth, the reaction of respectable / academics, who were confronted by rioting students, was an understandable alarm. Much of the reality-mugging (to use Irving Kristol's phrase) that sobered up anticommunist liberals took place on campus.

The campus "revolution" began, roughly speaking, with the Berkeley Free Speech Movement and crested with the violent shutdown of Columbia. Response among serious scholars varied. At Berkeley, a young professor, John Searle (now an eminent philosopher), saw little to object to in the Free Speech Movement, although he did point out that the political students utterly rejected the standard definition of the university as a place of teaching and research.[7] For Searle, and many others on both sides, the problem was not so much politics as academic order. The doctrine of *in loco parentis* was dead (at least at state universities), but, as Searle suggested, "so far no new ideology has really replaced" the older ideology.

If Searle was blasé, older scholars like George F. Kennan were appalled. Kennan's Swarthmore speech, "Rebels Without a Cause," was a harmless enough encomium on the ideal of academic detachment, but, when it was printed in the *New York Times,* it aroused such a storm of controversy that a book was made out of Kennan's speech and the hostile responses it had generated. (Martin Duberman at Princeton referred to "gross misrepresentation . . . barely a sentence . . . free of false accusation.")[8] Many distinguished academics like Nathan Glazer and Sidney Hook went farther than Kennan in deploring the threat to academic order at Berkeley and elsewhere. Their reaction marks a significant turning point in the creation of a neoconservative worldview.

Anticommunist liberals were deeply disturbed by the young barbarians who interrupted their classes, but many conservatives (if the truth be told) took a certain melancholy pleasure in the whole business. For years, Richard Weaver, Russell Kirk, and Thomas Molnar had been lamenting the disintegration of academic order and intellectual integrity. Now, their worst fears were being realized. Kirk's articles on higher education, which appeared regularly in *National Review,* took on an uncharacteristic briskness and topicality. In 1978 Kirk wove his speeches and articles into one of his most cogent books, *Decadence and Renewal in the Higher Learning.*

The conservative indictment against higher education was sweeping. Several points were made repeatedly: standards—of instruction and civility—had been lowered; the university had lost all sense of its original purposes; conservative ideas were excluded from most departments of political science, history, philosophy, English, and sociology. Russell Kirk saw the contemporary history of higher learning as the annals of "progressive decadence." The old classical vision of "justice, liberty, order, piety" was replaced, by 1955, with an "amorphous humanitarianism," which, "though it had badly damaged the old disciplines, had created no decent curricula to replace them. The unpleasant insecurity of many colleges by 1955 was produced, in part, by this very lack of form and purpose."[9]

For many conservatives, then and now, the principal problem was one of standards. Thomas Molnar, in a bitter and often brilliant book, *The Future of Education,* argued that despite the enormous gains in population since the nineteenth century, the actual number of educated Americans had, at best, remained constant. Throughout the fifties and sixties, Jacques Barzun—a liberal traditionalist—pilloried the follies and pretentions of *The House of Intellect* and lamented the fallen state of *The Teacher in America.* In the former work, Barzun recounts the failure of his graduate students to identify 20 common abbreviations or tell the difference between "i.e." and "e.g.": "What a commentary on so-called preparation for graduate study that these trifles . . . should not have been mastered long since. . . . One is tempted to conclude that our present 'approach' (for it is not a system) turns out with certainty only two products—complaints and cripples."[10]

Albert Jay Nock had made an even more extreme case for "excellence" years before and endorsed Jefferson's plan of public education by which "twenty of the best geniuses will be raked from the rubbish annually."[11] The expected answer to such reactionary criticism was, as Nock and Barzun knew, the charge of elitism. The disciples of John Dewey were educating children to be citizens in a democracy, while the conservative view of learning applied only to a small minority of aspiring aristocrats.

To some extent, conservatives accepted the charge. Russell Kirk, more generous than Nock (or Jefferson), pointed out that universal college education actually hurt both the bright and the dull student: "In the academic mob of 1967, the better students were frustrated, for general standards had been lowered beneath their interest and capacity. In this academic mob, the inferior students were bewildered and baffled, for even degraded standards were too high for them."[12] When the question of excellence began to be raised again in the 1980s, it was always expressed in democratic terms. The influential editors of a conservative blueprint for the humanities, *Against Mediocrity,* were content to couch their arguments in a prudently egalitarian style and speak of the humanities as "the strongest democratizing force that formal education can muster" and even as a "birthright" for all Americans.[13] In less than twenty years, the conservative argument had become, apparently of necessity, egalitarian.

The argument over standards reveals an essential confusion over the actual purpose and functions of higher learning, as Adam B. Ulam explained in his contribution to a *Daedalus* symposium on higher education.[14] The most popular vision of the university was that of University of California President Clark Kerr, who promoted the idea of the "multiversity." The vulgarity of Kerr's vision is summed up in the term he invented. Its popularity among academics—during the very period Berkeley was coming apart at the seams—was a clear indication of the identity crisis in higher education.[15] John Searle at Berkeley was willing to settle for the old formula of teaching and research, but (as Barzun and others were arguing) few universities wasted much time worrying about undergraduate teaching, which ranked near the bottom in a 1965 survey on "University Goals and Academic Power" conducted by the American Council on Education. (The highest ranked goals were academic freedom and institutional power.)[16] Beyond the two eminently worthy goals of teaching and research lay an equally serious matter: character development. What sort of men and women, what sort of citizens would be produced by a university education?

Two answers were given throughout the 1960s—one liberal, one radical. Harvard President Derek Bok, who presided over Harvard's "restoration," simply dismissed the problem of character development on the grounds that "we have no way of knowing." Academic virtues, he argued, include such things as intellectual skills, "qualities of mind," and developing something he calls "judgment and values," which a liberal arts education can encourage by, for example, offering "the opportunity . . . to experiment with a number of interests and life-styles."[17] A liberal education, with the accent on liberal, provides students with opportunities to become themselves, whether that "self" be Albert Einstein or Charles Manson.

Radical critics of the university, following in the footsteps of Marcuse, accused administrations of repressing creativity and individuality. Paul Goodman, in *Growing Up Absurd,* set the tone for much of the radical critique. One can almost hear Goodman's influence in the once-popular book *The Student as Nigger,* whose author, Jerry Farber, declaims against school as the place "where you let the dying society put its trip on you."[18] In their quest for liberation, such students were, in the view of psychologist Carl R. Rogers, creating "the person of tomorrow." The men and women of the future would reject all orthodoxies (including marriage) in favor of turning themselves on by whatever means they had. On the other hand, they would reject the liberals' dispassionate pursuit of truth. The Person of Tomorrow would be "active—sometimes violently, intolerantly, and self-righteously active—in the causes in which he believed."[19]

The Conservative Response

Conservatives were repelled by the violence and obscurantism of radicals and Marxists, but they agreed with them (against the liberals) that universities did, and should in principle, serve a moral purpose. The explicitly moral purpose of education is an ancient ideal, far older than Plato. The Roman rhetorician Quintilian summed up the ancient attitudes in his famous definition of the orator as "a good man skilled in speaking," that is, a man capable of moral judgment and public service. A handful of traditional scholars continued, right through the 1960s, to adhere to the old view, but they were rare birds in academic circles. In both issues of the *Daedalus* symposium, Gerald Else (a classical scholar) was one of the few to suggest that education's essential purpose was not to produce graduate students but "to train our students to make better moral and political choices."[20]

Apart from Russell Kirk, the conservative most identified with issues of higher education was John A. Howard, president of the tiny Rockford College and a member of President Nixon's Task Force on Higher Education. In the Task Force report "Priorities in Higher Education," Howard registered his dissent from the recommendation for increased federal spending. He who pays the piper calls the tune, he often warned. Rockford College under Howard, along with Hillsdale College in Michigan under George Roche and Brigham Young University, made valiant efforts to stem the rising tide of federal control over higher education. As Howard, Roche, and Kirk all warned, the dependence on government money eventually translated into acceptance of government priorities and guidelines that were set, typically, by bureaucrats and educationists who had no clear idea of the function of higher education.

In a debate with the Marxist H. Bruce Franklin, Howard insisted that it was a serious error to restrict the university's mission to "the pursuit of truth." There had to be a framework of principles, a system of "character education," if the other aims of education were to be reached.[21] While they disagreed on almost everything else, Howard and Franklin did agree that education had a social and moral purpose beyond mere intellectual and vocational training.

Few academics were listening to Howard's plea, although a number of groups like University Professors for Academic Order were founded to provide a conservative answer to the campus problems. Most serious professors, however, were too busy worrying about the threat to academic freedom posed by campus radicalism. Wayne Booth, who described the university as "the last true church," expressed strong indignation when he heard that New Left students were tampering with the University of Chicago library's card catalog. "The Shrines are under attack," he declared in his essay "The Last True Church."[22] Corroborative testimony was provided by three distinguished legal minds, including the future solicitor general Robert Bork, in their 1970 congressional testimony. Primarily concerned with the legal implications of campus politics, Bork and his colleagues went on to complain that the conditions for research were undermined by incivility and political polarization. Despite the divisions and tensions of academic life, they argued, "Politicization has . . . produced an opposite danger, that of conformity."[23]

Academic Freedom

In fact, throughout the sixties and seventies (and up to the present) conservative ideas and those who advanced them have often been shouted down by the radical opposition. After a 1971 *Atlantic* article on the genetic basis for I.Q., Harvard Professor Richard Herrnstein fell victim to a campaign against "racism" (the article never discussed race) by SDS. Other victims of the crusade against genetics and I.Q. included Arthur Jensen and the admittedly eccentric William Shockley. (A debate between Shockley and black activist Roy Innis was canceled in 1973 as the result of radical protest.) James Q. Wilson, a moderate liberal authority on crime and society, was subjected to a similar campaign, and his views may have cost him his chance to become Harvard's Dean of Arts and Sciences. During the same period, Harvard's economics department began caving in to pressures to hire more Marxists.

In some cases, the radical coercion turned brutal. Edward Banfield, author of the influential study of urban problems *The Unheavenly City*, was hounded from a chair he had accepted at the University of Pennsylvania and had to return to the comparatively civil world at Harvard. The neoconservative scholar (and ambassador to the United Nations) Jeane Kirkpatrick was driven off the stage by radical students in the course of her Jefferson lecture at Berkeley in 1983. Similar incidents have marred the academic serenity of Northwestern, Smith College (where a Kirkpatrick lecture had to be canceled), and Howard University, where ex-Black Panther Eldridge Cleaver tried to exhort black students to regard themselves as Americans. While most decent liberals deplored such disruptions, others preferred to ignore the discomfiture of their enemies. Even after the horror of the campus uprisings, University of Massachusetts President Robert Wood could find no threat to academic order on the Left. Instead, he complained against Jensen, Herrnstein, and Banfield on the grounds that they signified "the emergence of the first intellectually respectable school of conservative thought since the antebellum South's George Fitzhugh."[24] Wood's remark was all the more curious since he seemed totally unaware of such movements as the New Humanism, the Southern Agrarians, the "new" conservatives of the 1950s, and the free-market economics of the Austrian school and Milton Friedman. Such a degree of ignorance (or ideological passion) in a university president would seem to confirm the conservative impression that, to use Booth's phrase, the shrines were not simply under attack: they were already occupied.

The fear and hatred that greeted the hardheaded analysis of Herrnstein, Banfield, and James Q. Wilson was manifested, time after time, whenever "conservative" ideas disturbed the peace of college campuses. When the leading sociobiologist Edward O. Wilson attended the 1978 meeting of the American Association for the Advancement of Science, he was met with snarls of "racist" and "Nazi," before a bucket of water (or worse) was dumped on his head. The difficulties encountered by these scholars and scientists were predictable, since their research of the late twentieth century can be construed as a direct challenge to the liberal view of human life that held sway in the academic community.

Academic Heresy

In many ways, the postwar years were a period of extraordinary intellectual ferment in the United States and Europe, especially in the sciences that study man. Up through the forties and fifties, a sort of orthodoxy could be discerned in the social sciences and moral philosophy—an orthodoxy that would receive a series of powerful shocks from scientific rebels. The major schools of thought—behaviorist psychology, John Dewey's psychological and educational theories, Boasian anthropology, Sartrean existentialism, liberal and Marxist political theory—represented a high degree of consensus on the nature of man. Human nature was largely an open-ended affair, determined neither by biology nor history. The mind was viewed, by many social scientists, as essentially a Lockean "tabula rasa," a blank slate on which experience could create any conceivable message.

History became a sort of enemy, an obstacle to be surmounted in man's progress toward a better future. Democratic values—liberty, equality, and social justice—came to be viewed as things in themselves, rather than competing values, while the history of the United States became less and less a narrative account of previous generations and their accomplishments and more and more of a Hegelian search for meaning in the historical process.

Throughout the twentieth century, colleges and universities had been at work redefining their roles. What had been, in the nineteenth century, a community of scholars sharing the wisdom of the past with young students, was gradually transformed into an uneasy combination of research lab and indoctrination center. The classical academy and John Henry Newman's Christian concept of the university had come to be seen as largely irrelevant. A new democratic America required socially responsible citizens, not priests or aristocrats with a smattering of classics. By the early 1950s, colleges and universities had become the symbolic expression of the highest aspirations of industrial America. The reigning orthodoxy had survived challenges from the Left (Marxism) and the Right (the new humanism and agrarianism). Anticommunist progressive liberalism was *the* social and political philosophy of American intellectual life.

John Dewey, in many ways the most prominent American philosopher of the early twentieth century, combined a blank-slate psychology with a commitment to liberal democracy and social progress. He did not entirely rule out the effect of drives or instincts, but they were only "raw materials" for which "custom furnishes the machinery and designs." This meant, in effect, that human beings were capable of almost infinite progress toward a more just and humane society. A similar message was preached by the father of behaviorism, John B. Watson, and his disciple, B. F. Skinner. Watson reduced human instincts to three emotions: fear, love, and rage. Everything else was determined by environmental stimuli. Skinner advanced the behaviorist argument in several significant directions: First, he took up the question of language, which he treated as a simple case of stimulus and response, that is, language is only an instrument for satisfying desires; second, he promoted a utopian view of social and political life in his novel *Walden II* and in more theoretical works in which he argued that human social behavior could be improved simply by redesigning the environment.

These utopian psychological notions derived added force from the anthropological theories of Franz Boas and his students, Margaret Mead, Ruth Benedict, and A. L. Kroeber, among others. The Boasians emphasized the notorious variability of human cultures which gave the human species an "exemption from heredity."

Politically, these arguments gave support to Marxists, who repeated Marx's dictum that "man is the creature that makes his own history"; to existentialists, who argued that human beings created themselves; and to social reformers, who looked forward to endless vistas of humanitarian progress. In every real sense, then, the politics of the postwar welfare state was bound up with a scientific worldview that can be conveniently described as environmentalist.

An attack on utopian environmentalism was mounted in several disciplines: (1) the rise of cognitive science in linguistics and psychology; (2) the coalition of social science and evolutionary biology that came to be known as sociobiology; and (3) a new tough-minded approach to social problems that began to surface in sociology, educational psychology, and economics. In only a few cases were the rebels actually aware of any political implications to their work, but in each case, the scientists and scholars who put forward the new theories were attacked, sometimes physically, not so much on the grounds that they were wrong, but because it was morally wrong even to discuss certain questions.

The Cognitive Revolution

The rise of cognitive sciences has taken place in a number of separate, apparently unrelated disciplines: linguistics, psychology, computer science, and anthropology. The late forties and early fifties were a period of crisis for scholars and philosophers who concern themselves with the mind. None of the various schools of psychology had succeeded in establishing its principles as *the* main program for the discipline. The dominant school, behaviorism, focused almost exclusively on external patterns of behavior. This concentration effectively blocked any consideration of mental life. As Karl Lashley pointed out in a famous address, human beings, like all organisms, have a nervous system that responds *actively* and constantly to the stimuli it receives. Work on information theory (leading up to the construction of electronic computers) also emphasized the specific technique by which information could be processed, but it was Noam Chomsky who put cognitive science on the map. [25]

Chomsky made his mark early with a review of B. F. Skinner's *Verbal Behavior*. [26] Arguing against the mechanical view that reduces language to patterns of stimulus/response and networks of habit, Chomsky insisted upon the "creativity" of all human behavior, language in particular. Not long before his review, Chomsky had published his first major work, *Syntactic Structures*, in which he worked out the first version of his theory of generative grammar. In later works like *Aspects of the Theory of Syntax* and *Language and Mind*, he drew out the psychological implications. Going against the grain of most linguistic and psychological theory, Chomsky insisted that there are structures in language (syntax, for example) which are universal. What is more, he insisted, there are formal universals that underlie and determine the rules of native languages.

Chomsky has repeatedly revised almost every aspect of his theoretical work, but he has continued to emphasize the innateness of mental structures.

In psychology, Jerry Fodor comes close to representing the extreme "nativist" position. Fodor argues that the everyday language we speak— "natural languages"—cannot be the language of thought, because in that case we could not have had access to the thought processes we need to acquire a natural language. Put simply, learning English would be impossible if our minds did not somehow have a universal language built into them. Experiments conducted by cognitive psychologists, while they are not conclusive, do show that the mind tends to learn in some ways and not in others. [27]

Some of the strongest arguments against the blank state come from an unexpected quarter: color perception. Color terms do, in fact, vary from language to language. The general assumption has been that most cultures perceived color differently from Europeans and Americans. Studies, however, seem to show that color-vocabularies and color-perception are biased toward discriminating the four basic colors: blue, green, yellow, and red. What is more, even people without any color words are able to learn a "natural" vocabulary (i.e., one that discriminates the basic colors) twice as quickly as an unnatural. The naturalness of the basic colors is physiological, since the retina is designed to be roughly sensitive to the wavelengths that correspond to blue, green, yellow-green. [28]

Emotions are, perhaps, more obviously universal. Cross-cultural studies indicate a degree of agreement on interpreting facial expressions: happiness, anger, fear, surprise, and disgust can be correctly guessed from pictures of facial expressions. Even children born deaf and blind exhibit a standard repertory of expression. What is more surprising, many chimpanzee facial expressions can be correctly interpreted by students.

It now appears that such essential features of perception as constancy of shape and size and object permanence are present in newborn children, and cannot, therefore, be acquired by experience. Newborns also seem programmed to respond to the human face and voice (especially female), and children—when they are first beginning to talk—display a knowledge of grammar (with their very first words) never attained by chimpanzees that have been trained to communicate. [29] There are obvious implications for a conservative worldview. Human mental life and (by implication) social institutions are not infinitely plastic: they are rooted in the structures of the mind which is, itself, conditioned by the organic development of the brain. Few (if any) conservatives took note. Noam Chomsky was mentioned only in connection with his radical politics or, even more rarely, in attacks on the use of transformational grammar in the schools.

The New Synthesis

The implications of cognitive science were not lost on Edward O. Wilson, the Harvard entomologist who coined the term sociobiology.[30] For much of his career, Wilson has devoted himself to studying the social insects. Increasingly he came to apply the central insights of Darwinian natural selection to social behavior. In essence, modern Darwinists argue that every aspect of an organism—its body, sensory and mental abilities, and social behavior—evolved under the pressure of competition. Sharper teeth, better vision, and mating patterns are the result of a contest between individuals with different sets of genes. The winners are those which reproduce at higher rates; their genes eventually come to dominate or take over the population. Wilson was on fairly safe ground politically until, in the last chapter of *Sociobiology: The New Synthesis,* he turned his attention to the human species.

Obviously, Wilson was not the first writer to describe human behavior as the result of natural selection. It has long been believed that our distinctively human way of living is the result of a struggle for existence. The Christian view of human nature is very similar (although many Christians would prefer to speak of the old Adam or original sin). Even before Darwin wrote *The Origin of Species,* the philosopher Herbert Spencer was explaining human social life as the survival of the fittest. Ever since, "social Darwinists" have used what they knew (or thought they knew) of human origins to explain the current conditions of human life. Unfortunately, a corrupted version of social Darwinism got taken up by racial theorists whose works were exploited by the Nazis. The resulting contamination rendered the subject almost untouchable for nearly two decades. Serious interest in the human implications of evolutionary biology did not revive until the 1960s, with the publication of *On Aggression* by the ethologist Konrad Lorenz, *The Imperial Animal* by the anthropologists Robin Fox and Lionel Tiger, and the popular books of the playwright

Robert Ardrey: *African Genesis, The Territorial Imperative,* and *The Social Contract.*

Of these pioneers, Lorenz is by far the most important. Before taking up the human question, he had a distinguished career as a student of animal behavior—for which he received the Nobel Prize. *On Aggression* is a study of aggressive impulses in a number of species. Man, so Lorenz argued, was not by nature a particularly violent creature, especially against members of his own species. As a result, we lack the necessary mechanisms to regulate it. However, when men became hunters and warriors, they had to rely on their uncontrolled aggressive impulses. For this reason, according to Lorenz, we need such cultural institutions as clearly defined lines of authority (rank order or hierarchy) and rituals (sometimes religious) to defuse our violent impulses once they have been aroused.

Others of these early writers—most notably Ardrey, Fox and Tiger, and the zoologist Desmond Morris—compared human behavioral patterns with what is known of other primates, especially the baboons that live in large troops. They painted an unattractive picture of males domineering over females, fighting to establish pecking order, and defining and maintaining territorial boundaries. Man is, to use Desmond Morris's title, a "naked ape," or in Ardrey's phrase, the "killer ape."

The scientific community did not take seriously the writings of dramatists and anthropologists. Lorenz was a different matter, but—it was whispered—in his youth Lorenz had expressed sympathy for Hitler's eugenics policies and the German racial laws. However, by the early 1970s, a number of researchers were taking a new approach to certain facets of animal behavior. W. D. Hamilton, Robert Trivers, E. O. Wilson, and Richard Dawkins were looking at such phenomena as sex ratios among social insects (e.g., bees and wasps) and the question of altruism from the perspective of genetics. In principle, they argued, animal behavior should contribute to the reproductive success of the individual. This meant, in effect, that one set of genes was winning out in a competition with other sets. Therefore, the willingness of an animal to risk its life (or even sacrifice it) should be related to the amount of genetic material they had in common, that is to their degree of relatedness. (Years before, the geneticist J. B. S. Haldane had been asked in a pub if he would lay down his life to save a brother. No, he replied, not for *one,* but he would do it for three brothers or nine cousins. The point of his joke is simply this: I share with a brother—or parent or child—50 percent of the same genes and with a cousin 12.5 percent. By saving three brothers or nine cousins, I shall actually be enhancing the reproductive success of my genes.)

Richard Dawkins offered the most radical statement of this position in *The Selfish Gene* and *The Extended Phenotype.* For Dawkins, everything is in the genes. Organisms are simply vehicles that these replicating bits of DNA have adopted to ensure their survival and propagation. Dawkins and his colleagues were fond of quoting a witty remark of the Victorian novelist Samuel Butler that a chicken was just an egg's way of making another egg.

In the minds of most people, the single most important event in the development of this revolution was the publication of Wilson's *Sociobiology: The New Synthesis.* In the controversial last chapter of *Sociobiology* (and in the later *On Human Nature*),[31] Wilson applied the genetic insights of Trivers and Hamilton, as well as his own, to the problems of human society. The book was an overnight success everywhere, except in academic departments of sociology, psychology, and anthropology.

The most controversial question taken up by sociobiologists was the nature of human sex roles. By the 1980s, a great deal of research in psychology, anthropology, and sociology began to converge. Males and females, it began to be argued seriously, possess specialized mental aptitudes. Male students consistently outperform females in certain areas of mathematics, while females appear to excel in verbal skills. Men turn out to be, predictably, somewhat more aggressive, women more nurturant.[32]

This sexual distribution of mental abilities could be plausibly related to the sexual division of labor that was almost universally observed. Studies of family life and child-rearing revealed a greater uniformity than first appearances might indicate. In the view of many cross-cultural anthropologists, women are everywhere charged with primary responsibility for child-rearing and housekeeping, while men typically monopolize such activities as making war and hunting big game.[33]

Feminist scholars in the seventies began to make use of Sherry Ortner's observation that woman is to nature as man is to culture,[34] and a healthy interest in women's studies began to challenge certain liberal assumptions. Women were not always miserable in primitive or patriarchal societies; in fact, some feminists argued, women's place in the world had been seriously eroded by modernization, which laid such great emphasis on the more typically masculine qualities: specialized division of labor and analytical reasoning.[35] Increasingly, many feminists began to realize that the sexual revolution and campus radicalism amounted to little more than denial of women's special needs and rights.[36] Most seriously, liberalized divorce laws had the effect of impoverishing mothers with small children[37] and increasing the risks of child abuse.[38]

Most political feminists rejected such a line of reasoning, even though much of the research was conducted by women, indeed by feminists. Some conservatives, by contrast, were aware of the implications of this research and eager to use it in building up a case against the misapplication of sexual equality. Steven Goldberg, in a deliberately provocative book, argued for *The Inevitability of Patriarchy*. Women, he contended, should abandon their feminist pretentions and "follow their own physiological imperatives." In his view, "women have more important things to do" than compete with men. If feminists insist upon competition, then they will forfeit their right to protection.[39]

George Gilder, a former Republican liberal, argued from a paradoxically feminist perspective that men were the weaker sex because the male identity was a social invention, which could be undermined by feminism. Men, he suggested, had to be tamed by women or they would never make good husbands and fathers. On the other hand, men needed to find fulfillment in all-male groups where they did not have to compete with women.[40]

The Left was not slow to respond to the challenge of sociobiology and sex-role research. The attack on sociobiology reached its peak with the publication of *Not in Our Genes* by R. C. Lewontin, Steven Rose, and Leon Kamin. Jensen and Herrnstein were duly taken to task for their statements on I.Q., and Steven Goldberg was ridiculed for his "engagingly direct" arguments. The authors reserved their most powerful attacks, however, for sociobiology. After going over the usual slurs against Lorenz, Ardrey, and Dawkins, the authors delivered their verdict: "Inequalities of wealth, power, and status are not 'natural' but socially imposed," the standard Leftist position. As for the methods and research data of sociobiology, they are declared "fundamentally flawed."

Since the authors, especially Lewontin, were reputable scientists, their attack (endorsed by Stephen Jay Gould in the *New York Review of Books*) has to be taken seriously. However, resentment as well as research went into their arguments. The discussion of Richard Dawkins is, for example, patently unfair. They distort Dawkin's arguments and go so far as to present as part of his theory certain ideas that Dawkins introduces as the "entertaining speculations" of his colleagues.[41]

In fact, many of the criticisms made by Lewontin and others were previously addressed and answered by Dawkins. The most basic objection is to genetic determinism per se. Stephen J. Gould and now Lewontin, Rose, and Kamin apparently find it morally and intellectually reprehensible to think that there are several genetic constraints on human sexual behavior, although they have few reservations on the score of environmental determinism. On the surface, at least, distinction is political: if men were naturally violent and territorial, if human beings inevitably sorted themselves out in pecking orders, if male dominance really were a natural phenomenon and not just the result of social and cultural oppression, then certain elements of the Marxist political agenda might well have to be reconsidered.

Not in Our Genes (and all the essays and anthologies churned out in the late seventies) was a clear sign that implicitly conservative ideas were not covered by academic freedom. Few conservatives, it should be noted, took up the cudgels for E. O. Wilson or even bothered to examine the debate (Gertrude Himmelfarb is a distinguished exception). Well into the eighties, the conservative publication *Human Events* continued to print diatribes against "Darwinism." The one conservative philosopher who did make an effort to understand the new science was Thomas Molnar. At first he was attracted to the refutation of environmentalism, but, as he explained in an *Intercollegiate Review* article, he was put off by the scientists' philosophical naiveté and their hints at genetic planning. The "veterinarian" view of human life urged by Lionel Tiger would cancel any idea of moral responsibility: "Conduct for which not the free agent but the phylogenetic imprint is responsible is nothing but a mechanical act. On such an arid ground the moral judgment is pulverized and the political community joins the ant-hill."[42] Molnar's rejection of sociobiology (and Darwinism itself) would be echoed by many less erudite and less intelligent journalists on the right. On his own ground, the Christian view of men and society, Molnar was certainly prudent in rejecting any form of materialism. What he did not see, or rather what he was less interested in seeing, was the full implications of a scientific view of social and cultural behavior that restored a sense of the "givenness" of human nature. Paul Johnson, a British moderate conservative, was one of the few to be deeply impressed. He begins his history, *Modern Times,* with an account of Einstein, whose relativity disturbed the peace of the universe, and he concludes with Edward Wilson, whose sociobiology restored man to his place in nature. Johnson ends his remarkably influential book on a sanguine note: "Was not human planning to produce a 'classless society' not only intrinsically unattainable but positively harmful, in that it conflicted with the hidden but magisterial plans of nature itself? It might. The experience of modern times, when human activism led so often, and on so grandiose a scale, to inhuman destruction, suggested as much. On the other hand, it might not. It was possible human improvement could be used to reinforce natural selection. The essential thing was to find out." Thus by the 1980s, the wiser minds among us had returned to Alexander Pope's conclusion: "The proper study of mankind is man."[43]

Sociological Reaction

A biological reconstruction of sociology was unlikely to win many conservative adherents (apart from racialists); however, sociology itself was another matter. The roots of the discipline, as Robert Nisbet has demonstrated, go deep into the counterrevolutionary thinking of the nineteenth century. While conservatives have generally regarded sociology as an upstart discipline and a willing participant in schemes for social engineering, more than a few important postwar sociologists could be regarded as conservative or even reactionary.

Robert Nisbet is the most obvious example. Both as the philosopher of his discipline in *The Sociological Tradition* and in his works on community and authority, Nisbet revealed himself as one of the most thoroughly conservative scholars in America. There were others. George Homans, one of the founders of small group sociology, pursued an implicitly traditionalist line of research both in his study of medieval England and in his attempt to discover the roots of social cohesion. In his autobiography, Homans finally declares his conservative principles without reservations.[44]

In many ways, Homans's nemesis at Harvard was Talcott Parsons, the most influential American sociologist. Parson's work is often opaque to the point of unintelligibility, but in the main he supported the postwar restoration of the bourgeois order, endorsing the nuclear family and traditional sex roles, and some of Parson's students have carried on his affirmation of "the American way of life."[45]

One of the earliest classics of sociology was Emile Durkheim's attempt to relate suicide rates to religious affiliation, and Robert Nisbet and Peter Berger (among others) have recognized the profoundly conservative implications of Durkheim's research. Mention should also be made of Mircea Eliade's magisterial writings on non-Western religions and, more recently, studies by Steven Stack and Rodney Stark, which improve upon Durkheim's original work: belonging to a church now appears to significantly lower an adolescent's chance of committing suicide.[46]

In the sixties and seventies, many noted sociologists were particularly interested in questions of social and political organization. Seymour Martin Lipset became famous not only for his classic study, *Political Man*, but also for his discussions of union politics, big business, and higher education. Lipset, along with Irving Kristol (and later Nathan Glazer), was coeditor of the *Public Interest*. From its inception in the sixties, the new journal displayed a deepening distrust of utopian politics and the revolutionary claims put forward by radicals. Even the title conveyed a new respect for the public interest of the nation as a whole, which distinguished it sharply from Marxist and radical sectarianism.

Dismantling the Welfare State

By the 1970s the *Public Interest* had become a rallying point for disaffected sociologists and political scientists who recognized, with Nathan Glazer, the increasing social and economic costs of social engineering. Mention has already been made of Edward C. Banfield's difficulties. His book, *The Unheavenly City*, while it was not written from a conservative perspective, outraged the Left and delighted the Right. Banfield showed, among other things, that many social programs, ostensibly aimed at improving the whole of society (especially the disadvantaged), actually were designed to benefit the relatively affluent: "The expressway program and the FHA and VA mortgage insurance and guaranteed programs in effect pay the middle-class white to leave the central city for the suburbs. . . . These government programs . . . aim at problems of comfort, convenience, amenity, and business advantage, not at once involving the essential welfare of individuals or the good health of the society."[47]

Banfield's criticism of urban planning was shocking enough, but even more controversial was his argument that most racial problems were, in fact, class problems. Each immigrant group has gone through a lower-class phase from which it has worked its way out. The riots of the sixties, which were supposedly in response to racial discrimination, were actually conducted "for fun and profit."

A good liberal on most social questions including race, Banfield's book was offered as a progressive criticism. One by one, other honest liberals were to come forward with similar criticisms. In *Visible Man* and *Sexual Suicide* (1973), the still-liberal George Gilder documented the effects of the welfare system on poor blacks, an insight developed a decade later by Charles Murray into a thoroughgoing critique of poverty programs, *Losing Ground,* a book that became the primary topic of conservative conversations in 1984–85.

The works of Gilder, Murray, and Harvard professor (later United Nations ambassador and senator) Daniel Patrick Moynihan drew attention to the plight of female-headed black families. Many black scholars, somewhat surprisingly, were already making similar arguments. In *The Declining Significance of Race,* University of Chicago sociologist William Julius Wilson provided compelling evidence that as upwardly mobile blacks separated off from the community, class was becoming a more important factor than race. Thomas Sowell, a black economist, has repeatedly pointed to the paradoxical effect of social policies. Sowell, like Walter Williams and activist Robert Woodson, has argued that government programs designed to help the urban poor (blacks especially) have proved to be the greatest obstacle to black social progress. By creating habits of dependency, removing the rewards for effort, and providing disincentives for family stability, federal and state governments have served to establish a permanent underclass.

Economics is the cutting edge of social analysis, and it is in economics that the impact of conservative ideas has been greatest. The success of Milton Friedman and George Stigler, among many others, is all the more surprising when the apparently universal triumph of Keynesian economics is taken into consideration. In the mid-1930s, Friedrich von Hayek was engaged in a losing struggle against Keynes. For the next 50 years he took refuge in the obscurities of capital theory and, increasingly, devoted his best efforts to political philosophy. Both classical economics and the Austrian school, with their emphasis on individual decision-making, seemed dead beyond hope of recovery. By the fifties, however, Milton Friedman was giving a twist to the Keynesian tail in such works as *A Theory of the Consumption Function.* By the early sixties he was reaching a broader audience, which he initiated into the values of free men in free markets. Friedman seemed tireless, not only in reviving the "quantity theory of money" but also in promoting his own favorite alternatives to the planned society: a voucher system for education and a negative income tax.[48] His study of monetary policies led him to conclude that the federal reserve brought on the Great Depression by its incompetent tinkering with the money supply.[49] Friedman's sometimes simplistic social philosophy is summed up in the title of his television series, *Free to Choose.*

Free choice became a unifying theme of much economic theory in the sixties and seventies. James Buchanan and Gordon Tullock, first in their book, *The Calculus of Consent: Logical Foundations of Constitutional Democracy*, and later through their journal, *Public Choice*, attempted to apply economic theory to decision-making outside the marketplace. In their view, much of what government does is an illegitimate usurpation of individual choice. At times approaching close to libertarian anarchism, the Public Choice school has hammered on the need to constrain the role of government. Buchanan has pointed out that economic theory, by using maximizing models of analysis, encourages planners in their assumption that the economy can be managed. Markets are, in fact, less precise than textbooks suggest. More importantly, interventions into the market must be based on some social philosophy of common good—a philosophy generally rejected by individualists.

George Stigler, like Friedman, a Nobel Laureate, also contributed to the critique of social planning. In papers and lectures on economic regulation, he maintained that regulatory agencies inevitably act in the interest of producers, rather than consumers, while suggesting more than once that students of economics were inexorably attracted to conservative ideas.[50] Other prominent economists who began to unravel the seamless garment of the welfare state included economic historian Douglass North and Armen Alchian; on a more abstract level, Robert Nozick exerted a powerful influence in the direction of free choice and responsible citizenship. While Nozick's libertarian ethics were unlikely to appeal to older social conservatives, his *Anarchy, State, and Utopia* served as a rallying point for intellectuals disenchanted with the growing power of the state.

On several fronts—psychology, sociobiology, social analysis, economic theory—conservative ideas were on the advance in the postwar years. Ironically, many conservatives were at the same time abandoning the field to their enemies. Some conservative intellectuals were forced out by the new McCarthyism; others chose careers in politics or political journalism. Few of them seemed very concerned with passing on the torch to another generation. In a letter to *Chronicles,* one of the rare birds—a real conservative with a successful academic career—Grace Goodell, expressed her misgivings:

As a "conservative" social scientist now with tenure in a major academic institution, I have found that the stultifying intellectual atmosphere—institutionally and interpersonally, though certainly not in print—which the older generation of mature conservative thinkers have themselves created for the younger generation coming along, has been far more discouraging at almost every step of my own development than have liberal and leftist antagonisms. . . .

Listening to conservative students at various of the leading college and university campuses, one is tempted to generalize that the most antisocial professors teaching young people today are almost invariably those of conservative persuasion—especially of that generation. In my years at college and through graduate school, even on post-doctoral grants, from campus to campus conservative professors stood out as a group for their closed doors and intolerance even toward genuinely conservative students. Rather than seeking out or at least welcoming young minds of sincere inquiry, like Solzhenitsyn, many of our mentors seem to us to have retreated with undiscriminating arrogance—perhaps self-protection, self-pity, and bitterness?—behind a siege blockade, while we, the young seeking to prepare ourselves to carry on the challenge of our age, were left on the outside of the barricades.[51]

Of greater significance, perhaps, was the steady withdrawal of conservative scholars (apart from economists and neoconservatives) from the mainstream of academic debate. As time went on, more and more seemed to devote their energies to writing articles in conservative magazines, fewer and fewer to carrying on the fight within their disciplines.

There were, of course, conspicuous exceptions, such as Lino Graglia in law, Stanley Rothman in political sociology, the cold war historian John Lukacs, constitutional scholar Forrest McDonald, American intellectual historian Aileen S. Kraditor, and Southern regionalists Ludwell Johnson, Clyde Wilson, and Grady McWhiney. Another example of a respected conservative academician is Jacob Neusner, one of the best-known scholars on the political Right. An ordained rabbi and an outspoken patriot, Neusner has virtually created an entire academic discipline, Judaic studies. Among his more than 200 painstakingly researched volumes are explications of Rabbinic Judaism and, more recently, of the theological similarities and discrepancies between the Rabbis and the primitive Church. He has also served with uncompromising candor on both the National Humanities Council and the National Arts Council.[52]

Despite the important work carried out by these academic luminaries, by 1980, the year of Ronald Reagan's accession to the presidency, conservative scholars of rank and influence were in short supply. Among the many reasons for this development is the postwar American Right's embarrassing indifference to the life of the mind, which (alas) is rooted in a long history of anti-intellectualism and a surprising tolerance for low standards among movement stalwarts. In his first book, for instance, *God and Man at Yale,* William Buckley had scolded his alma mater for nurturing opinions that he regarded as un-American. In Buckley's view, universities existed in order to transmit and defend a set of attitudes, particularly Christian piety, an appreciation for free enterprise, and a belief in democracy. While some critics of higher education were to lament the imposition of leftist orthodoxy in the universities, Buckley called for the establishment of his own orthodoxy, which he believed could be accomplished by putting the alumni in charge.[53] Yale professor and future *National Review* editor Willmoore Kendall, both admired and criticized his onetime student's bold proposal to bring to American universities a style of populist politics that Kendall himself recommended to conservatives in government but not to those in academic life.[54]

Despite the justice of many of his censures, Buckley failed to understand the peculiar nature of a university as a corporate union of scholars sharing the fruits of their learning with a younger generation. Unfortunately, the inquisitorial ring of Buckley's attack on academic freedom was to reverberate through the next several decades, as the American Right prepared to do battle with a generally hostile university community.

Matters were complicated by the fact that many of the conservative critics were less than honest about their own education. While most neoconservatives who remained in the academy had respectable though not outstanding reputations in their fields, neoconservatives on the outside worked to enhance their academic image by funding and coopting scholars who were open to persuasion. Some of the more popular writers among the neoconservatives attempted to combine professorial and journalistic careers with less than complete success. Irving Kristol, for example, who did much to popularize the idea of the "New Class," held an Olin Professorship without benefit of doctorate or evidence of academic work.

For some time now neoconservatives, particularly the Straussians among them, have been creating their own publishing and reviewing network in the face of a, for the most part, unreceptive academic establishment. Straussian manuscripts are especially welcome, for instance, at Basic Books and by the academic presses at Cornell University, Johns Hopkins University, and the University of Chicago. Moreover, *National Review, American Spectator,* and certain other conservative magazines bend over backward to praise Straussian scholarship—though the noticeably fulsome tribute that one Straussian critic lavished in the pages of *National Review* on a book written by another elicited harsh comments from some conservative readers.[55]

This drawing together of wagons has produced a condescending attitude toward Straussians from scholars outside their group. In *Political Theory,* for example, the renowned Locke commentator Richard Ashcraft offered a devastating attack on Thomas Pangle's *The Spirit of Modern Republicanism: The Vision of the American Founders and the Philosophy of John Locke,* noting Pangle's "remarkable arrogance and narrowness of vision in his commentary of others."[56] Ashcraft contends that Pangle misrepresents John Locke—who for Straussians was the progenitor of the "American regime"—by dismissing all competing views about the philosophical origins of American republicanism and advancing the questionable notion that Locke was an atheist who did not really believe in the sanctity of private property. Ashcraft accuses Pangle of reconstructing Locke to accord with his own Straussian notion of an American materialist and egalitarian regime. Though stated with less ridicule, the same type of observations appeared in the *American Political Science Review,* and in several other journals, which likewise lamented the "rigid Straussian grid" evident in *The Spirit of Modern Republicanism.*[57] These criticisms are notably free of leftist bias, unless one adopts the characteristically Straussian tack of identifying any historical approach to textual analysis with the enemies of liberal democracy.

What makes the charges of partisanship hurled by neoconservatives against American universities all the more suspect are the academic credentials in particular of many of the accusers. Indeed, a dissertation could be devoted to the fudging or inflation of doctoral studies by neoconservative cultural critics and Reaganite connoisseurs of learning. At least three supposed conservative exemplars of academic accomplishment, who have been touted as such in the national press, have done graduate work that leaves much to be desired.[58]

During the Reagan years conservatives came to realize that the pursuit of political influence exacts a price: the loss of energy otherwise devoted to scholarship. A new Republican administration was, at times, hard put to locate conservative appointees with solid academic credentials. When qualified conservatives were suggested for positions at the National Endowment for the Humanities or the Department of Education or for the National Archives, they were quickly shot down by the overwhelmingly liberal academic community. The most prominent casualties included M. E. Bradford, who failed to win nomination as director of the NEH (and later as national archivist).

The Bradford case became a cause célèbre on the Right, not only because of the attempt by Irving Kristol to characterize Bradford as a scholar of no importance, but also because of the role played by Edwin Feulner of the Heritage Foundation. Originally a supporter of Bradford, Feulner was persuaded to defect during a meeting of the heads of prominent philanthropic foundations who followed Kristol's lead in making the entirely erroneous assertion that Bradford could not possibly prevail in the confirmation process.[59] (In fact Bradford already had the public backing of a great many senators—Democrats and Republicans—as well as sufficient private assurances to guarantee confirmation.) The affair was the first clear sign of the neoconservative hegemony over the American Right, and although Kristol in later years is reported to have wished he had never got involved in the case against Bradford, the damage was done.

By 1986 it was clear that Reagan supporters of the highest distinction would not be allowed to serve in any position requiring Senate confirmation. Among those rejected for National Humanities Council positions were Charles Moser, a professor of Slavic languages and literatures with solid credentials, and E. Christian Kopff, an important classical scholar with an outstanding publishing record. Both were dropped by the White House for their conservative views on such matters as Marxism, homosexual rights, education, and feminism. Despite the success on campus of at least some ideas with conservative implications, conservatives themselves had become embittered from having to fight unsuccessful wars.

In the course of the 1980s a group of neoconservative and liberal academics, disturbed by what they perceived as leftist intolerance on campus, began gathering in Manhattan for discussions. The group, which included Peter Shaw, Herbert London, Carol Iannone, Steven Balch, Nelson Ong, and Michael Levin (among others), was incorporated in 1985 as the National Association of Scholars. By 1987 the NAS had set up an office in Princeton and was publishing a journal, *Academic Questions*. By 1991 it listed 2,300 members from chapters in 27 states.[60]

The NAS does not claim to be a conservative organization per se; rather, its director Steven Balch defines the association as "an academic reform organization, conservative only in a small 'c' sense of wanting to preserve the traditions that animate our culture." Seeing itself as something other than part of a broad conservative coalition, the NAS has sought to attract the interest of persons who disagree politically but share a concern for academic freedom and the preservation of liberal education. By 1991 the NAS had succeeded in drawing the fire of such prominent radicals as Stanley Fish, who not only attacked the goals of the organization but also tried to blacklist its members in promotion and tenure decisions. When NEH chairman Lynn Cheney nominated NAS board member Carol Iannone for a position on the National Humanities Council, the battle was joined. When Iannone's nomination was rejected, however, the decision had less to do with her politics than with her lack of scholarly writings.

The fight over Iannone illustrates both the virtues and the weaknesses of the NAS. Although Iannone was unquestionably an intelligent and prudent professor who could have made a valuable contribution to the National Humanities Council—the principal function of which is to review grant proposals—she was not above reproach. Most of her published writings had been in political magazines, particularly *Commentary* and the *New Criterion,* rather than in refereed academic journals. When conservatives leaped to Iannone's defense (as they had not in the earlier dispute over E. Christian Kopff and Charles Moser), her defenders (e.g., William McGurn in *National Review*) may have done more harm than good to the Right by denigrating the value of academic publishing and claiming equivalent status for the *New Criterion.* Samuel Francis of the *Washington Times* was more cautious in his consideration of the nominee, challenging Iannone's supporters to bring forth solid evidence of academic distinction.[61]

Similar questions about the Right's academic agenda followed the publication of Dinesh D'Souza's *Illiberal Education* in 1991, a tirade against what came to be known as political correctness on campus. Consisting, for the most part, of anecdotes about left-wing excesses among the professoriate and academic administrators, the work was neither original nor well researched. Its author, a young Republican journalist, had none of the academic training required for a study of postmodern intellectual trends. Yet the book's manifest failings meant nothing to the conservative press, which celebrated it for its supposed erudition and investigative thoroughness.[62] Curiously, the work received almost as much praise in mainstream liberal publications as in establishment conservative circles. Unlike the brash call for alumni control of universities found in *God and Men at Yale, Illiberal Education* prescribes nothing that might offend the academic powers that be. Rather, it criticizes racial and gender-based quotas, and proposes replacing them with a system of government subsidies based on the relative social disadvantage of the applicants. In a plea for American togetherness, D'Souza also insists that university administrators take action against ethnically distinct groupings on campus that militate against democratic pluralist solidarity.

It is hard to see how this work represents an assault on egalitarian social engineering in higher education. D'Souza in fact provides a defense of such an undertaking, together with lurid, if not always well-documented, accounts of lunatic Left activities, in at least some universities.

It may be possible to argue that the war against academic political correctness has itself become a subgenus of the same correctness. This might in fact illustrate the theory of cooptation popularized in the sixties by the godfather of the New Left, Herbert Marcuse, albeit with one crucial difference: In this case it is the journalists, and not big business, who shape the political culture. The publicized opponents of academic radicalism produce massively subsidized books that receive advance hype in the *Atlantic Monthly,* the *New York Times,* and the *New Republic.* The liberal press, which overflows in its praise of the worthy opposition, prints Dinesh D'Souza, Charles Sykes, and other commentators on the American university's descent from the sound liberal doctrines of the early sixties into the multiculturalism of the nineties.[63] As an added fillip the National Endowment for the Humanities, through its passionately neoconservative leaders—Lynne Cheney, Celeste Colgan, and John Agresto—have agitated for the same positions. Cheney in particular has used her office as NEH director to highlight the problem of academic decline since the sixties, or from whatever point university power was seen to pass from moderate liberals. Martin Luther King, Sidney Hook, and Allan Bloom have been raised to contrapuntal icons in this New York–Washington-based war against "radical feminism" and multiculturalism.[64] In the present exaggerated cultural war, major foundations have kept their side financially comfortable. Clearly, neither they nor the journalists wish to open the political or cultural conversation to unwelcome guests.

Chapter Four

Revolt of the Intellectuals: The Neoconservatives

The seventies were a decade of severe crisis for American conservatives. The landslide reelection of Richard Nixon, which was supposed to usher in a new Conservative consensus, quickly provided the opportunity for liberal Democrats to take the offensive during the Watergate hearings and their aftermath. In the mid-seventies the dissolution of the Republican party was being confidently predicted, as conservatives turned increasingly to Ronald Reagan and moderates attempted to regroup around safe party leaders like Jerry Ford and Howard Baker.

What hardly anyone expected to see was the emergence of two new conservative forces that would influence the presidency of Ronald Reagan, while at the same time alarming the remnants of the Old Right. These two forces were the neoconservatives and the populist and religious New Right (discussed in the next chapter). Both groups created or refashioned institutions and publications to articulate their views, and both have been remarkably successful—albeit in different ways—at raising money and attracting the attention of the press.

Breaking Ranks

It is true but simplistic to state that as American academics and journalists moved Leftward during the civil rights crusade and the Vietnam War, the conservative mainstream drifted in the same direction. The reality is more complex. As American universities, literature, and art became increasingly radicalized from the mid-sixties on, cold war liberals, those dissatisfied with black power politics, and, finally, critics of what became known as the "counterculture" all disengaged from the Left. This process of disengagement among incipient neoconservatives has been described exhaustively from different angles, by Peter Steinfels and Alexander Bloom on the Left, by an admiring English scholar Gillian Peele, by George Nash in his survey of the conservative movement, and by two leading neoconservatives, Norman Podhoretz and Irving Kristol, in their autobiographical writings. The critical moments in this flight from the Left are related by major commentators in a similar fashion. Although Kristol (often described as the neoconservative "godfather") has had the greatest success in formulating the movement's aspirations in a set of formal doctrines, it is Norman Podhoretz, editor of *Commentary,* who has become its most representative figure.

As a culturally conscious young intellectual, Podhoretz had temporarily abandoned his Truman-Democratic (cold war liberal) politics to become a protester against the Vietnam War. As an editor of *Commentary* in the sixties, he had pulled a magazine that had been founded in the early fifties as a pro-Israeli, anti-Soviet publication toward the emerging New Left. In *Making It* and *Breaking Ranks,* Podhoretz dwells on his onetime fascination with Freudian critics of capitalism, such as Norman O. Brown and Herbert Marcuse, and with other heralds of the counterculture.[1] His break with the Left occurred by stages, which are documented in his editorials for *Commentary*. Podhoretz rediscovered the evils of Communist rule and expansion and, furthermore, grew disgusted with the Left's attacks on academic standards and the principle of merit (as illustrated by its demand for preferential treatment of blacks and women). Podhoretz also turned against the revolution in sexual and social relations that counterculture writers were advocating in the sixties and seventies. The effect of the new morality on family life and already confused adolescents was a theme Podhoretz and his talented wife, Midge Decter, discussed with increasing urgency throughout the seventies. A *Commentary* leitmotiv for the seventies was established in the December 1970 issue, which included several articles criticizing such spokesmen for the counterculture as Charles Reich and Theodore Roszak, both of whom had written against repressive, middle-class morality.[2]

Among the factors that led Podhoretz and many other neoconservatives to disengage from the Left, their Jewishness was certainly significant. From 1969 on, *Commentary* included strongly worded polemics that presented the "Movement," particularly black radicalism, as a danger to American Jews.[3] Critics like Earl Raab and Nathan Glazer stressed the inevitably anti-Jewish character of the policies advocated by the New Left and its liberal followers. An anti-Israeli policy closely keyed to Arab revolutionary organizations, the willful neglect of Jewish victims of Soviet oppression, and the catering to black demands for preferential hiring in the New York City school system and elsewhere were all features of the movement that Podhoretz and his associates castigated. Isidore Silver has made an observation about the Jewish consciousness of neoconservatives, which Alexander Bloom, in *The Prodigal Sons,* has recently drawn out at length:

Although psychohistorical explanations have substantial, built-in limitations, it is apparent that the development of neoconservatism in the last twenty years has consisted of a reaction to one major trauma—the fear of anti-Semitism. Since, of course, not all Jewish intellectuals are neoconservatives nor are all neoconservatives Jewish, a conventional disclaimer of universality should and must be entered. Despite the caveats, however, there can be little doubt that the Holocaust constituted the seminal event not only for European Jewry but for many American Jews not far removed from their East European or German heritages.[4]

Silver makes the argument that the neoconservatives were impressed by Hannah Arendt's *Origins of Totalitarianism,* particularly by her discussion of the populist and tribalist roots of modern anti-Semitism. Arendt had traced both totalitarianism and anti-Semitism to the inability of the ruling classes in France, Germany, and the Slavic countries to retain their legitimacy in the face of upheaval and mass political movements. To the neoconservatives who had fought their way to the top academically, while being confronted with professional obstacles, the danger lay exactly where Arendt had claimed it was, in lower-class populist jealousy.

But anxieties over populist upheaval have not always led to the same political views. Though similar concerns can be ascribed to other American Jews, most of the American Jewish community, and particularly its more affluent and better educated elements, continues to identify with the liberal Left. The majority of American Jews may see their enemy in a Christian rural America from which it seeks protection through an enlightened managerial state and progressive judiciary. The Jewish neoconservatives, in any case, have not yet swayed a critical mass of Jewish voters, however much they and their coreligionists may agree about specifically Jewish issues.

Despite the close and enthusiastic identification of *Commentary* with the Reagan administration (Norman Podhoretz's son-in-law, for example, served as an assistant secretary of state), President Reagan obtained a smaller percentage of the Jewish vote in 1984 than in 1980. The 70/30 split of the Jewish vote between Walter Mondale and the president did not at all reflect the electoral preferences of Jewish neoconservatives.[5] Moreover, a poll conducted by the American Jewish Committee (which sponsors *Commentary*) in 1984 revealed that 70 percent of the Jewish respondents oppose silent meditation in schools, 87 percent favor "gay rights," and 80 percent support federally funded abortions. None of these positions coincided with the dominant *Commentary* views, though the respondents and Jewish neoconservatives may both have experienced problems related to their Jewish identity.[6]

Many Jewish neoconservatives found themselves in unfamiliar circumstances, as the unavoidable allies of a political movement that previously had been predominantly Christian. In this situation they were justifiably sensitive to any outbreak of anti-Semitism on the Right. In the summer of 1986, an acrimonious quarrel erupted between several New York–based neoconservatives—most prominently Norman Podhoretz, Midge Decter, and Dorothy Rabinowitz, a columnist for the *New York Post*—and Joseph Sobran, a senior editor of *National Review*.[7] Sobran, for some time, had published critical statements about the role of Zionists in American political life and about Jewish hostility toward Christian society. Sobran had even had the tenacity to praise *Instauration*, a journal devoted to scientific racism, for its willingness to broach risky opinions about social relations. The neoconservative reaction was predictably impassioned: It ranged from demands to have Sobran professionally blacklisted to cries about virulent anti-Semitism on the Old Right.

Fighting on Two Flanks

In fact, the fight did reveal understandable tensions between the neoconservatives and some elements of the Old Right. While the neoconservatives generally added luster to conservative organizations, one effect of this alliance was to shift the parameters of conservative respectability toward the center. Positions significantly to the right of *Commentary* were increasingly regarded as suspect. Southerners and Christian traditionalists were particularly suspect to the neoconservatives, who during Reagan's first term fought successfully to keep M. E. Bradford from becoming director of the National Endowment for Humanities.[8]

If some members of the Old Right came into conflict with neoconservatives, the far Left was at least intermittently hostile to the same group. Sidney Blumenthal of the *Washington Post* produced a book in which he sought to document the careerism of those neoconservatives prominent among pro-Reagan journalists and within the Reagan administration. Though Blumenthal claimed to be examining the rise of the entire "conservative counterestablishment," it is obvious that his deepest interest, if not strongest dislike, was directed toward neoconservative renegades from the Left.[9] Christopher Hitchens covered much of the same ground, without anecdotal embroidery, in a biting article in *Mother Jones,* where, amid caricatures of neoconservative celebrities, he details the political and professional honors and connections of Norman Podhoretz and his family.[10] At the height of their institutional power in the mid-eighties, Podhoretz and his kinfolk held positions extending from the publishing world into government. One Podhoretz son-in-law, Steven Munson, served as a director of the Committee for the Free World, edited the influential neoconservative periodical the *Public Interest,* and worked as press counselor for the celebrity Jeane Kirkpatrick while she was U.S. representative to the United Nations. Currently Munson is news specials chief for the Voice of America. The other Podhoretz son-in-law, Elliott Abrams, worked on the staff of Senator Daniel Moynihan. Later he was an assistant secretary of state for human rights and then the highly visible assistant secretary of state for inter-American affairs.

The power and connections of what their enemies sometimes called the "*Commentary*-crowd" appear even more impressive as the family tree moves to Irving Kristol, former managing editor of *Commentary,* coeditor of the *Public Interest,* and publisher of the *National Interest.* Hitchens notes Kristol's ties to the American Enterprise Institute, the *Wall Street Journal,* and the Committee for the Free World, and his former association with Basic Books and the English journal *Encounter.* However, he misses Kristol's ties to the Olin Foundation, including his occupancy of the Olin chair at New York University, given almost entirely for his private research. Ernest van den Haag, Kristol's friend, occupies another lucrative Olin chair in the Fordham University Law School. Hitchens extends the neoconservative family tree to Jeane Kirkpatrick, Ben Wattenberg, Max Kampelman (the former chief U.S. negotiator at the Geneva arms talks), and other prominent public figures. Such neoconservative political influence can still be seen at the present time in the role of Kristol's son William as chief adviser to Vice President Quayle.

Despite the well-established concentration of power in the neoconservative camp among the members and retainers of great families, the real exercise of influence may have had less and less to do with dynastic ties: The Podhoretz and Kristol families still control vast financial and publishing resources. They can place their younger members in any number of journalistic positions, and many bitter jokes can still be heard at the *Washington Times* and the *New York Post* about parental attempts to push "mini-cons" seeking employment on the editorial staffs of these and other papers. The movement to which the neoconservatives have tied their fortunes, however, came to embrace more than midtown New York Jewish intellectuals breaking from the Democratic Party. Neoconservatism became the journalistic mainstream and the source of much of the political rhetoric of recent times. The locus of rhetorical and moral authority in that movement, however, has shifted steadily away from *Commentary* to other magazines, particularly the *New Republic,* which state neoconservative positions in a more lively and less ethnically coded manner. Meanwhile other neoconservative journalists such as Charles Krauthammer, Paul Gigot, and Morton Kondracke have begun to share the limelight with Podhoretz and Kristol. Neoconservative positions on many issues have come to overlap so much with the contiguous Left (a point treated at length in the closing chapter), that neoconservatives can no longer be seen as politically distinctive. Even the socialist Left, which once viewed neoconservatives as renegades, now treats them as preferable to the hard Right, presenting them as a counterforce to nativists and religious bigots. Since the late eighties the only serious battle that neoconservatives have fought is against the rallied and revitalized Old Right. In that struggle they have steadily enjoyed the support of liberal and far-Left journalists.

Creating a Counterestablishment

It is certainly fair to say that neoconservatives have created their own opportunities. To their great credit, Kristol and the Podhoretzes turned *Commentary* from a culturally parochial New York periodical into one read and discussed by the president, his advisers, and foreign heads of government. The journal's prestige can be seen from the appointment of Jeane Kirkpatrick as U.S. representative to the United Nations, which occurred after Ronald Reagan had read her November 1979 *Commentary* essay, "Dictatorships and Double Standards." President Reagan's repeated calls for the establishment of liberal democracy throughout the world closely paralleled a theme that *Commentary* has played up.[11]

In the seventies and eighties Kristol, Podhoretz, and Wattenberg managed to surround themselves with impressive academic talents. *Public Interest* and *Commentary* featured in every issue such outstanding scholars of public policy as Daniel Bell, James Q. Wilson, Edward Banfield, S. M. Lipset, Aaron Wildavsky, and Nathan Glazer. Daniel Patrick Moynihan remained closely attached to friends at *Commentary* from the time he was professor of sociology at Harvard until his election to the Senate in 1976. Although Moynihan subsequently veered to the Left, he nonetheless hired incipient and declared neoconservatives—such as Chester Finn, Joshua Muravchik, and Stephen Miller—to work on his senatorial staff. The senator has also published blasts against anti-Zionists and the Old Right in *Commentary* and *Public Interest*.

The bicentennial issue of *Public Interest* testified to the academic luster that neoconservatives brought to their enterprises. The issue included essays by Bell, Glazer, Lipset, Wilson, and S. P. Huntington, all scholars with Harvard connections, another essay by Moynihan, and a study by the constitutional scholar and political neoconservative Martin Diamond.[12] Kristol, Wattenberg, and Podhoretz were able to channel much of the same talent into other neoconservative publications, especially *Public Opinion, This World,* and the *Wall Street Journal.* They helped Hilton Kramer launch the *New Criterion,* a journal that expresses their cultural and political approach to aesthetics. This elegantly produced periodical has featured highly gifted interpreters of art and literature such as Joseph Epstein, Samuel Lipman, Bruce Bawer, and Kramer himself. Its defense of what might be described as anticommunist, prodemocratic modernism has brought down charges upon the editors of being crass political reductionists. The *New Criterion* is well-edited and includes such notable academic contributors as Robert Nisbet and Edward Banfield. Moreover, unlike other journals devoted to interpreting art, music, and poetry, it is admirably open about its political values.

At their best, neoconservatives have brought to the intellectual Right a critical intelligence that has proved useful in political discussion. Although members of the Old Right grappled with legal theory and economics, they rarely sought the kind of statistical information that neoconservative academics produce for their positions. The editorial staff of *National Review* opposed court-ordered busing in the 1960s by appealing to the original meaning of the Fourteenth Amendment and by arousing popular resentment against the government's interference with established community life. The neoconservatives, Glazer and Banfield, criticized the same experiment by documenting its failure to achieve the intended result. Busing did not lead to increased racial harmony or to improved scholastic performance for black or white children.[13]

In an incisive commentary written in the mid-eighties on the differences between the paleo- and neoconservatives, Edward Shapiro stressed the critical importance of their methodological points of departure. The paleoconservatives drew their insights and convictions from a humanistic and religious heritage. Although they studied economics and law defensively, in order to protect inherited institutions, their hearts remained in literature and theology.[14] The neoconservatives, by contrast, revel in statistics and computerized information. They believe that social problems are amenable to rigorous investigation that can throw light on them and thereby contribute to their solution. While not all neoconservatives were better trained than all paleoconservatives in the methods of the social sciences, Shapiro was correct about the dominant attitudes of both groups. What paleoconservatives often attribute to human frailty, or to the failure to deal adequately with that condition, neoconservatives treat as problems for which there exist right and wrong solutions. Neoconservatives may cry out in despair about the intractability of anti-Semitism or terrorism, and railed until recently against the Soviet empire. They may, as Irving Kristol did in an essay for *Partisan Review,* praise T. S. Eliot's later, Christian poetry. Yet, their position is not entirely incompatible with modern state planning. Almost all neoconservatives, and certainly the distinguished academics among them, remain qualified defenders of the welfare state. This loyalty is understandable in light of their study of society as sets of problems, which may or may not call for state action. One need not search far in the work of Glazer, Moynihan, Lipset, Wildavsky, or Wilson to find proof of what Michael Oakeshott calls "rationalism in politics." All of them believe that social problems can be properly managed if the state acts on the basis of knowledge.

This line of thought crops up occasionally even in Irving Kristol, whom Russell Kirk describes as "not a neoconservative at all . . . but a Conservative." In his *Reflections of a Neoconservative* and elsewhere, Kristol lists among neoconservative doctrines the support of a "conservative welfare state." Kristol distinguishes this kind of regime from both the night watchman state advocated by libertarians and democratic and non-democratic forms of socialism. It is obvious from his descriptions that he is referring to the present American model of a mixed economy and a bureaucratically managed democracy. Kristol defended that model in his acidic commentary on David Stockman's *The Triumph of Politics,* published in the *Wall Street Journal.* He scolded Reagan's former budget director for the simpleminded belief that the Reagan revolution originally aimed at rescinding the welfare state.[15] The proper task of the current administration and of any other conservative one is to prune the overgrowth of an essentially sound form of government. George Will, a close friend of Kristol's and a self-declared Tory Democrat, has noted scornfully of the Old Right that "people who preach disdain for government can consider themselves the intellectual descendants of Burke, the author of a celebration of the state." Further: "Two conservatives (Disraeli and Bismarck) pioneered the welfare state and did so for impeccably conservative reasons: to reconcile the masses to the vicissitudes and hazards of a dynamic and hierarchical industrial economy."[16]

The same belief in the welfare state shaped the neoconservative defense of the family and of other intermediate institutions between the individual and the state. Identified in the eighties with, among others, Peter L. and Brigitte Berger, Michael Novak, and Allan Carlson, neoconservative plans to assist the family were based on the view of the welfare state as being a useful as well as necessary condition of life. The battle to preserve the family from disintegration is to be waged through the state, by revamping taxes and transfer payments to favor two-parent families, natality, and domestic stability. In all fairness, it must be said that Allan Carlson, one of the most vigorous defenders of the traditional family allied with the neoconservative camp argued against the welfare state as well as "the ideological corruption of social work." Carlson arrived at the view that the welfare bureaucracy is irreversibly opposed to established social morality. Family services, he has argued, must be "reprivatized" in order to save what remains of lower-income families from total restructuring at the hands of social engineers. Carlson's pessimism about the family under the managerial state has driven him toward the Old Right and away from neoconservative sociologists. In a November 1985 essay for *Commentary,* Peter L. Berger, perhaps the premier sociologist of religion and emphatic defender of the nuclear family, extolled the "gigantic political efforts to ensure that no group within it [America] is excluded from the cornucopia of industrial capitalism." Looking toward the future for even further progress, Berger called for "a specifically American version of the welfare state" without the bureaucratic obstacles that have hindered similar enterprises in Europe.[17] This statement is particularly illuminating in view of the fact that the Bergers have been relentlessly critical of most family assistance programs that have originated on the Left.[18]

Undoubtedly, the neoconservative view of the welfare state stems partly from a recognition of the historically given. It seems unlikely that the system of transfer payments, poor relief, and extensive commercial regulation that operates in American society, with bipartisan political backing, will ever be substantially reversed. Kristol may indeed have been correct in his interpretation of the support Reagan got for his pledge to "get government off people's backs." The voters took this pledge, says Kristol, as a promise to trim government and lower taxes, not as a restatement of Goldwater's plan to rescind the welfare state. But if George Gilder was correct in describing neoconservatives as principled, not merely calculating, defenders of a mixed economy and managerial state,[19] then the neoconservatives' belief in the welfare state has been both a permanent aspect of their ideology and a characteristic that distinguishes them from the older Right.

Neoconservatives of the eighties also distinguished themselves from older American conservatives by their vision of a global democratic order. Although this vision is one that Irving Kristol views critically and Jeane Kirkpatrick approaches with reservations, it was nonetheless basic to the thinking of other neoconservatives. This neo-Wilsonian focus was evident in the foreign policy pronouncements of Norman Podhoretz, Ben Wattenberg, and Elliot Abrams and may have moved from them and other *Commentary* writers into the speeches of President Reagan. Some of the younger neoconservatives, most notably Joshua Muravchik, Michael Ledeen, and members of the National Endowment for Democracy (which serves as a bridge between organized labor and the neoconservative camp), advocated a global democratic revolution.[20] Such a revolution is to lead to a worldwide secular, politically egalitarian community. In the short run, non-Western governments are to be encouraged to hold democratic elections and to undertake land reform, unionization, and capital formation. The entire world is to be brought into conformity with the American regime that has developed in the twentieth century. A November 1985 *Commentary* symposium on America since 1945 made abundantly clear that prominent neoconservatives (Kristol was the most notable exception) did not typically search for their ideals in the past. Whatever problems they found in present-day America, they marveled at how far it had come since 1945 in achieving more democracy and social justice. This was the point of a series of television lectures by Ben Wattenberg several years ago; it was also the theme of a book of his that describes high divorce rates and other apparent signs of social decay as more or less the fruits of newly won freedoms.

Neoconservatives presented themselves as political centrists who deplored the lack of moderation on both sides of the spectrum. In *Breaking Ranks* Podhoretz depicted himself as supporting the moderate progressive candidate for the Senate, Daniel Moynihan, against the left-wing extremist Bella Abzug and the equally extremist incumbent Senator James Buckley.[21] Diane Ravitch, whose writings on educational problems appeared in *Commentary,* claimed to occupy the same middle ground. Ravitch sought to save public education from the Right, which demands "ideological and moral purity," and from the Left, which promotes "far-out ideologies of sexual liberation."[22] Although her writings were usually more critical of progressive educators and sex education than of creationists and anticommunists, her sense of symmetry was characteristically neoconservative. Neoconservatives, who may have learned from Arthur Schlesinger's book by that title the value of claiming to be the vital center, never abandon, at least rhetorically, the *juste milieu.* Recent neoconservative broadsides against Patrick J. Buchanan, Russell Kirk, and other figures identified with the unreconstructed Old Right always stress extremism as well as anti-Semitism.

Moral and tactical reservations about their association with the older Right led neoconservatives into producing their own account of a conservative movement that is anticommunist and patriotic but also humane and moderate. Such a conservatism, according to this account, did not arise through *National Review.* In fact, William Buckley had to tame his own magazine to bring under control the "seedbed infested with racism, chauvinism, and paranoid looniness" that Suzanne Garment in the *Wall Street Journal* identifies with the older Right.[23] Although, according to this view, "you can still hear an echo of the Right's more distasteful origins" in the pages of *National Review,* Buckley and his associates have "pried conservatism from the fingers of its more demented followers." In this sense, that journal and its editors are seen as the beneficiaries rather than sources of sound political teachings.

Few neoconservatives ever admit to being deeply influenced by a paleoconservative. Neoconservatives are, however, rich in praise of those mentors with whom they wish to be identified. Irving Kristol pays tribute to Leo Strauss, the German political philosopher, but not to James Burnham, as a father of his movement.[24] Kristol's concept of political realism has much in common with Burnham's, and he has praised *Suicide of the West* in conversation, though not in print. Moreover, Kristol may have been overgenerous to Strauss in attributing to him his own preference for Aristotle over Plato and for Locke over Rousseau. Lionel Trilling, a distinguished longtime professor of English at Columbia, enjoys an almost legendary status among older neoconservatives. Norman Podhoretz, who was Trilling's student at Columbia, invariably describes him with reverence; what is more, Trilling's widow, Diana, has been a respected contributor to *Commentary*. Podhoretz and Bell see Trilling as someone who incarnated civility, one of the values considered indispensable for discourse in a democratic society. Podhoretz is particularly impressed by Trilling's attempt to combine in his own life democratic beliefs and cultural refinement. Although Trilling was a Jewish intellectual long mesmerized by Marx and Freud, he wrote critically about the "liberal mind" and warned against the beginnings of the counterculture.[25]

Alexander Bloom has tried to argue that it was not Trilling so much as the less elegant and certainly pluckier Morris Raphael Cohen who helped to shape the neoconservative style. Cohen never made it out of City College of New York into the more prestigious philosophy department at Columbia. Though he blamed his professional frustrations on anti-Semites, his real problem may have been his combative personality. In this sense, Cohen may have had more in common with Bell, Lipset, Kristol, and other neoconservatives than did the aloof and oracular Trilling. Moreover, Cohen was a fierce anticommunist while Trilling, despite his stately demeanor and Victorian prose, took years to extricate himself entirely from Marxism.[26]

In light of the growing war between neo- and paleoconservatives, it may seen remarkable that many traditionalists originally welcomed the neoconservative newcomers. Part of the answer may be the quest by postwar conservatives for intellectual as well as political respectability in the face of electoral defeat and isolation from the academic community. The disengagement of prestigious academics and political journalists from the Left opened up the possibility of an advantageous alliance for "policy-oriented" conservatives. By ignoring the divisive issues, pragmatic conservatives hoped (and still hope) to entice into their camp great names from Harvard, Berkeley, and Columbia. Conservatives have also developed more positive attitudes toward Trilling, Adlai Stevenson, and Harry Truman. *National Review* has extolled all three since the early seventies as neoconservative heroes who, had they lived long enough, would by now be on the American Right. Some old conservatives also believed that the entire Right might benefit from neoconservative arguments against the Left and the libertarians. During the late sixties and early seventies, traditionalists were battling anarcho capitalists who, like Murray Rothbard, called for a minimal state and for an end to defense spending. The old conservatives, Russell Kirk and Robert Nisbet, long remained more critical of libertarians than of neoconservatives.

The old conservatives of the eighties were being swallowed up by the alliance that they initiated and sustained. From the mid-sixties on, many of them became convinced that by going into politics or by running foundations, they would promote their ideas more effectively. They began to look to others to represent them both in institutions of higher learning and in highbrow culture. A division of labor was to occur—at least in the minds of some old conservatives. The new breed of conservative activists would pursue political place and lay the financial foundations of a conservative counterestablishment, while academic and literary converts from the Left would fight the intellectual battles.

Conservative activists eventually lost the power to distinguish conservative from nonconservative reasons for the very policies they advocated. In opposing the Equal Rights Amendment, for example, one writer in *Policy Review,* like President Reagan, avoided the quintessentially conservative argument that sexual roles are necessary for the functioning of a stable society; and prohibition of their political and public recognition is therefore harmful to humanity. Others embraced Nathan Glazer's critique of minority quotas as inconsistent with the 1964 Civil Rights Act and with the individualism that Glazer associates with American democracy. The conservative humanistic perception of the same problem (which can easily be drawn out of the essays of Kirk, Nisbet, and Gertrude Himmelfarb) is much different: It is based on a view of unchanging human nature and on various authorities, from Aristotle to Burke. Conservatives (excluding libertarians) believe in the corporate nature of man; and though they may oppose the further intrusion into society by social engineers in the form of minority quotas, they defend traditional group identities as necessary for the nurture of the individual.[27]

The relationship between the Old Right and neoconservatives has nonetheless grown increasingly bitter since the mid-eighties. The symposium on America since 1945 that appeared in *Commentary*'s November 1985 issue stirred latent resentment among old conservative intellectuals. The *Commentary* symposium included people of the Left but, with the exception of Robert Nisbet, featured no one to the right of the neoconservatives. Most of the neoconservative contributors emphasized social progress, even while deploring high crime rates and the Soviet military buildup. The symposium elicited two stormy responses. One was in an issue of *Intercollegiate Review* published by Intercollegiate

Studies Institute; here old conservative intellectuals, including Russell Kirk, M. E. Bradford, and George Panichas, the literary critic, presented their predominantly bitter assessment of the neoconservatives. The Southern conservative historian Clyde Wilson expressed a dominant theme when he wrote: "First of all, we have simply been crowded out by overwhelming numbers. The offensives of radicalism have driven vast herds of liberals across the border into our territories. These refugees now speak in our name, but the language they speak is the same one they always spoke."[28]

An even more dramatic sign of Old Right revolt against neoconservative hegemony came in April 1986 at the annual meeting of the Philadelphia Society in Chicago. The Philadelphia Society had originally been set up as a forum for debate and discussion among conservatives. The early meetings had often resonated with lively exchanges between libertarians and traditionalists. Frank Meyer and Russell Kirk, surrounded by their followers, had held forth on their differing views of liberty and authority. In the seventies, Philadelphia Society sessions became more subdued; and except for some of the regional meetings at which Harry Jaffa and M. E. Bradford debated the status of equality as a basic principle of the American regime, the organization, and certainly its leadership tried to give the impression of a broad consensus on the Right. During the Reagan presidency, this theme of consensus became particularly important; conservatives of all kinds saw an opportunity to rule that they were not about to sacrifice as the result of internal division.

In 1985, however, M. E. Bradford became president of the Philadelphia Society and thereafter served a two- rather than one-year term. The gesture seemed harmless enough since the organization had ceased to generate controversy, and, in any case, conservatives who had deserted Bradford for the neoconservative candidate Bennett during the race for the NEH directorship were hoping to conciliate an old friend. But in 1986 Bradford did the unexpected. He staged a debate between conservatives and neoconservatives at the Philadelphia Society at which blood was drawn. Harsh words were exchanged by the participants; and the moderate representatives on both sides were overshadowed by the more combative ones. Stephen Tonsor, a Catholic conservative, declared that Christian Aristotelianism was integral to any true conservative perspective; he deplored the arrogance of former Marxists and radicals dictating policies and beliefs to those who had never strayed from the truth. On the other side, R. E. Tyrrell, the editor of the *American Spectator*, lashed out against "phony conservatives" who had come to divide the Right. Such people, said Tyrrell, had no idea of how much "neoconservatives were suffering for the cause." But that, argued the paleoconservatives, was the point at issue. In their view, neoconservatives had received mostly benefits from their hesitant and qualified identification with the political Right. On the other hand, the Christian Aristotelianism—or neo-Thomism—that Tonsor considered essential to the intellectual Right had never been more than a minority position among postwar conservatives. The exchange at the Philadelphia Society did, however, yield one truth: The growing tension between paleo- and neoconservatives could no longer be disregarded.[29] It would flare up again, even more dramatically, several years later.

The Counterestablishment

By the late eighties the most frequently reiterated complaint against the neoconservatives came down to the simple questions of money and power. For years conservatives had wandered in the wilderness, but now, just as they were about to reap the reward for their suffering, a set of Johnny-come-latelies were taking the lion's share. From the early 1970s, the American Enterprise Institute, the Hoover Institution, and the Heritage Foundation began to include neoconservatives among their trustees and resident scholars. Significantly, all three of these think tanks, which have multimillion dollar annual operating budgets, started out as vehicles for more traditional conservatives. Originally their publications and the speeches of their staffs represented the foreign and domestic policies associated with *National Review* and with the Goldwater presidential bid. How that situation changed is taken up in Chapter 6; however, some of the early phases in that transformation are outlined here.

The American Enterprise Institute, founded in 1943, initiated the new direction for conservative think tanks. In the seventies it began offering support and fellowship to liberal academics whose collaboration it sought in presenting certain policy positions. Then, as now, its council of Academic Advisors and the editors of *Public Opinion*, its chief periodical, worked hard to maintain a reputation for academic respectability and political moderation. Ben Wattenberg and Seymour Martin Lipset, longtime editors of *Public Opinion*, exemplify the American Enterprise Institute's changed orientation. Both came from urban intellectual environments and combine principled anticommunism with strong residual sympathy for social democratic ideals.

The Hoover Institution, which is tied through an increasingly problematic relationship to Stanford University, made similar efforts to obtain centrist respectability. Starting in the 1970s, and perhaps even in the 1960s, when W. Glenn Campbell became its president, it aimed at incorporating main-line academic support. Hoover also offered generous and extended fellowships to anticommunists of the old moderate Left, such as Sidney Hook. The Heritage Foundation, under the direction of Edwin J. Feulner, formerly with ISI, searched even more resourcefully for new allies. From the late 1970s, Feulner together with the editors of *Policy Review,* a quarterly published by Heritage, highlighted foreign, economic, and administrative policies (particularly eschewing divisive philosophical and ethical questions).[30] In this tendency, Feulner and his staff did not break entirely new ground. Certainly a "policy-oriented conservatism" could already be seen in Goldwater's presidential campaign and among postwar libertarians of the Right. Heritage, moreover, maintained at least cosmetic ties to the Old Right by naming Russell Kirk one of its senior scholars. (AEI bestowed a similar honor on Robert Nisbet.)

Heritage used the avoidance of theoretical issues to broaden its appeal among groups that were offended by the Old Right. It did this while continuing to enjoy the financial backing of Joseph Coors, Jr., and of other staunchly Old Right benefactors. The result of this quest for academic friends on the part of conservative foundations led inescapably to a new ideological mix; although some foundation leaders persist in treating the postwar conservative movement from 1945 to the present as a seamless robe, even a cursory reading of *Public Opinion* or *Policy Review* would have tempered their confidence. Proposals for "trimming" the welfare state replaced plans to dismantle the New Deal. The model for dealing with the Soviets became Truman's "containment policy" or the Wilsonian vision of world democracy, not James Burnham's program of rolling back the Soviet empire by appealing to historic nationalities. Harry Truman, FDR, and Martin Luther King, Jr., were treated with respect, while, by contrast, such heroes of the Old Right as Edmund Burke, Richard Weaver, and Robert Taft were hardly mentioned. Joseph McCarthy survived only as an object of obloquy.[31]

In the 1980s neoconservatives began to face opposition in their handling of foundations. This happened most noticeably in the case of the American Enterprise Institute, which in 1986 was forced to reduce its full-time staff from 154 to 110.[32] AEI had initiated its opening to the Left under its founder and first president, William Baroody, who had actively sought the collaboration of neoconservative academics for what Baroody has assumed were essentially conservative policies. Under his son and successor William Baroody, Jr., the foundation had tried to build bridges to political celebrities of all types, and it became known as a meeting ground between neoconservatives—such as Jeane Kirkpatrick, Irving Kristol, Ben Wattenberg, S. M. Lipset, and the legal expert Walter Berns—and those further to the Left. Unfortunately for AEI, the organization became progressively less distinguishable from more liberal foundations such as the Brookings Institution. Brookings opened its door to neoconservative policy experts and thinkers precisely as AEI was drifting Leftward. In 1986, a decision supported by the younger Baroody to invite Vladimir Posner, the Soviet spokesman, to speak at the institute as a guest, angered conservative benefactors. The John M. Olin and Smith Richardson foundations expressed unwillingness to give further support to the straying institute. Although both of these foundations were willing to befriend the neoconservatives, Baroody's behavior had become so distasteful to those who provided the funds for AEI that a financial crisis occurred, which required Baroody to leave his post.

Despite the defunding of AEI and the flareup of old conservative resentment against the neoconservatives, it seems premature to speak of a waning neoconservative influence in the formulation of policies. Adam Meyerson, the current editor of *Policy Review,* has made the useful observation that no group on the Right will likely soon replace the neoconservatives as framers and exponents of policy positions.[33] The old conservative activists of the seventies and early eighties fell between two stools: abandoning the theoretical interests of the founding generation of postwar conservatism, they then failed to achieve authoritative status as policymakers or policy experts. Thus those who in the eighties went into government or foundations played second fiddle to neoconservatives or to authentic New Rightists.

George Panichas, the editor of *Modern Age,* a Christian Platonist, and a morally committed interpreter of modern literature, has warned against the "contaminating" obsession with making it in Washington. He has stressed the distinction between Plato's attempt to spiritualize the political and the modern tendency to reduce spiritual questions to political ones. In his contribution to the *Intercollegiate Review*'s symposium on the state of conservatism, Panichas laments the "sad paradox that conservative leaders and thinkers often fail, in the present climate of their political victories, to recognize or implement their spiritual identity and responsibility. No authentic conservative metaphysic can be operable when the discipline of God and the discipline of the soul have been ceded to the *doxai* the dialectical structures and superstructures of modern life."[34]

Panichas was issuing an appropriate warning to Old Right activists of the eighties who made misguided professional and strategic judgments.

What must now be asked, however, is whether their neoconservative successors have remained—as Adam Meyerson suggested several years ago—on the cutting edge of policy issues. Again, though Chapter 6 will discuss such questions at some length, a few closing observations are called for in this chapter.

Neoconservative policy examinations have become in recent years increasingly less interesting and increasingly more prescribed. On some matters, such as Israel, global democracy, immigration, and the appropriateness of using public education to instil "democratic" values, neoconservatives are tiresomely predictable—and establishment-sounding. Whereas in the seventies and eighties neoconservative publications produced perceptive policy assessments by, among others, Banfield, Wilson, and Lipset, they have come to depend heavily on a stable of youthful polemicists, all of them pro-Zionist, proimmigration, and anti-isolationist. Daniel Pipes, Joshua Muravchik, and David Frum are three of the most reliable—and most abrasive—of these polemicists. The charges of racism and anti-Semitism they routinely level against anti-immigrationists and neoisolationists, however, are no substitute for serious argument.[35]

In general, neoconservatives seem to be losing their interest in politics broadly defined. Their major political concerns have become holding on to and promoting political celebrities whom they have been able to influence, such as Jack Kemp and Dan Quayle, and moving into federal bureaucracies, particularly NEH and the Department of Education, which they can staff with their followers. It may even be argued that neoconservatives have pushed the otherwise idle debate about the "end of history," through the *National Interest, New Republic,* and other magazines they control, to get back to the cold war liberal "end of ideology" discussion of the fifties. Both then and more recently Americans were told that all significant political and ideological struggle was drawing to a close. In the fifties Daniel Bell declared that the struggle was soon to be at an end in the United States; in 1990 neoconservative Francis Fukuyama, writing in *National Interest* and by then already enjoying neoconservative subsidies, announced the imminent end of the struggle everywhere. For neoconservatives the only major struggles now to be waged, outside of the battle to contain Israel's Muslim expansionist enemies, are cultural: converting humanity, starting with American educators, to global democracy. While there are other reasons that neoconservatives now prefer educational and cultural discussions over wide-ranging political debate, it is clear that they wish others to believe that they have already resolved all significant political questions. They have supposedly achieved this feat by laying down the proper policy positions and by offering themselves as administrators. Though this dogmatic approach to the end of ideology may wash for many liberal as well as neoconservative journalists, it has not settled any aspect of the ideological quarrel on the American Right. By the end of the eighties the neoconservatives would see a renewal of ideological war by determined right-wing opponents.

Chapter Five

Populist Rebellion: The New Right

The political movement known as the New Right has a great deal in common with neoconservatism. Both movements took formal shape in the 1970s, although their antecedents are much older. Both arose in reaction to what was regarded as a betrayal of purpose. For the neoconservatives, it was Democrats and young radicals who corrupted the great liberal tradition; for the New Right, the villains were moderate Republicans who betrayed the interest and principles of the great majority of ordinary Americans. Both have been remarkably successful at raising money and establishing public-policy organizations, and both are accused of taking over organizations.

For many political analysts, the New Right amounts to little more than "a collection of general-purpose political organizations" in alliance with conservative politicians.[1] These analysts cite groups like the Conservative Caucus headed by Howard Phillips, the Moral Majority (now Liberty Foundation) led by Jerry Falwell, the Committee for the Survival of a Free Congress under Paul Weyrich, the National Conservative Political Action Committee under Terry Dolan, and, to a lesser extent, the Heritage Foundation, which had its origin on the border between Old and New Right, but which has grown over the years into a central conservative organization.

If there are many similarities between the two groups of new conservatives, there are also profound differences. For one thing, many (if not most) of the New Right leaders were previously involved in conservative politics: Richard Viguerie worked for YAF, which he helped to put back on its feet economically; Howard Phillips was an assistant to the chairman of the Republican National Committee and headed the Office of Economic Opportunity under President Nixon; Paul Weyrich had been an aide to Senator Gordon Allott, a conservative Republican; and Phyllis Schlafly was the author of *A Choice, Not an Echo,* a book that galvanized many in the Draft Goldwater movement. Some have gone so far as saying that the difference between the Old and New Right is "purely chronological"[2] or only a matter of the personalities involved.

The continuity is significant. Both groups oppose communism, support free enterprise and limited government, and respect (although they do not always practice) religion and "traditional values." But while the Old Right continues to emphasize anticommunism and free enterprise, the New Right has learned how to emphasize themes that are more populist than conservative: the fear and resentment of the Eastern "establishment," defense of family and conventional morals, popular control over schools and churches. They also display a greater willingness to use single-issue campaigns, like the Panama Canal treaty or abortion, as the basis of external fund-raising.

Richard Viguerie, long the symbolic leader of the New Right, views style and strategy as the binding forces of his diverse movement. He lists four common characteristics of the New Right: technical ability in promotion and politics, a cooperative spirit, a commitment to principle over and above loyalty to the Republican party, and, finally, the optimism displayed in his own title, *The New Right: We're Ready to Lead.*[3] Viguerie is a suitable symbol for the movement he heads: a hardworking, self-made man from the Sunbelt, he is distinguished neither by his learning nor by his literary style. Compared with a William Buckley or Jeffrey Hart, Viguerie resembles a car salesman attending, uninvited, a formal dinner.

Perhaps the single most important element in the success of the New Right coalition was the involvement of Evangelical Christians, including the prominent Evangelists Jerry Falwell and Pat Robertson. The Christian Right contributed more than religious fervor and moral commitment: by the 1980s Christian broadcasting was reaching millions of television viewers and radio listeners, who responded to its appeal for moral revival and patriotic dedication. The impact of religious broadcasting is especially strong in Southern states, which increasingly play a key role in elections.

Origins of the New Right

Richard Viguerie dates the formation of the movement he has midwived to August 1974, when Gerald Ford selected the liberal Republican Nelson

Rockefeller to be his vice-president. It was not simply that Ford had passed over a number of attractive conservatives, but that in picking Rockefeller, Ford had "revealed the true colors of so-called 'moderate' Republicanism by choosing the very symbol of everything we Conservatives had always opposed." Viguerie assembled a group of friends to discuss ways of stopping the appointment. Though they failed to stop Rockefeller, they did succeed in launching a new political movement. This incident and its aftermath underscore several New Right themes: the feeling they had been betrayed by the Eastern establishment; a willingness to oppose the Republican leadership—even in the very difficult days after Watergate; and the use of strategic planning sessions.

The major actors in the early days were Paul Weyrich, Howard Phillips, Terry Dolan, and Viguerie himself. Weyrich had been instrumental in creating the Heritage Foundation and, with the backing of brewing magnate Joseph Coors, established the Committee for the Survival of a Free Congress in 1974. He had previously been active in the American Legislative Exchange Council (ALEC) and the Republican Study Committee. Weyrich's Free Congress was instrumental in supporting the election of conservative candidates in the late seventies and early eighties, while disseminating ideological materials through the Free Congress Research and Education Foundation.

In the first decade of his operation, Weyrich succeeded in attracting several valuable collaborators to his banner. Kathleen Teague, a former YAF activist and executive director of the American Legislative Exchange Council, became his board chairman, and conservative Catholics Patrick Fagan, Joseph Piccione, and Patrick McGuignan have all played a significant role in socially oriented projects like the Child and Family Protection Institute.

Connaught Marshner, also a Catholic conservative activist like Weyrich himself, played an important role in focusing attention on issues of education and the family. Author of *Blackboard Tyranny,* coeditor (with Weyrich) of *Future 21: Directions for America in the 21st Century,* chairman of the National Pro-Family Coalition, and an executive with Free Congress, Marshner emerged as a tireless spokesman for the traditional values espoused by the New Right. She is also a relentless and passionate debater. As a result of their varied activities (conducted in a maze of interlocking organizations), Weyrich and his staff had established themselves by the eighties as the ideological center of social conservatism.

Terry Dolan, the chairman of the National Conservative Political Action Committee (NCPAC), may have been the most controversial New Right leader. Under Dolan, NCPAC devoted its energies to unseating liberals by any possible legal means. Charges against Dolan ranged from slander to blackmail to attacks on his private life. Whatever the substance of the allegations, NCPAC became a symbol of New Right political successes in mobilizing the politics of resentment. Alan Crawford, a self-styled conservative and author of *Thunder on the Right,* records part of a conversation in which Dolan explained his strategy: the key phrases include, "Let's get rid of the bastards," "Stir up hostilities," and "The shriller you are the better it is to raise money."[4] In a 1977 campaign to defeat the Democratic gubernatorial candidate in Virginia, Dolan's tactics were shrill enough for the Republican candidate to disassociate himself publicly. In the 1986 North Carolina Republican primary contest, Dolan even refused to concede defeat when the conservatives lost but threatened to continue his advertising campaign. North Carolina's New Right Senator, Jesse Helms, was not amused, and some Republicans were quick to blame their candidate's defeat on the divisive primary campaign. However, there was no denying NCPAC's successes. In 1978 alone, it made financial contributions to 200 conservative candidates and provided $440,000 worth of campaign services. In 1980 Dolan's organization reported raising $7.6 million and spending $3.3 million on independent expenditures aimed at unseating liberal Democrats,[5] although by 1986 NCPAC was in serious financial trouble.

In its rise to prominence, NCPAC was an important client of the Richard A. Viguerie Company (RAVCO), a fund-raising and promotion empire that mushroomed in the late seventies. Viguerie learned the business of fund-raising as Marvin Liebman's account executive for YAF, a job that he obtained in 1961 after answering a classified ad in *National Review.* A shy man, Viguerie found it difficult to ask for contributions directly and hit upon the expedient of writing letters. In 1964 he set up his own direct mail firm and built his original list by hand-copying the names of Goldwater supporters. (There does not appear to be a great deal of substance to the allegation that he stole the YAF list.)

Viguerie is a bundle of strange contradictions: a Catholic (like Weyrich) who is closely identified with Christian Fundamentalists; a sincere and committed ideologue (few who know him seem to doubt this) whose company is frequently accused of raking off the lion's share of funds raised for conservative causes; a simple populist who lives in great style in McLean, Virginia. As Viguerie tells his own story, many of his most fateful decisions were made in emotional reaction to some slight, real or imagined. In 1971, for example, he actively sought the Committee to Re-Elect the President (CREEP) account. When he failed, Viguerie began to turn against Nixon and rejected an offer, later that year, to do mailings. He attributed his decision to Nixon's shift to the left: "I decided I wanted no part of Nixon. . . . I realize that Nixon may never have had any deep-rooted belief or goals, except those that furthered his particular personal ambition."

Viguerie and his colleagues supported—only to reject—a number of Republican politicians: Barry Goldwater, Richard Nixon, John Connally, George Wallace, and Ronald Reagan. Reagan was not the New Right's prime candidate for president—the less conservative but more outspoken John Connally of Texas was the candidate the New Right supported. After Reagan's 1980 victory, it was hoped that the new administration would treat the Heritage Foundation's *Mandate for Leadership* not merely as a blueprint—which it did—but also as a detailed agenda to be followed to the letter. When Reagan proved to be as much politician as ideologue, the cry went up: "Let Reagan be Reagan." And it was not long before Viguerie began to offer alternatives, like Jesse Helms, to the press. At first, the attacks were mostly directed against White House advisers, particularly James Baker, a George Bush Republican accused of blocking conservative appointments. A 1981 Heritage Foundation report on the administration's first year attributed Reagan's mixed performance to "a lack of political sensitivity in the personnel staff." In February of 1982, conservative leaders met with Reagan to discuss their complaints, but by the end of Reagan's first term, New Right leaders were discussing the formation of a third party. For hostile critics, this refusal to "play ball" was a sign of instability in the New Right leadership. In the words of an English chronicler of American conservatism in the Reagan era, Gillian Peele: "The New Right showed an element of self-destructiveness and sectarianism which has perpetually marked much of the thinking and testimony of the Conservative movement."[6]

The sense of betrayal runs deep in New Right circles, and few political leaders have demonstrated an ability to command their loyalty for more than a short period. Conservative politicians, on the other hand, developed doubts about RAVCO's methods. The most frequently heard complaint was that Viguerie's fees practically bankrupted Representative Phil Crane's presidential bid as well as the campaigns of Iowa Senator Roger Jepsen. In his defense, Viguerie was to point out the enormous start-up costs involved in building a list of contributors, a list that only begins to pay dividends after the fund-raisers had left the scene.

Religious Right

From almost the beginning, the New Right's tactics were controversial. Its image was tarnished in the press, and its coalition sometimes seemed like an unstable assortment of alliances. At least the alliance with Evangelicals proved to be popular among many Americans. By the 1970s politics was hardly a new concern for Evangelical Christians. Much of the support for William Jennings Bryan's populist crusades had been drawn from the Evangelical churches, and the 1950s and 1960s were treated to anticommunist political sermons by the Reverend Carl McIntire and even Billy Graham. Still, the Fundamentalist mainstream, represented by the Bob Jones dynasty in South Carolina, avoided politics and did not hesitate to criticize politically minded preachers.

Jerry Falwell himself used to preach sermons against marching ministers. The key event in waking Falwell and other Fundamentalists from their apolitical slumbers was the 1973 Supreme Court decision on abortion. Most Evangelicals had not given a great deal of thought to what was regarded as a typically Catholic issue, but *Roe* v. *Wade* changed all that by turning a personal moral question into a national political issue. The failure of the main-line churches to oppose the decision and the political escapades of the World Council of Churches contributed to the growing unease of Falwell and others. As Dinesh D'Souza, his biographer, puts it: "Abortion politicized, even radicalized Falwell, but as he began to be interested in politics, other issues arose."[7]

In the late 1970s, a number of Christian political groups began to attract attention, particularly the Christian Voice, led by Gary Jarmin, an organization that rated congressmen. The National Christian Action Coalition (NCAC) was another prominent Christian political group. NCAC was particularly engaged in efforts to prevent the IRS from interfering in religious schools. Outside the Evangelical spectrum, Catholics for Christian Political Action focused on the evils of abortion, homosexual rights, and the national defense.

The largest and most conspicuous group on the religious Right was the Moral Majority. Established after a May 1979 meeting, its founders included Robert Billups (former director of NCAC), Howard Phillips (Conservative Caucus), Richard Viguerie, Ed McAteer (Christian Roundtable), Paul Weyrich (Free Congress), and, most significantly, Jerry Falwell of the Thomas Roads Baptist Church in Lynchburg, Virginia. As an obvious sign of Falwell's centrality, the meeting was held in his office—although it was actually Weyrich and McAteer who came up with the name.

In a brief but stormy career, the Moral Majority and its leader were attacked from all sides of the political spectrum. On the left, black leader Julian Bond, George McGovern, and Norman Lear (People for the American Way) pronounced it dangerous and drew comparisons with the Ku Klux Klan and Nazi Germany. On the right, Barry Goldwater suggested it was every American's patriotic duty "to kick Jerry Falwell in the ass." The critical abuse rose to a crescendo when MM began a campaign against network television and raised the possibility of boycotting certain programs. A similar uproar was created in 1985 when a letter-writing campaign put pressure on Southland Corporation (7 Eleven Stores) to remove *Playboy* and *Penthouse* from their magazine racks.

Falwell's response to accusations of bookburning and bigotry was a friendly assertion of democratic pluralism. Old-fashioned Christians and Jews, he repeatedly argued, are entitled to have opinions and to act upon them. "Liberals have been imposing morality on us for the last fifty years,"[8] he declared, and there was nothing wrong in fighting back. On rare occasions, Falwell may have lived down to the stereotype presented in the press. In the beginning, he was not always properly briefed on political questions and had to fall back on scriptural quotations. As time went on, however, he became an adroit politician, affable and deft in handling hecklers and willing to sit down and talk pleasantly with opponents like Ted Kennedy. While it is hard to measure the success of the Moral Majority's efforts, pollster Lou Harris attributes the 1980 election of Ronald Reagan partly to the vote of the awakened Evangelicals. It is an unquestionably large group. Of the 30 million or so estimated Evangelicals in the mid-eighties, one survey suggested at least a third regularly tuned in to religious programming on television.[9] However, estimates of Evangelical strength often include large numbers of Catholic and black voters who do not quite fit the Moral Majority mold. Perhaps this diversity helps to explain why the Christian Right has not, by and large, succeeded in realizing its ambitions. Despite a few victories, "the record," as Kenneth Wald suggests, "has been one of failure. Under Ronald Reagan, abortion was still legal, while school prayer was not."[10]

Hostile critics Alan Crawford in *Thunder on the Right* and John Saloma in *Ominous Politics* describe the New Right almost exclusively in the terms of campaign technology and "interlocking directorates": who raises money for whom, who gets appointed to which job through whose influence, and so on—a technique the John Birchers used against the Left. Such an approach deals, however, only with the surface. On a number of important subjects, especially social issues connected with the family and education, the New Right represented a distinctive and fairly consistent position that made it, in the view of the authors of *Neopolitics*, "the most significant new force in American politics in half a century, and quite possibly the full one hundred years."[11]

The precipitous decline in political influence and even visibility of the Religious Right since the eighties is something that the first edition of this book failed to foresee. Whereas in the 1980s Pat Robertson was a contender for the Republican presidential nomination and Jerry Falwell a celebrity frequently interviewed on TV and by print journalists, in 1992 no Religious Right leader commands national attention. Indeed, Robertson still runs a TV network, and he and Falwell are cited as supporters of George Bush, but neither is seen any longer as controlling electorates. The politicized Evangelicals and antiabortion Catholics who together formed the Religious Right of the eighties have now been absorbed into other groups, particularly neoconservative-funded institutes, which will be discussed in a later chapter.

There are several reasons for the decline of the Religious Right. One is the devastating effect to its image of the exposure of the financial misdeeds and other crimes committed by Jim Bakker and the revelations concerning the sexual misconduct of TV evangelist Jimmy Swaggart. The resulting loss of confidence in these high-profile revivalists has affected the public and financial standing of others in this line of work, even of those who have not been touched by scandal. Like ancient ritual pollution, guilt by professional association has hurt Falwell, Robertson, and other TV ministers once numbered among the leaders of the Religious Right.[12]

A second reason for the weakening of the Religious Right has been its loss of autonomy through incorporation into beltway activist and neoconservative front groups. Religious Right spokesmen have moved into the organizations run by Michael Novak, George Weigel, Paul Weyrich, and R. J. Neuhaus, as supernumerary advocates of "democratic capitalism." Even the culturally and economically libertarian Cato Institute has put on its staff the evangelical free-enterpriser Douglas Bandow. Most on the Religious Right have hardly resisted such cooptation, having perhaps nowhere else to go financially, politically, or professionally. Their Washington-based neoconservative and libertarian sponsors have been eager to take them in because of their usefulness in advertising certain issues.

Political Evangelicals, who are predominantly Protestant Dispensation-alists, are strong supporters for theological reasons—albeit by now for career considerations as well—of the Zionist Right in both the United States and Israel. Moreover, the Catholic Right has produced advocates for less restrictive immigration, particularly from Latin America, a posi-tion neoconservative foundations have consistently backed. By now the Religious Right has become a force for others to manage; for example, Republican presidents hosting prayer breakfasts and giving speeches op-posing abortion, and Washington activists offering token staff positions. Given the current weakened position of the Religious Right, it seems unlikely that it will be a major player in the conservative movement for the foreseeable future.

Social Issues

Older conservatives were not insensitive to the social and moral ques-tions that agitated the New Right, but the old "fusionist" coalition included a libertarian strain summed up—albeit crudely—in the expres-sion, "You can't legislate morality." Throughout the sixties and seventies, conservatives depicted the federal government as an oppressive agent of moral enforcement through the Civil Rights Act, forced busing, and affirmative action policies. It was inevitably more convenient (and less divisive) to attack existing policies than to offer alternatives. While this alliance against a common enemy helped to keep the "fusionist" coalition together, it also hindered the development of positive vision that went beyond political antistatism and economic freedom.

From the very first, however, the New Right took the offensive on a whole range of controversial issues: sex education, homosexual rights, abortion, school prayer, and the Equal Rights Amendment. At the center of all these issues is the traditional Judeo-Christian conception of the family as a divinely ordained institution. In their view, homosexual be-havior is not only unnatural, but contrary to God's will. Marriage exists, especially in Protestant theology, for both companionship and procrea-tion. Homosexuality is, as one Christian Voice appeal for funds put it, part of "a master plan to destroy everything that is good and moral here in America." On this issue, the Religious Right took the lead, and Jerry Falwell went so far as to attack Coors Brewing (a major funding source on the Right) for advertising in a homosexual publication. While Anita Bryant became the symbol of opposition to gay rights, the most serious discussion was provided by Enrique T. Rueda of Paul Weyrich's Free

Congress Committee. Rueda cited evidence of government support for the homosexual movement, which he portrayed as a kind of conspiracy against conventional morality. Unlike most attacks on homosexual rights, Rueda's *Homosexual Network* avoided hysterical language and attempted to document its indictment.

When they are accused of imposing their personal morality, Christian activists reply that all laws are a matter of "values." For example, commitments to protection of life and property are not self-evident givens; they are derived from specific cultural and religious traditions. When liberal and Christian traditions collide, the principal question becomes, as Carl Horn expressed in a book title, one of *Whose Values?*: "The conflict is between those who believe that law and public policy derive from religious belief and those who reject such an assumption."[13]

Social conservatives maintain that homosexual rights threaten the family by legitimizing alternative life-styles. For the same reason, an even more serious danger is posed by women's rights. Phyllis Schlafly and her Eagle Forum were successful in preventing what seemed to be the inevitable passage of the Equal Rights Amendment—a victory that caused George Gilder to refer to her as "one of the most effective political leaders ever to emerge in America."[14] Schlafly was herself far from hard line on women's issues. She supported as "benign discrimination" the privileged legal status enjoyed by women in a society that enforced equal rights under the law.[15] Critics on the Left (and even a few radicals on the Right) complained of the inconsistency in having one's cake and eating it too, but Schlafly was an activist rather than philosopher. Her concern was to defend women, not to draw up a system of political ethics. The efforts of Eagle Forum and of countless state and local anti-ERA organizations caused the Republican party to drop its support in 1980.

There was—and still is—a single issue campaign even more explosive than stopping ERA or homosexual rights ordinances: abortion. It was an issue that united Evangelical Protestants with traditional Catholics and Orthodox Jews against what columnist Joseph Sobran called "the abortion sect," a materialist worldview that sees man, so critics say, as only "an animal whose destiny is a life of pleasure and comfort."[16] Opposition to abortion ranged from the dignified essays in the *Human Life Review* (edited by J. P. McFadden) to the disciplined and well-coordinated efforts of the National Right to Life Committee all the way to the pugnacious tactics of Joseph Scheidler, who declared open war on abortion clinics.[17] Perhaps the most striking development has been the gradual shift (partly under the influence of the late Francis Schaeffer) from Catholic to Evangelical domination in the movement, although many Evangelicals continue to be more flexible than Catholics (Falwell, for example, considers it a tactical mistake to insist upon a federal law forbidding abortion in every case including rape).

Early in the Reagan years, Senator John East, on Old Right political scientist, held hearings on when life begins, but even a Republican-held Senate was not about to take on a politically explosive topic. By the mid-eighties, however, the subject would not go away. What little traditional Catholic support Geraldine Ferraro brought to the Mondale ticket began to melt away as her "prochoice" position became generally known. Her conflict with Cardinal John O'Connor, archbishop of New York, did little to reassure Catholic voters of her fidelity. Catholics differed little from other Americans who opposed abortion except to save the mother's life or in cases where rape or incest was involved. What had seemed to be the safe, middle course of the seventies—"I'm against abortion personally, but do not wish to impose my views on others"—began to seem, by the eighties, a proabortion argument.

Opposition to ERA, homosexual rights, and abortion was part of what the New Right regarded as a crusade to save the American family. Liberalized divorce laws and a general air of permissiveness had spawned a wide range of "alternate life-styles" that resulted in spiraling rates of divorce, abortion, and adolescent suicide. The tax code, itself, in the view of Allan Carlson, offered massive disincentives for family life. In a series of reports on the family,[18] Carlson argued that Social Security was a scam for breaking up intergenerational family ties, that tax deductions for day care amounted to a subsidy for mothers who neglected their children, and that inflation-eroded personal exemptions constituted an assault on traditional families burdened by the expense of rearing children on a single income.

Carlson was not alone in his concern for family issues. Weyrich's Free Congress established the *Family Protection Report,* a political newsletter on family issues edited by Connaught Marshner and Patrick Fagan. Later Weyrich founded the *Journal of Family and Culture,* edited by Joseph Piccione, as an alternative to more liberal academic publications, particularly the *Journal of Marriage and the Family.* Other prominent participants in the profamily coalition included John Whitehead of the Rutherford Institute and James Dobson, who put out a monthly *Focus on the Family.*

While there was no denying the sincerity of the family's defenders, many of them were severely limited in their approach. Ignoring a mass of evidence from social history, anthropology, and psychology, much of the profamily literature is a series of almost hysterical reactions to events. Some of the writing was fueled by a nostalgic wish to return to the golden age of a simple America. The nuts-and-bolts approach to family policy, characteristic of Weyrich's Free Congress publications, was eminently serviceable in rallying the profamily forces around specific issues, but it failed to attract and convince serious psychologists, family historians, and sociologists. Allan Carlson, who had connections both with the neoconservatives and the New Right, was a conspicuous exception, but not even he could always avoid the major pitfall of the New Right family coalition: the conviction that the nuclear family was a fragile product of bourgeois society that needed political support from the government. Inevitably, this would invest the government with the power to "protect" the family. This sort of family policy was more typical of European social democrats than American conservatives.

Strange ideas began to emanate from conservative quarters. Both George Gilder and Joseph Piccione came out for government subsidies for children on the model of European social democracy. Previously, conservatives had only sought to reduce government intrusions into private life. The call for government support was uncharacteristic and seemed to call into question the conservative claim that the family was a universal requirement for stable society. If conservatives came to view the family as unable to survive without financial rewards from government, Leftists would have reasons for stepping up their attacks on the family as a "patriarchal" institution.

This paradox became clear in discussions of parents' rights. Much of the debate on the subject has been concerned with a minor's right to an abortion, the parents' role in sex and values education, and child-abuse legislation. Until the twentieth century, families were generally responsible for the moral instruction (and behavior) of minor children. Increasingly, however, schools and social work agencies have come to define what is in the children's interests.

By the late 1970s, the idea of children's rights began to surface. Sex education, contraception, religious and racial tolerance, and mental health began to be seen as human rights to be guaranteed by law. The process was encouraged by the United Nation's International Year of the Child and a similar program in the United States. Decent treatment for children seemed to be an unimpeachable idea to many people, but conservatives viewed it as one more stage in the state's usurpation of family responsibilities. In fact, much of the proposed child protection legislation (especially child-abuse laws) bypassed the ordinary civil rights of accused persons and acted against parents on the presumption of guilt.

There was an obvious conservative strategy illustrated in the writings of Mary Pride[19]: This was to challenge the child-abuse statistics and to document the sufferings of innocent parents in the grip of a coercive legal system. The Leftist Christopher Lasch, in his book *Haven in a Heartless World,* also deplored the therapeutic state that has grown at the expense of families. Here was a rare chance for a Left/Right antigovernment consensus.

But many conservatives went further. Not content with attempting to undo the misuse of government power, many argued that such power must be used to defend and build up the power of the family. John W. Whitehead of the Rutherford Institute based such an argument on the dubious claim (derived from Alvin Toffler!) that the fragile family structure is breaking down.[20] Fears of widespread family dissolution served as a pretext for activists on the Right and social workers on the Left to uphold governments' claims to be the ultimate authority on social and ethical questions. In the end, at least some profamily arguments may have had the effect of diminishing family autonomy.

The more sensible and intelligent profamily activists were not unaware of the tension between their resentment of big government and their desire to use that same government to buttress the family. Earlier, Connaught Marshner explained the government had been working to undermine the family, but a New Right State could do a number of useful things: exclude alternative living arrangements from the legal definition of family, give financial protection to mothers in need, make divorce more difficult, and recognize the historic rights of parents in the education of their children.

The New Right's education campaign had been aimed primarily at questions of ethics and religion. At stake was the right of schools to decide on curriculum as against the right of parents to determine what sort of moral and religious values their children will be taught. The focus of much of the criticism had been on sex education and values clarification (what is sometimes called ethical reasoning). In 1984 the Department of Education held hearings on the Protection of Pupils Rights Amendment. Edited (and widely distributed) by Phyllis Schlafly,[21] the testimony was used to demonstrate the immorality and underhanded techniques of values-education classes. What Evangelicals called "secular humanism" was being taught, while references to God and religion were being excluded from textbooks and curricula. In a study supported by the Department of Education, Paul Vitz made a detailed examination of social studies text-books and found virtually no mention of such momentous religious events as the Great Awakening. [22] Elementary school reading books do inculcate values, Vitz concluded: They are against patriotism and business but support feminism, and "serious Judeo-Christian religious motivation" is featured nowhere. [23]

Since the Scopes trial in the 1920s, education has been a battleground between the forces of academic liberalism and middle-American populism. Issues like busing in South Boston or textbooks in West Virginia and Tennessee were able to galvanize support for a New Right agenda. Reagan's head of the U.S. Department of Education, William Bennett, defused some of the growing antagonism, but the hostility ran too deep for any rhetorical solutions. By the 1980s New Right and religious activists were on the offensive, demanding full support for their views. *Washington Times* columnist John Lofton, for example, in interviewing Secretary Bennett, refused to be placated by general reassurances. What Lofton and others insisted on was (1) the primacy of revelation and (2) the unconditional right of parents to determine what their children are taught. Bennett, on the other hand, was willing to grant only a qualified support for the importance of religion and the need for parental involvement.

While the New Right was most prominently identified with social issues, it did not shy away from other political questions, particularly on foreign policy. Jerry Falwell and Pat Robertson regularly made statements on South Africa, the Soviet occupation of Afghanistan, and Nicaragua. It was conventional politics that brought into prominence Viguerie, Weyrich, and Phillips, all of whom appeared opposed to President Carter's 1977 proposal to democratize political campaigns. [24] Ironically, several aspects of Carter's proposal, for example, his plan to abolish the electoral college, were populist in nature and deserved New Right support.

On foreign policy, the New Right organizations worked against the Panama Canal treaties, arms limitation agreements, and economic sanctions against South Africa. On the other hand, they supported aid to "freedom fighters" in Nicaragua, Afghanistan, and Angola. The Angolan rebel Jonas Savimbi became a favorite cause; and an article appeared under his name in the Heritage Foundation's *Policy Review*. Howard Phillips was particularly active in demanding that U.S. companies pull out of Soviet-dominated Angola—a conservative version of "disinvestment." [25]

Agenda or Social Philosophy?

The New Right/Religious Right had staked out positions on a broad array of subjects. They were against abortion, gun control, sex education, ERA, dealings with Communist regimes, and high taxes; while they favored censorship, restoration of religious values, support for anticommunist guerrilla movements, and self-determination for states and municipalities. Hostile critics saw this coalition of single issues either as the opportunism of fund-raisers or the symptoms of a reactionary backlash. One question that was rarely asked was whether the New Right possessed anything like a positive vision of social life that could be called a political philosophy. The answer may be no and yes: No, if we are looking for a systematic exposition of first principles of the type offered by Thomas Hobbes or Karl Marx, but yes, if we mean an implicit set of assumptions that can be stated systematically.

Few New Right representatives would have expressed interest in political philosophy. Viguerie, on his own account, was never a diligent student. Weyrich and Phillips, by contrast, are intellectually quick but preferred to avoid most first-principle discussions. The reason for this was neither lack of conviction nor educational deficiency. Pat Robertson of Christian Broadcasting Network is among the best-educated political figures in the United States, but he shares with other Fundamentalists a certain suspicion of abstract analysis. When solid academics joined forces with the New Right, they almost invariably chose to work on the everyday level of policy questions. Charles Moser, for example, is a distinguished scholar in Slavic studies who worked closely with Weyrich's Free Congress Committee; his work for them, however, was unrelated to his groundbreaking scholarship in Bulgarian and Russian literature.

One effort was made to work out a New Right philosophy in a volume of essays edited by Robert W. Whitaker entitled *The New Right Papers*.[26] Whitaker himself was an eccentric populist and author of *A Plague on Both Your Houses,* a provocative work predicting the overthrow of the liberal elite of *both* political parties. *The New Right Papers* included statements from the leadership—Viguerie and Weyrich—as well as contributions from sympathetic members of the Old Right like William Rusher and Jeffrey Hart of *National Review*. However, the three essays that drew the most fire from reviewers were made by three relatively unknown scholars, all with University of North Carolina Ph.D.'s. Their essays were controversial, precisely because they attempted to articulate a set of New Right political principles that combined a populist/Jacksonian defense of the common man with the respect for tradition and order characteristic of the Old Right.

The emphasis was strongly on what the writers regarded as the authentic republican tradition of the American people. "Liberty," as historian Clyde Wilson argued, "was a by-product of membership in good standing of a free community, not a grant from government." Wilson opposed the false democracy of managed elections and rejected what he called the "imperialism" of a government that ruled in its own interest: "The New Right, it seems to me, may best be understood as a largely spontaneous and as-yet-imperfectly-articulated defense of the American community (or rather communities, for there are several) against the inroads of imperialism." Wilson rejected equally the exaltation of the state and the celebration of individual freedom, while locating the political center in family and community. The American system of civic responsibility, he insisted, was not derived from abstract proclamations of rights. It was a living inheritance bequeathed by European (especially British) and American ancestors. It was real and rooted but not universal.[27]

Another essay, "Old Rights and the New Left," was even more explicit in rejecting both the individualist tradition of natural rights and the statism that inevitably ensued.[28] In defense of "the Southern tradition" in politics, the authors rejected not only natural rights but any ideology of freedom that eroded family and community: "The destruction of the family began long ago in the apparently innocent decision of state and local governments to provide for schools. Public education . . . has turned out to be the principal weapon used by the enemies of the family." Not only government provoked the Southern apologist's fire; big business capitalists were held just as accountable for teaching equal opportunity at the expense of family integrity and for "turning a blind, libertarian eye" to the moral questions of divorce and pornography. Free enterprise was a positive good, but, as Clyde Wilson warned, only as "part of the genius of the American people." It was "not an absolute"; he insisted: "It is a means, not an end. New Rightists, including those who devoted their lives productively to free enterprise, did not intend to establish a religion of the dollar bill."[29] The Southern apologist agreed. Free enterprise was "the best of all economic systems" but certainly not "a way of life":

Our social vision, it must be argued, is not limited to a choice between economic theories of political life—capitalism and socialism—both reflexes of the same degraded, aluminum coin, both sound as the paper dollar.

. . . The hardest tasks for conservatives will be to convince our capitalist allies that the common rights of humanity, as embodied in the family, and our civil rights as Englishmen and Americans take precedence over our desire for profits and productivity.[30]

The New Right's hostility to sex education, the ERA, forced busing, and no-fault divorce might be plausibly explained as a rejection of the liberal philosophy that has evolved in our time. The values of ordinary Americans were to be taken seriously not so much because they were reactionary or because as individuals they possessed rights. It was rather that families, communities, and regions were by nature suited to carry out certain functions that were spelled out in the doctrine of natural law. In the natural law tradition or Aristotle, Cicero, and medieval Catholicism, God had inscribed his will in the heart, or as we now say, the instincts of the human species. Mothers did not have to be told to take care of children or forgo sexual relations with male offspring, since they were naturally so predisposed. What instinct failed to inculcate, the faculty of right reason would. Without really employing the language of natural law, the New Right agenda took much of it for granted.

All that was lacking to this potent combination of reactionary political theory with single issues voting blocks was a practical strategy for taking power. Such a plan was worked out by Kevin Phillips, William Rusher, and perhaps most interestingly by Samuel T. Francis in his contribution to *The New Right Papers.* Borrowing the term "Middle American Radicals" (MARS) from Donald Warren's *The Radical Center: Middle America and the Politics of Alienation,* Francis integrated the idea into the conceptual framework of Italian political theory (i.e., Mosca and Pareto) and James Burnham's *The Managerial Revolution.* The task, as Francis saw it, was "to dismantle or radically reform the managerial appetites of social control" and to strive for "the localization, privatization, and decentralization of the managerial apparatus of power."[31]

There were foreign policy implications to this thesis. Francis appealed to American "nationalism." From the perspective of Middle American entrepreneurs, "the military and economic preeminence of the United States" would become the primary objectives. A new mercantilism was proposed that would provide "some measure of protection for domestic producers." New Right politicians would win support by standing up for American interests against "Third World arrogance, aggression, and barbarianism." A president who learned to apply such a strategy might practice an American "Caesarism" and dismantle the managerial apparatus.[32]

Populists or Conservatives?

By the beginning of 1984, Richard Viguerie and his friends were already discussing the formation of a populist party alternative to both the Democrats and Republicans—a shift predicted by Robert Whitaker several years earlier. They were against big government, big labor, and most significantly, big business. Viguerie advanced these populist themes in his book *The Establishment vs. the People*. While a reviewer in *Fortune* was both amused and alarmed,[33] the New Right populists were in serious danger of alienating mainstream Republicans and of losing the support of conservative businessmen.

Viguerie proclaimed his populist creed in the bastion of Old Right/pro-business conservatism, *National Review*. In "A Populist and Proud of It"[34] he claimed both Jefferson and William F. Buckley as precursors for "opposition to the elitists." His arguments did little to reassure moderate Republicans in Virginia, who overwhelmingly rejected Viguerie's bid for the Republican nomination for lieutenant governor. Voters may have short memories, but stalwart Republicans might still remember Viguerie's tepid support for Reagan and his willingness to work for conservative Democrats. The campaign cost Viguerie months of time and effort that could have been directed to his business. It also cost about a half million dollars of his own money.

Although Viguerie was often accused of avarice and unscrupulous business practices, it was ironically his idealism and generosity that brought his empire to the brink of ruin in 1985. His insufficient loyalty to the Republican party helped to sour his primary fight and his willingness to extend credit to financially dubious causes resulted in a cash crunch that forced him to sell *Conservative Digest,* his main publication, and to lay off most of his work force. The whole technique of direct mail fund-raising began to be called into question as response rates and average contributions went down. Not just RAVCO, but also NCPAC and even Weyrich's political action committee were in serious danger. By early 1986, however, Viguerie was back in business with new clients and a less optimistic business strategy.[35]

Viguerie's populist rhetoric alarmed the Republican mainstream at the same time that Paul Weyrich was attempting to build bridges to the Republican Center and even to the Democratic Left. Late in 1985, Senator

Robert Dole agreed to host a $250-a-plate dinner for Weyrich. (Dole also hired conservative Donald Devine to run "Campaign America.") In building coalitions, the object is either to articulate a set of common principles or at least to identify a common enemy. The New Right had already exploited the negative campaign attack. It seemed that the time had come for a more positive method.

By 1986 Weyrich was promoting what he called "cultural conservatism" and employing the talents of William S. Lind.[36] While Lind and Weyrich seemed to oppose the rationalist skepticism of the French Enlightenment, Lind, at least, refused to embrace either revelation or natural law as the basis for cultural conservatism. Lind's creed endorsed "Western Judeo-Christian values" but didn't require anyone to believe traditional values are true *absolutely,* that they derive from God, from natural law, or from some other source outside secular human experience." He went on to add: "Politically, it does not matter whether an individual sees traditional values as absolutely true or only functionally true. Either belief leads to the same political actions, actions intended to reaffirm and reinforce those values, to lead the nation and the government to advocate them, and to make them once again define the political center. . . ."

Cultural conservatives view themselves as the precursors of a revived conservative movement that embraces Old Right intellectuals, New Right activists, neoconservative policy analysts, and liberals concerned with civility and serious literature. Nonetheless, obstacles to this alliance do remain.

In the first place, few New Rightists have displayed much interest in literature, the arts, or philosophy. It is all very well to talk of traditions and values, but problems arise over details. Are Rousseau and Hume both skeptics, part of the preferred tradition? What of the pagan classics that many Evangelical Christians object to? What will cultural conservatism say on the subject of modern art?

Of far greater seriousness is a problem that Lind deliberately built into his creed: neutrality on the subject of divine will and natural law. While it is possible to argue that Fundamentalist Christians and atheist sociobiologists possess a common view of human nature, it is harder to broaden that agreement to include those who think the family only *happens* to be functionally important. It is hard to imagine the Religious Right fighting under the same flag with well-intentioned secular humanists.

Chester Finn, assistant secretary of education under Ronald Reagan, attempted to take up the challenge of filling in the blanks of cultural conservatism. In an *American Spectator* essay, Finn listed ten tenets and the strategies that flow from them. The first is respect for Western civilization and the Judeo-Christian tradition, which requires us to redesign school curricula to include "cultural literacy." Other tenets include recognizing the importance of beliefs, sanctity of the individual, democracy, the safety and liberty of individuals, a patriotic mythology, etc.[37]

There are two main problems with Finn's recommendations: by themselves, they are neither cultural nor conservative. By employing the usual language of rights ("No one may invade another's rights"), Finn explicitly endorsed a political philosophy alien to most conservative thought; by setting up democracy as the ideal, he loaded the dice both against the authoritarian and the libertarian strains of American conservatism, and by erecting a national pantheon and patriotic calendar ("Independence Day, Memorial Day, Martin Luther King's birthday, Easter"), he ran the same risks as the social architects of the Eisenhower years. A vital culture cannot be designed by federal bureaucrats or created by popular magazines, and it may be too much to hope that Middle American Christians will both celebrate Easter and learn to venerate the memory of Dr. King.

There is more than a little presumption in any attempt to define a culture. Magisterial literary figures like Samuel Johnson, Matthew Arnold, and T. S. Eliot command our respect in such matters, precisely because they had already established themselves as important writers before they began laying down the law. In the United States of the 1980s, there was no Arnold or Eliot in a position to pronounce an American culture. Indeed, no great poet or novelist was willing to identify himself as a conservative, although Walker Percy, the Catholic novelist, did admit to voting for Reagan.

A Senescent New Right

It now seems increasingly likely that the New Right is on its deathbed. New Rightists who have stuck by their principles, particularly Phillips and Viguerie, suffer from both declining fortunes and a growing indistinguishability from the resurgent Old Right. For instance, Phillips and Viguerie took the initiative to break with Republican regulars and neoconservatives in backing Patrick J. Buchanan as their presidential candidate.

The New Right's problems, in part, go back to a lack of issues that it can claim for itself alone. One issue New Rightists would like to monopolize is opposition to abortion. Now that the Supreme Court has allowed states to restrict abortion rights, thereby departing from the benchmark *Roe* v. *Wade* decision of 1973, a window of opportunity has opened for advocates on both sides. Prochoice and prolife groups have vied with each other to sway the votes of state legislatures.[38] Yet, the New Right has not had the prolife side to itself; significantly, it has had to share that issue with the National Republican Party and George Bush, both now on record as being against liberal abortion laws. Because Jerry Falwell, Pat Robertson, and other Religious Rightists defend George Bush as a good Christian and fine president, it has been harder still for New Rightists to present themselves as the most effective antiabortion front in an effort to attract more money from prolifers.

Another issue that the sinking New Right and the associated Religious Right might well have viewed as a lifesaver was the fury aroused in 1990 and 1991 by the National Endowment for the Arts. The generous support bestowed by that organization, and defended by former director John E. Frohnmayer, on Andres Serrano, Robert Mapplethorpe, and other producers of what many considered unabashedly blasphemous art, created a grim and sustained public outcry. Objections were heard from the Congress on down to the man on the street, about turning tax monies to obscene and impious purposes.[39] But the issue was not readily convertible into New Right dividends. For one thing, there were too many groups quickly springing to battle, from neoconservative presidential hopeful, William Bennett and North Carolina Senator Jesse Helms to taxpayer associations that advocated dumping the NEA. New Rightist opposition to Mapplethorpe and Serrano as well as Frohnmayer was hardly noticed—at most perfunctory, it came from a group without the financial means to survive as an independent force.

Its onetime representative Paul Weyrich, driven by the instinct for survival, has now repackaged himself as a Catholic neoconservative. Viguerie has made a less-entangling but also compromising alliance by accepting millions of dollars in support from the World Unification Church. Unlike Weyrich's benefactors, however, Viguerie's do not seem to have attached strings to their gift. Howard Phillips, the most cerebral of the New Right organizers, has moved from one issue to another, from opposition to the Gulf War to limiting taxes, without being able to recapture his financial or political base of 15 years ago. A highly literate as well as deeply engaged activist, Phillips would certainly find a place among top presidential advisers, if the highly improbable occurred and Patrick J. Buchanan became the next U.S. president.

Chapter Six

Funding an Empire

The Benefactors Acquiesce

The Left has consistently characterized the conservative movement as representing the interests of big business, a portrayal that goes back at least to the turn of the century, when the protection of monopolies and cartels was typically described as "conservative." In the period between the two World Wars, however, many businessmen and corporate executives, even those of a progressive or liberal stripe, came to the conclusion that Roosevelt's foreign and domestic policies were undermining the economic and political stability of the nation. Such thinking brought them into partnership with the so-called conservatives, who believed that any restrictions on business were an invasion of property rights.

In the thirties newspaper magnates Robert R. McCormick, Joseph Patterson, W. R. Hearst, and Frank Gannett, together with prominent industrialists grouped around the American Liberty League (founded in 1934), openly led the battle against federal control of the economy. The defense of the free market that evolved in this period came "from the effort of corporate wealth to assume public leadership of opposition forces." According to one Marxist critic, this strategy proved to be a "political blunder," causing the public to associate opposition to the welfare state and the growing power of organized labor with corporate interests.[1]

Despite the presence of earnest columnists on the Right, including George Sokolsky, Westbrook Pegler, and Fulton Lewis, Jr., the anti–New Deal forces were seen to be led by "big money." Among Liberty

League benefactors were members of the DuPont family, J. Howard Pew of Sun Oil, Alfred P. Sloan of General Motors, James H. Rand of Remington, and Ernest T. Weir of National Steel. Beside pouring money into league publications, all these defenders of an unfettered free market worked to steer the Republican party into principled confrontation with New Deal Democrats.

The press magnates of the period also pushed their chief newspapers—Hearst, The *Journal-American;* McCormick, the *Chicago Tribune;* and Patterson, the New York *Daily News*—into opposing, step by step, the economic interventionism of the Roosevelt administration.[2] Intellectuals also played a role in the war waged by conservative businessmen in the thirties, with some of them joining the American First Committee to take a stand against American entanglement in European and Asian wars. But well into the postwar period the theorists and ideologues on the American Right remained in a subordinate position to political and business figures who sponsored anti–New Deal positions and represented them within the government.

Anti-Roosevelt corporate families, some associated with the American Firsters, like the Richardsons, Pews, and DuPonts, continued to underwrite conservative activities after World War II, with this crucial difference: By the fifties businessmen were funding foundations and scholars in order to influence society. The new direction in funding was apparent from the earmarking of Pew money for education and the arts and from the heightened emphasis among conservative businessmen on promoting "free enterprise thinking." The owners of Sun Oil were now awarding substantial sums to the Intercollegiate Society of Individualist, a group founded by the libertarian Frank Chodorov. Anti–New Deal philanthropies, particularly the Kemp and William Volker funds were also responsible for subsidizing the scholarship and teaching of laissez-faire economists. Both Friedrich Hayek's professorship in the Graduate Committee on Social Thought at the University of Chicago and the original post held by Ludwig von Mises as visiting professor at the New York University Graduate School of Business came about through Volker funding; Mises subsequently received further financing of his chair from the advertising executive Lawrence Fertig.[3] Fertig, who admired Mises's social ethics as well as his economic theory, not only paid most of his mentor's salary but also provided funds (demanded by NYU) to pay the rent for Mises's seminar room.

This effort of business conservatives to shape popular thought has a long tradition, going back to educational mission statements made by

Andrew Carnegie and John D. Rockefeller. In the conservative movement of the eighties and nineties, successful entrepreneurs continued to
back the advocates of congenial ideas. Both William H. Simon's fund-
raising work as head of the John M. Olin Foundation and the help of
Henry Salvatori, a California industrialist, in promoting the teaching of
democratic values at the Claremont Institute and Heritage Foundation,
exemplify the continued reaching out by conservative businessmen for
intellectual and cultural influence.

Despite the apparent continuity in conservative philanthropy, the past
20 years have also witnessed a shift in the focus of conservative influence
toward New York- and Washington-based think tanks. The claims of
these institutions to being in the business of producing and supporting
scholarship may be overstated however. In an article in the *Boston
Phoenix,* Lawrence Soley argues that: "The annual budget of any
one of the big conservative thinks exceeds the combined budgets of all
left-of-center think tanks. With so many resources available, the right-
wing think tanks should be able to conduct serious research. But according to their critics, not just on the left but among trained social-science
researchers of all stripes, they generally do not; most just disseminate
opinions."[4]

By the seventies the commercial benefactors of most conservative
think tanks had come to view the objects of their philanthropy as so many
tax write-offs. This, Soley insists, has become especially true for the
"conservative fat cats" who patronize the Heritage Foundation. Indeed,
specific funding allocated by "conservative thinks" no longer results from
decisions by individual benefactors; rather, the families of the anti–New
Deal business coalition have turned to philanthropic managers to oversee
their gifts. What is more, this funding is no longer directed at efforts to
rescind the New Deal or dismantle the Great Society. Now benefactors
speak of making an educational investment, by teaching the values of
freedom, democracy, and patriotism. If Robert McCormick and James
H. Rand took appropriate steps to control their beneficiaries, Randall
Richardson, an anti–New Deal Republican and scion of American Firster
H. Smith Richardson, has allowed the directors of the foundation to dis-
pense his family's money to Humphrey Democrats.[5] It is now the philanthropic staff that keeps its grant recipients on a short leash, without
having to answer to the families who fund their programs.

The Heritage Foundation will typically consult with the staff—not the
benefactors—of the Harry and Lynde Bradley Foundation in seeking approval of a candidate for a Bradley Fellowship in the humanities. To be

successful in securing financial support, an applicant for funds from the John M. Olin Foundation needs to establish the appropriate relations with the former University of Pennsylvania junior faculty member James Piereson, who directs funding. Similarly, a scholar would gain little advantage by currying favor with William H. Simon, though Simon does endow the Olin chairs, and it would be a mistake for a conservative academic seeking support to bear too close a resemblance to John Merrill Olin (1892–1982), who established the foundation as part of a rearguard action against the New Deal.

The direction and control as well as size of the current conservative philanthropy need to be stressed, inasmuch as some commentators exaggerate the links between prewar and contemporary conservative philanthropies. Thus Jerome L. Himmelstein, in his monograph *To The Right*, notes that the families of J. Howard Pew, John M. Olin, and Sarah Scaife, daughter of Andrew Mellon, contribute millions of dollars to conservative institutions. Himmelstein focuses special attention on Richard Mellon Scaife, who took over his family's extensive philanthropy in 1973. We are informed that by 1980 the son of Sarah Scaife, drawing money from depositories of family wealth, such as the Scaife, Allegheny, and Carthage foundations, had bestowed $5 million each on American Enterprise Institute, Georgetown University Center for Strategic Studies, and the National Strategic Information Center. Scaife also donated $4.1 million to the Hoover Institution, and another $2.1 million to the Heritage Foundation during its formative stage. Himmelstein makes much of the presence of Scaife, Joseph Coors, and other conservative philanthropists on the Heritage board to demonstrate the persistence of certain families and corporations in funding "the Far Right."[6]

In fact, none of the institutional recipients of Scaife or Pew money can any longer be reasonably described as far Right. Almost all of them are cold war liberals with soft libertarian wrinkles. The opposition to both a welfare state and an interventionist foreign policy that was characteristic of the prewar Right has disappeared from the think tanks and groups now receiving conservative funding. Survivors of the prewar anti–New Deal tradition, such as Auburn University's Ludwig von Mises Institute and The Independent Institute in Oakland, California, exist as virtual outcasts on the margins of today's conservative movement. Equally important, family benefactors no longer exert the ideological control that Himmelstein ascribes to them. Although Soley's "conservative fat cats" may be wined and dined whenever they come to New York or Washington, the role they play in formulating positions for their philanthropies and beneficiaries is not more significant than the involvement of Republican trustees and alumni donors in the affairs of Yale University.

Himmelstein and other leftist critics of the American conservative movement would do well to notice how little those they study embrace the views associated with the conservatism of the thirties or even the fifties. Too often critics present entirely static pictures of both conservatism and big business, reflecting their own static demonology. In the thirties J. Howard Pew gave money unstintingly in support of constitutionally restricted federal power and an isolationist foreign policy. In the eighties and nineties his descendants are payrolling foundations that call for a further consolidation of the New Deal presidency and the spread of American-type democracy abroad.

Even from a strictly Marxist perspective, one might observe that capitalists have gone from excoriating the New Deal to defending a redistributionist federal government (though admittedly not one radical enough to please socialists) and the export of present-day American democracy. It may even be argued that contemporary conservative think tanks supported by certain big business interests have no more in common with the Liberty League than do leftist commentators now deploring conservative influence. During the recent Gulf crisis, movement conservatives joined liberals as the war party, while remnants of the prewar and early postwar Rightists were calling for American disengagement from the Gulf.[7]

Big business philanthropists may well have a greater awareness of their interests than a superficial reading of the evidence might suggest. At the very least, there have always been some capitalists who were willing to forestall future hostilities by placating potential revolutionaries. It is good insurance to finance democratic globalists and welfare state theorists in a world rushing toward social democracy. It is equally true that multinational business has never been interested in the provincial loyalties and rooted traditions advocated by conservatives. International markets imply international economic and political systems whose object is the elimination of all national and ethnic barriers to economic growth. Despite former associations, conservative philanthropists no longer subsidize the policies that defined their worldviews in the thirties or as late as the fifties. Positions they now support financially, on foreign policy and income redistribution, are dramatically different from those that conservatives, including conservative businessmen, were once likely to hold.

The neo-Marxist James Weinstein explains the change by citing the evolving economic interests and perceptions of those within a corporate capitalist economy.[8] From this interpretive perspective, Liberty Lea-guers may well have taken an anachronistic view of their true interest as corporate capitalists, which by the thirties was to build an alliance with the managerial state and organized labor. The corporate backers of Her-itage Foundation, which include Chase-Manhattan as well as the Pew, Scaife, and Olin families, see the present age more realistically. Thus they support a welfare state with an expansionist foreign policy that tilts toward big business. Even though few of the present corporate backers of conservative think tanks are as cunning as Weinstein assumes corpo-rate capitalists are, his argument does take into consideration the inver-sion that has occurred in conservative positions. The charge made by some, that conservative foundations and philanthropies have been "more of the same" since the thirties, is simply counterfactual when looking back even 20 years.

The staffs of philanthropic foundations are sometimes accused of at-tempting to take over conservative organizations that are open to their positions, of denying funds to (or attempting to destroy) groups found guilty of being independent, and of establishing institutions for narrow ideological purposes. One example might serve to underscore the depth and penetration of foundation influence.

In *Time* magazine, a detailed report is given about the comings and goings of Vile Bodies, self-identified cultural conservatives who meet in New York to exchange ideas.[9] The group, which includes, among others, Roger Kimball, Richard Brookhiser, Bruce Bawer, and (depending on his schedule) John Podhoretz, has published with Poseidon Press an anthol-ogy of its broadsides against the "adversary" culture. What *Time* over-looks is that all 14 participants in the group represent magazines and other interests receiving steady, indispensable subsidies from one or more of the four recognizably neoconservative foundations. The *New Criterion,* to which most of the group's members contribute and which employs several of them, drew a subsidy of $125,000 from the Sarah Scaife Foundation in 1989; the journal has also received annual grants of $100,000 from the John M. Olin Foundation and at least $50,000 from the Milwaukee-centered Bradley Foundation since the mid-eighties.[10]

Two other publications that claim Vile Bodies as contributors, *National Review* and the *American Spectator,* are also recipients of regular subsi-dies from neoconservative foundations. Like the *New Criterion,* the *American Spectator* (an ever faithful organ of neoconservative opinion) is one of the publications on the Right most often in straitened circum-stances. Until recent years Bradley and J. M. Olin jointly provided it with more than $200,000 per year, while Bradley made a special grant of $50,000 to the *American Spectator*'s editor in 1986 to help relocate offices in Arlington, Virginia.[11] The decline in foundation subsidies in recent years may be related to the general perception that the magazine's influence has been steadily declining, partly because some leading conservatives have lost confidence in the *Spectator*'s editor, R. E. Tyrrell.

Without the administrative staffs of Bradley, Olin, Smith-Richardson, and Sarah Scaife, there would be no operative agenda of "cultural conservatism" being implemented in New York and Washington. While cultural conservatives—i.e., critics of modern society—would undoubtedly still have a forum, there would be no organized activity for positions that foundation heads have decided to call "culturally conservative"—e.g., preferring Jackson Pollock to Robert Mapplethorpe or Martin Luther King to Jesse Jackson.

The shaping of cultural conservatism is now bringing economic benefits to political activists who have discovered a market for "values." For example, the head of the Free Congress Foundation, Paul Weyrich, receives hundreds of thousands of dollars annually from the Bradley, Olin, and Roe foundations. In return, Weyrich goes beyond functioning as a mere congressional lobbyist and serves as a spokesman for an activist political agenda based on "Judeo-Christian values."[12] Breaking with the traditional conservative emphasis on limited government, he calls for governmental programs to promote cultural conservatism across the country. In one memo to conservative leaders, Weyrich even sketched out a program for an organized youth corps to clean up the streets.

An even greater amount of annual funding from Bradley, Olin, and Smith-Richardson goes to the Institute for Educational Affairs. Under the institute's recently departed head, Leslie Lenkowsky, its staff worked to further "democratic values," which was seen as the neoconservative foreign policy of aiding both the A.F.L.-C.I.O. and the Reagan State Department in their drive for global democracy.[13] In late 1988 Bradley conferred $475,000 on the James Madison Center, which was subsequently incorporated into IEA.[14] The center was organized as a forum for William Bennett, who, together with Jack Kemp, has emerged as one of the preferred presidential candidates of the neoconservatives. Bennett's decision to become drug czar made it no longer necessary to furnish him with a think tank staffed with like-minded constitutional and educational theorists. In the last two years Bradley has also spent several hundred thousand dollars annually to dress up the image of the Heritage

Foundation. Having long presented itself as "pragmatic and action-oriented," Heritage offered its donors "an active role in influencing legislation."[15] However, it too has now moved, with neoconservative resources, into the fostering of culture through its politically approved Bradley fellows and its own humanities directors.[16]

Although conservative cultural rhetoric has obvious political implications, neoconservative philanthropy serves ideological as well as pragmatic ends. Neoconservative-controlled foundations are subsidizing a particular worldview that may be inferred both from their editorials against the Old Right and from recently published essays on conservative wars. Neoconservatives, who have defined the conservative movement in the New York–Washington corridor since the early 1980s, stand generally for open immigration, civil rights as they were understood before some of their advocates turned against Israel and in the direction of quotas, the welfare state without Jimmy Carter's additions to it, the imposition of "democratic values" in public and private schools, and "American democracy" throughout the world.[17] The view of recent American social reform is of a train that became derailed at the time its neoconservative passengers elected to get off. Those on their Right are dismissed as racists and anti-Semites for failing to board the same train; those too far over on the Left are viewed with contempt for staying behind too long. Only those who rode the train of Progress for the proper time span and left with the right people are entitled to the redemptive label "democrat."

In their own view neoconservatives and their allies have seized foundations to influence culture and in turn shape politics.[18] Observing the Left's "long march through the institutions," neoconservatives have begun their own march, producing official positions on educational, religious, and aesthetic questions and hiring or coopting advocates to publicize their stands. Michael Novak's *Crisis* and Richard John Neuhaus's *First Things* have provided the Christian or Judeo-Christian counterparts to *Commentary:* Both magazines are lavishly funded by Olin and Scaife. As part of the same strategy, Olin and Bradley earmarked $200,000 for *This World,* and Neuhaus, then an employee of the Rockford Institute, filled that periodical with hymns to democratic capitalism. Funds from the same sources have also gone to support the politically proper Institute on Religion and Democracy, and in 1989 Scaife bestowed $100,000 on Neuhaus's Institute on Religion and Public Life in New York and $125,000 on the Ethics and Public Policy Center in Washington.[19] Now led by George Weigel (a Neuhaus disciple), the Ethics and Public

Policy Center underwent abrupt change from the top in the late eighties. Its founder, Ernest Lefever resigned as head, after board member Richard Neuhaus persuaded other board members to make administrative changes. Lefever had been insufficiently responsive to neoconservative directives and had mocked the idea of a global democratic crusade.[20] The center and other related organizations show distinctions without differences, having interlocking boards and advertising the same point of view: that Judeo-Christian morality requires "democracy" and "democratic capitalism."

The heavy concentration of funding from neoconservative philanthropies on the same activities and programs has two explanations. One is the attempt by neoconservatives to rivet public attention, particularly in downtown Washington, on salient ideological positions. Thus it is possible, while walking on Connecticut Avenue in Northwest Washington, to encounter a phantasmagoria of neoconservative magazines and advertisements for lectures, all with titles that include the word "democracy" or "democratic." The four sister philanthropic foundations have funded, singly or jointly, all the following advocates of world democracy: Institute on Religion and Democracy, Institute for Democracy in Eastern Europe, Bradley Institute of Democracy and Public Values, Institute for Liberty and Democracy, the partly public National Endowment for Democracy, the Friends of the Democratic Center in the Americas, Gregory Fossedal's tribute to global democracy titled *The Democratic Century,* a center for "democratic" journalism at Boston University, and the magazine *Studies in Democracy.* The vision of a democratic state with a mixed economy and unlimited immigration radiates through these and other objects of neoconservative philanthropy, particularly programs done through Radio Free Europe and Voice of America, the (now defunct) Committee for a Free World, Freedom House, and academic chairs set up by the Olin Foundation for the study of democratic civilization.

In the maiden issue of *First Things,* Richard John Neuhaus castigates his Old Right opposition for expressing too many reservations about "democracy."[21] This charge could not be properly leveled at Neuhaus or his friend and ally Michael Novak, who has invoked democratic capitalism as the true incarnation.[22] The charge would apply even less well to the four sister foundations and to the dominant figure who coordinates their combined philanthropic activities and has been executive director of both Olin and Bradley—Michael S. Joyce.

Joyce, who has characterized himself as a Martin Luther King liberal, is bitter about the direction taken by the civil rights movement in abandoning King's vision of a color-blind society. As a student at Cleveland State, he had thrilled to King's "I have a dream" speech, and like most white liberals Joyce cannot understand why blacks and other minorities refuse to be satisfied with legal guarantees of equality. As a means to bring about the visions of Martin Luther King and John F. Kennedy, Joyce went to work for Irving Kristol at IEA and later for William Simon at Olin.

As head of the Bradley Foundation, Joyce has remained loyal to his patrons. He has also cooperated with Leslie Lenkowsky of Smith-Richardson, IEA, and, more recently, the Hudson Institute. Through the Philanthropic Roundtable, these two cold war liberals have pulled grant-making foundations behind "democratic initiatives" both at home and abroad.[23] For Joyce and Lenkowsky, the National Endowment for Democracy has been a critical instrument for "doing something about democracy" in Central America. Also, despite traditional identification of conservative foundations with free enterprise, both Joyce and Lenkowsky have been happy to throw support to the National Endowment for Democracy, two-thirds of whose budget goes to labor union activities.[24]

What Neuhaus, Novak, and Joyce mean by democracy, however, has never been made clear. Since they strongly object to populist movements of any kind and oppose the doctrines of states rights and local control, the neoconservative vision of democracy has nothing in common either with the Jeffersonian tradition or with the contemporary Left's insistence on what Benjamin Barber calls "strong democracy."

The foundations may be fuzzy about their ideology, but they are very clear on the subject of personal loyalty. In 1988 Olin granted $376,000 for a three-year fellowship to Irving Kristol at American Enterprise Institute.[25] The grant was mere pocket money for someone who has been called the neoconservative godfather and who numbers among admiring proteges Joyce at Bradley, James Piereson, director of Olin, and Richard Larry at Scaife.

Kristol has always professed himself an admirer of Leo Strauss, and understandably Olin and Bradley have done particularly well by the Straussians. Joyce particularly admires Harry Jaffa and his work on equality as the highest American value, but he has given stipends with equal alacrity to other disciples of Strauss. Among these are Clifford Orwin and Thomas Pangle at the University of Toronto, Ralph Lerner and Allan Bloom at the University of Chicago, Walter Berns at Georgetown University, and Berns's student James H. Nichols at Claremont. Between

1986 and 1989 Berns also received from Olin $500,000 for his endowed chair at Georgetown.[26]

The appointment of Berns's son-in-law, Hillel Fradkin, as senior program officer at Bradley in 1986 (after a stint at Olin) brought a certain balance to its funding operations. Fradkin's superior, Joyce, was a Western Straussian, a follower of Jaffa and his Claremont circle; Fradkin, by contrast, took his cues from the Eastern Straussians centered around Bloom and Berns. Since 1986 supporting scholarship has meant for Bradley dividing at least a million dollars annually between two doctrinaire sects, each looking for the roots of Reaganite democracy in Locke, Montesquieu, and Rousseau.

The equally sectarian and personal focus of Olin funding came out in a 1987 *Chronicle of Higher Education* article that describes James Piereson's annual expenditure of more than $5 million to provide "seed money" for the *New Criterion* and to set up "campus-based centers," most prominently for Allan Bloom.[27] In 1986 Olin set aside close to $4 million for Bloom and his fellow-Straussian, Nathan Tarcov, at the University of Chicago–based John M. Olin Center for Inquiry into the Theory and Practice of Democracy. Though Jon Wiener of the *Nation* does not distinguish between personal and operating budgets, he has come up with the noteworthy figure of over $2 million as the total gift from Olin for Bloom's center. Most of these funds, which were made available to Bloom and his associate Tarcov, eventually rose to over $3 million. Wiener also reports that Samuel Huntington, a neoconservative political scientist, has received $1.4 million from the same benefactor for *his* institute at Harvard.[28] The grant, which has been given for lectures and seminars rather than buildings and capital equipment, is a gift package, with seemingly few restrictions.

A smaller but nonetheless interesting award was a 1988 Olin Fellowship for $36,856 that went to the Catholic University of America historian Jerry Z. Muller, an otherwise undistinguished junior professor.[29] Muller had *Commentary* connections and was apparently willing to oppose the appointment of his sponsors' critics to posts within the university.[30]

Three circumstances have combined to produce the neoconservative ascendancy over the four sisters and over conservative foundations generally. The first is the gradual withdrawal from foundation leadership of the actual benefactors at Olin, Bradley, Scaife, and Smith-Richardson in favor of neoconservative staffs. This occurred most extensively at Bradley, which underwent two related revampings. The elevation of the Milwaukee business tycoon I. Andrew (Tiny) Rader as the Lynde and Harry

Bradley Foundation president in 1985 came during the first of two organizational changes. A local philanthropic arm of the Allen-Bradley Company, the national foundation was formed in 1985 when Rockwell International Corporation acquired the parent organization.[31] Once placed under Rader's direction, the foundation departed from precedent by funding "scholarly activities" nationwide, at $23 million annually, and by paying generous salaries to its board members. Rader himself received $77,220 during fiscal year 1987–88 for working part-time as board president.[32] Soon after his arrival, Rader brought in Joyce and Fradkin from Olin and then Amy Crutchfield, a sometime Bloom student at the University of Chicago, as program assistant to Fradkin. Though the charter for the revamped foundation speaks of its being "dedicated to strengthening American capitalism, its institutions, principles, and values," the appeal to the free market contained therein has little relevance for current funding practices.[33] Almost all the recipients of Bradley as well as Olin foundation scholarly grants support a mixed economy and a highly aggressive approach to exporting American democracy.

The board of governors of Smith-Richardson, which includes Robert Bork, Jeane Kirkpatrick, and James Q. Wilson, are all loyal neoconservatives with the appropriate social and/or political connections. Though Bork is not a grantee of Smith-Richardson, he does receive an annual fellowship of $162,000 from Olin.[34] As director of Scaife, Richard Larry has been able to manage his own board, which now includes Edwin Feulner. Several million dollars out of Feulner's $18 million annual budget is generated by the four sisters, and—seemingly out of deference to his benefactors—Feulner has arranged for the appointment of Midge Decter to the Heritage board.[35] He and Paul Weyrich also dominate the small board of the Roe Foundation in Greenville, South Carolina, and award funds from that foundation's annual budget for grants, which now total roughly $533,000.[36]

Neoconservative activists have largely succeeded in centralizing both the collection and distribution of funding from right-of-center philanthropies. With the assistance of Piereson, Larry, and the Philanthropic Roundtable, Joyce and Lenkowsky have been gaining control over the form and content of movement conservatism. Though the Roundtable has not been able to silence all mavericks, its leaders can isolate some of them, while bestowing on their own allies over $30 million in annual patronage. Lenkowsky, who worked briefly for the United States Information Agency (now heavily staffed by neoconservatives) before moving on to IEA, has stressed the need to maximize the public impact of grantmakers.[37] Such phrases are interpreted less charitably as a cover for Lenkowsky's democratic globalist fixations. Though it may be hard to isolate entirely personal factors, Lenkowsky's career thus far has been dedicated to a single ideal, which he has promoted through a rapid succession of high-paying positions.

James Taylor, president of the World Youth Crusade and a self-described Old Rightist, believes the Philanthropic Roundtable was never intended as a mere "clearinghouse." It was, from the outset, an "attempt by neocons to search out all conservative funds and direct them toward their own friends."[38] The Old Right Fund for American Studies, Taylor's own World Youth Crusade, the Young Americans Foundation, the Conservative Caucus of Howard Phillips, and even the black conservative Lincoln Institute (whose leader Jay Parker dared to dress down HUD Secretary Jack Kemp for defending the welfare state) have all either been deemed unfit for funding at Roundtable discussions or repeatedly discouraged from applying for grants.

In the meantime, Lenkowsky has moved on to become director of the Hudson Institute in Indianapolis, an organization now enjoying heavy support from both Olin and Bradley as well as from the Indianapolis-based Lily Foundation. Lenkowsky has added Aaron Wildavsky and other familiar neoconservatives to his board, while receiving Olin money to invite Elliott Abrams to be a Hudson Institute Visiting Scholar. Here again, the term scholar must be interpreted broadly to refer to public personalities whose genealogical and ideological credentials may weigh in favor of their interest in learned pursuits.[39]

The executives of the principal conservative foundations have labored to control a critical mass of the funding of groups that did not start out as neoconservative but have been pushed in that direction. They denied funds to the National Humanities Institute, once having convinced themselves of that group's lack of political usefulness. A scholarly organization that defends the humanism of Irving Babbitt and has been contemptuous of "democratist sentimentality," the NHI also bears another liability: its cofounder Claes Ryn has made light of Straussian scholarship in print.[40] By contrast the four sisters and the Feulner-and-Weyrich-controlled Roe Foundation assist the Intercollegiate Studies Institute, making a joint contribution of almost $200,000 annually to what has been an essentially Catholic Old Right organization. Such restricted generosity, however, has not enabled ISI, with an annual operating budget that now exceeds $1.5 million to end its perpetual struggle for funds.[41] ISI has kept itself going by making calculated concessions to the conservative movement's

power brokers; for example, by accepting Edwin Feulner as the permanent head of its board and by having as board members Feulner's subordinate at Heritage, Charles L. Heatherly, and Richard Larry.

Like the old Communist party, conservative philanthropic foundations
have found it necessary to mobilize front groups in order to gain public
credibility. Such proliferating front organizations include the National Legal Center, the Georgetown Center for Strategic and International Studies, Institute on Religion and Democracy, Center for International
Relations, and Bradley Institute of Democracy and Public Values, all of
which are run almost entirely by doctrinaire neoconservatives. The organizations each operate to publicize a particular aspect of the neoconservative worldview or policy agenda: for example, the National Legal
Center advances the ideal of presidential supremacy over Congress and
keeping alive the tradition of presidential activism typified by Lincoln,
Wilson, and the two Roosevelts; and the Bradley Institute of Democracy
at Marquette University emphasizes "democratic values" as understood
by the benefactors.[42]

The Neoconservative/Libertarian Realignment

For at least several years now libertarian think tanks and publications
have reflected the growing power of neoconservative views. This tendency can be seen in the policies of libertarian foundations, which are
cutting ties with members of the American Old Right while bestowing
honors on neoconservative dignitaries. Of all libertarian groups, the Social Philosophy and Policy Center in Bowling Green, Ohio, under its present director Jeffrey Paul, has moved farthest in this new direction. For
instance, the center's deputy director and editor of publications, Ellen
Frankel Paul, a former graduate assistant of Sidney Hook, has written a
book defending moderate feminism against "comparable worth legislation."[43] The center's published authors, like Aaron Wildavsky, Michael
Novak, and Herman Belz, its editorial and other boards, and, finally, its
choice of guest scholars leave no doubt about its ideological core.[44] When
European visitors have asked, perhaps naively, why the center did not
invite Old Right scholars, the question has occasioned visible embarrass-
ment among the staff.

Another aspect of the neoconservative/libertarian realignment can be
glimpsed in recent issues of *Reason,* a publication of the once libertarian
Reason Foundation in Santa Barbara, California. Under its feminist and
ardently pro-Zionist editor, Virginia Postrel, *Reason* has moved conspic-

uously toward crusading interventionism abroad. In March 1991 Postrel presented a symposium embracing five *soi-disant* conservatives on foreign policy issues. After expressing her own impassioned backing for a new world order, Postrell led a discussion with global democrats distinguished only by varying degrees of faith—Joshua Muravchik, Daniel Pipes, Charles Krauthammer, and Glenn Frankel. The only dissenting voice to the general interventionist line came from Ted Carpenter of Cato Institute.[45]

On the evidence, most libertarian foundations have drifted toward the neoconservative camp, but few can be described as having been taken over financially. Doctrinal is not the same as financial control. A few illustrations might illuminate this critical distinction.

The publications of the Washington Times Corporation—especially *Insight* magazine, and the Commentary and Life sections of the *Washington Times*—all betray the marks of neoconservative political correctness. The former editor of the *Washington Times'* Life section who assumed the directorship of *Insight* before falling out with the Reverend Moon and resigning his post, John Podhoretz, culled from his section—including book reviews—any text that might offend his influential parents.[46] The Commentary section, minus a few Old Right columnists, remains a redoubt of Scoop Jackson Democrats. Most of the columns celebrate global democracy or deplore right- and left-wing isolationism and Jesse Jackson's betrayal of the civil rights movement. The recent elevation of John Podhoretz's former college roommate Todd Lindberg to the editorship of the editorial page may further tighten the neoconservatives' hold on the paper—and should offset the departure of Podhoretz.

Despite their political orientation, the publications of the Washington Times Corporation do not, in fact, depend on neoconservative financing, but rather on the unstinting generosity of a controversial religious movement originally based in South Korea. The Unification Church, which runs the corporation, distributes tens of millions of dollars annually among neoconservatives. The disciples of the self-proclaimed Korean divinity Sun Myung Moon do this in spite of the "Moonie"-bashing from neoconservative journalists—some of whom are beneficiaries of the church's largesse—that crops up in *National Review,* the *American Spectator,* and the *New Republic.* The Unification Church finances its taunters out of a belief that neoconservatives share their vision of a globalist politics leavened by anticommunism.[47]

Generally speaking, it is difficult to correlate the amount that a foundation or publication receives from one or more of the four major neoconservative philanthropies with the intensity of its adherence to neoconservative positions. The Federalist Society for Law and Public Policy Studies receives almost $500,000 annually from Smith-Richardson, Olin, and Bradley. By contrast, Reason Foundation was awarded only $34,000 from Olin and $23,000 from Smith-Richardson in 1990.[48] One can only conclude, after looking at the positions taken by these groups, that there is no simple equation between the magnitude of foundation support and the degree of neoconservative influence.

Despite their mounting influence over some libertarian enterprises, neoconservatives have not been as generous in subsidizing libertarians in general as they have in assisting their own organizations. From the neoconservative perspective, it makes tactical sense to create their own libertarian vanguard, as they may now be doing with the Acton Institute. Established by Michael Novak, an advocate of welfare state capitalism, and the "free market" priest Robert Sirico, the Acton Institute for the Study of Religion and Liberty has already benefited from neoconservative munificence. Notably, the institute has blurred the distinctions between democratic capitalism and social democracy, conveniently discovering a "tremendous overlap" between them.[49]

On the whole, the four sisters give sparingly to most of their libertarian beneficiaries. In 1989 the Sarah Scaife Foundation bestowed on Heritage $800,000, but only $100,000 on the Cato Institute (the largest of the libertarian think tanks).[50] The order of funding going from John M. Olin to the two institutions was about three to one, until Olin dropped Cato entirely from its rolls for making impolitic foreign policy statements.[51] No libertarian think tank draws as much from the four sisters as Freedom House (about $500,000 annually), a predominantly social democratic anticommunist lobby.

The neoconservative relationship to libertarian politics has always been fraught with suspicion. Though neoconservatives and most of today's libertarians agree on liberal immigration and free-trade policies, neoconservatives are still not comfortable with slighting references to "big government." The phrase popularized by George Will, Irving Kristol, and Edward Wilson about a "fiscally conservative welfare state" may be oxymoronic. But it does express the neoconservatives' favorable view of the present American regime and their continuing hope of winning for their own wing of the Republican party a segment of minority support. In international relations, again in stark contrast to traditional libertarians, neoconservatives are irrepressibly hawkish, favoring crusades for democracy intended to help "friendly" nations and organized labor and to engage their own foreign policy experts. There is, in short, little common ground between the two sides, save for small talk about deregulation and changing proposals for educational vouchers and enterprise zones.

Then, too, the neoconservatives have little patience with the social projects advanced by the Cato Institute and the Libertarian party, such as legalizing the use of mind-altering drugs, recognizing legal equality between homosexual and heterosexual marriages, and removing all governmental bans on pornography. The recent undignified attack unleashed by Ed Crane, director of Cato (in his *Liberty* interview of November 1990), against the "intolerant attitudes among people like Rothbard and Rockwell, in ethnic and cultural matters, and even on the question of sexual diversity" would have to apply a fortiori to the *Commentary*-circle.[52] Neoconservatives consistently defend laws against drugs and pornography and call for social sanctions against homosexual life-styles. One of the most favored individual recipients of Olin funding has been the Straussian constitutionalist and Great Society Democrat Walter Berns. In his writings on free speech and virtue going back at least 25 years, Berns has put forth the view that both censorship and government surveillance of popular morals are needed to make democratic regimes workable. Berns also views government administrators as appropriate instruments for imposing virtue on the American "polis."[53]

The distribution of funding to libertarian groups by neoconservative philanthropies in fiscal years 1989–90 confirm the generalizations offered above. In each of those years Cato's combined funding from Bradley, Scaife, and Olin came to approximately $250,000. Among libertarian recipients of neoconservative funding, Cato found itself in third place. Though behind the Institute for Humane Studies and the Social Philosophy and Policy Center, Cato was still ahead of the Manhattan Institute, which has always combined neoconservative and libertarian staff workers and has attracted Nathan Glazer to the editorial board of its publication, *The City Journal*. Some idea can be had of the priorities of neoconservative philanthropic staffs if one considers the following: In 1990 Bradley gave the surprising sum of $80,000 to an obscure Straussian and former student of Walter Berns, James Nichols, to write a doctrinally correct study of Plato's rhetoric. Bradley's highest grant to a libertarian foundation in 1990 went to Cato and amounted to only $25,000.[54]

Of all libertarian think tanks the Institute for Humane Studies may be the most successful at attracting neoconservative and other funding. It is awarded over $350,000 annually from Olin, more than any other libertarian organization, while doing less to adopt the proper protective coloration than its counterparts elsewhere. IHS can also count annually on $250,000 from the David H. Koch Foundation, which is one of Cato's mainstays but gives as much to IHS.[55]

Another Wichita, Kansas, philanthropy, which the Koch family controls, the Claude R. Lambe Foundation, makes its own yearly gift to IHS of $200,000.[56] The Charles G. Koch Foundation, under David's anarcho-Randian brother, bestows an additional $15,000 to the same coffers.[57] This success with its benefactors may be related to the way IHS distributes awards, by funding individual researchers and individual projects. And though staff members, particularly Leonard Liggio, have attacked the welfare state frontally, the institute nonetheless does not have enough of a paper trail to offend the neoconservatives. Nor has it published anything that would upset the socially permissive libertarians who contribute funding from Kansas. IHS may be prospering by being different things to different people. It also provides a resting place for neoconservatives making job changes in Washington.

Significantly, most libertarian groups have not been sufficiently supportive of the one overriding concern of all neoconservative philanthropies: maintaining an activist foreign policy guided by cold war liberal prescriptions. Between 1973 and 1991, the Scaife foundations and their affiliates have paid out more than $18 million to "conservative" grantees.[58] Of those recipients the most generously treated has been the National Security Program, identified with the late Frank Traeger at New York University, which has attracted $6 million; second on the list is the Georgetown Center for Strategic Studies, with $5 million from Scaife and considerably more from Olin. Heritage, which has drawn $3.8 million, and Hoover, receiving around $3 million, have not fared as well at the hands of Scaife as the activist organizations that are more exclusively focused on foreign policy. All recipients are expected to espouse the same positions, from support for Israeli West Bank settlements to National Endowment for Democracy propaganda initiatives.

The foreign policy focus among neoconservative philanthropies may help to throw into relief the perils confronting Cato Institute. With an annual operating budget of more than $3 million, Cato has made itself the most visible libertarian think tank in the country. While IHS may in fact be receiving more money, it has not attracted as much attention as Cato, whose research fellows appear on television and publish in the national press. In expanding, Cato has undoubtedly been helped by its steady funding sources. Beyond the recent annual allotments of $250,000 from

Olin, Smith-Richardson, and Scaife, it has also benefited from Ed Crane's past exemplary relations with the Koch family. Charles and David Koch, friends from Crane's days as a Libertarian party activist, provide him with over a million dollars a year for his institute in Washington. The Claude R. Lambe Foundation, over which Charles Koch functions as the only trustee, seems particularly inclined toward supporting the work of Crane. Out of the $1.7 million it disburses annually for "the arts and civic affairs," over $800,000 go to the Cato Institute, according to the available 990 PF forms.[59] But Cato has now slipped in its dealings with Olin, which may have repercussions elsewhere. In spring 1991 Olin dropped Cato as a grantee, and its president, William Simon, explained the reasons to Crane in a letter full of harsh words. The failure of Cato to rally behind the war effort in Iraq showed that it was unpatriotic and unworthy of funding.

Securing Control

The neoconservative ascendancy over policy institutions has occurred most demonstrably in Washington. There conservative foundation heads seem always in a hurry to express agreement with fixed neoconservative positions. In 1989, the sociologist Charles Murray suffered the consequences of stepping out of line when he was released from a fellowship by the Manhattan Institute, even though the Bradley Foundation was willing to continue financing his research. Murray, it was discovered, had extended his work on the culture of the underclass too far by investigating racially based differences in I.Q. testing. The only foundation that stepped forth to provide office space for the displaced scholar, long a neoconservative darling, was the politically centrist AEI. Ed Crane, president of the Cato Institute and Murray's longtime fishing partner, commented on Murray's current project by saying that "sometimes taboos serve a legitimate social function."[60] Such a remark may seem particularly surprising, coming from a figure and institute that claim to oppose social taboos, especially prohibitions against homosexuality and mind-altering drugs.

Yet Crane made a costly decision when he moved his predominantly academic think tank from San Francisco to Washington in 1981. Thereafter his institute became identified almost exclusively with public policy, and the need for both increased funding and media accessibility may have impelled Crane to move leftward on both social and cultural questions in order to win mainstream respectability for his pamphlet crusade for deregulation and privatization. In recent years, for instance, Crane has judged paleoconservatives to be "neo-fascist in the social arena" and has scolded Patrick Buchanan for trying to "reinforce our Euroethnic heritage" by encouraging the integration of Eastern Canada into the United States.[61]

None of the charges raised by Crane was buttressed by evidence, but his outburst might have been calculated nonetheless. For a long time Crane has depended on the goodwill of the Washington media and the deep pockets of his left-leaning libertarian benefactors, David and Charles Koch. Henceforth he will have to rely on them even more, seeing that Olin, Bradley, and Smith-Richardson have stopped awarding more than $200,000 in funds. Ever resourceful, Crane has begun to speak openly of a new alliance that might steer affluent friends in his direction. In both his self-defense to William G. Simon of Olin and in his public addresses he has offered plans for a coalition, brokered by the Cato Institute, that would be broad enough to embrace both multinational corporate interests and the social concerns of the American Civil Liberties Union.[62]

In a similar fashion, Edwin Feulner of the Heritage Foundation sounded more Catholic than the Pope with his attacks on the Rockford Institute at a 22 January 1990 neoconservative summit in New York. "Rockford is digging itself a hole and cutting itself off from the mainstream conservative movement," Feulner complained apropos of a controversial essay on Lincoln written by the editor of *Chronicles* but published in *National Review*.[63] Feulner has also written letters to prominent journalists, including Rowland Evans and Robert Novak, calling for total war against *Chronicles*.[64] He has threatened to send "ICBM's" against the institute if executives refuse to muzzle their editor.[65]

Like other Washington foundation heads, Feulner and, before his resignation this year, the outspokenly neoconservative vice president B. Y. Pines, have been justifiably concerned about their financial future. Thirty-eight percent of the institute's budget now comes from philanthropic foundations, and along with Coors, Pew, and a few other major donors, Scaife, Olin, and Bradley are at the top of its list of backers.[66] Feulner could not survive a sea change in his relationship to the neoconservatives; and by now his own board, which includes William G. Simon and Richard Scaife, would likely get rid of a rebellious Heritage president even before Michael Joyce took action.

In any case, it would be risky for Feulner or for any Foundation head dependent on the neo-conservatives to challenge that solidarity. To his credit, this experienced Washington operator has been a superb fund-raiser. In the late 1970s he and Paul Weyrich organized the Council on National Policy, sometimes described as the barn where conservative cash cows go to be milked.

Partly at the initiative of the CNP, the Roe Foundation has passed under the combined control of Feulner and Weyrich. In a more controversial step, Feulner positioned himself in 1983 to take over the assets and records of the Aequus Institute. The chairman of the board, Alan Mansfield, had set up his institute to defend the principles of capitalism and Christian Science, and established an $11 million endowment. Mansfield invited Feulner and two professed free-marketeers, David Keyston and Patrick Parker, to join his board of directors (all three were members of the Mt. Pelerin Society). To his surprise Mansfield soon discovered that he was being ousted by his new directors, who charged him with mental incompetence and urged him to hand the endowment over to the more capable directors. In a subsequent meeting Feulner and his friends voted to strip Mansfield of control over his own endowment, which allowed them to distribute a large part of the funds among foundations of their choice.[67]

The Heritage Foundation has also benefited from Feulner's profitable relations with governments and businessmen in the Far East. Beyond the trips and honoraria that the Unification Church provided to his staff, Feulner has drawn substantial assistance from South Korean and Taiwanese business interests, much of it earmarked for Heritage's Asian Studies Center. Heritage has reciprocated by giving Asians generous honoraria, some of them instrumental in defraying expenses for Feulner's travels.

Much of Heritage's support from the Far East is obviously in response to Heritage's aggressive advocacy of free trade; namely, policies that discourage retaliation against what are widely regarded as unfair trade practices carried out by Korea and Japan. In October of 1990 *Heritage Today* published an account of its series of meetings and conferences bringing together U.S. and Japanese government officials, businessmen, scholars, and journalists. The meetings were aimed at dispelling concerns on both sides about the possibility of a trade war, particularly American anger of "Japan's refusal to open its markets to U.S. businesses."[68] Heritage has also been enthusiastic in the way it has backed increased immigration to the United States from the Third World. In 1986 it took sides with Hispanic activists in opposing sanctions against employers of illegal immigrants. Noting the efforts of Heritage and other like-minded foundations to increase Third World immigration to America,

Dick Kirchten in *National Journal* offered the opinion that "immigration is a growth industry in the think tanks of the Right."[69]

More complicated and harder to track are Feulner's activities as director (along with longtime associate Richard Allen) of the Credit International Bank in Washington.[70] Feulner has made money from his association with Credit International, for which he has solicited investments while serving as president of Heritage. A three-part story on Feulner's finances and his handling of the Heritage Foundation was spiked by editor Arnaud de Borchgrave (ironically, the coauthor of *The Spike,* the novel that gave to this form of censorship its catchy name), but then appeared in the *Washington Times* in a shortened version on 2 December 1991. The report combines information about Feulner's earnings with comments about the waning political influence of his foundation. The first half of the report seems more convincing than the second.

In view of the funding achievement of the four sister philanthropies, it would seem that an imposed peace could hold the current conservative movement together. John B. Judis's references to "the conservative crackup" and to the "movement's disunity and disintegration" in an essay in the *American Prospect* nicely sum up the contemporary situation.[71] Judis depicts a conservative movement reduced to clashing armies of right-wing populists, Wall Street internationalists, and competing Washington hustlers looking for money and not being overly scrupulous about where they find it. He insists that the Heritage Foundation has marginalized itself. Like Jack Kemp, Heritage conservatives have "encountered a chilly reception from other conservatives" by backing "increased state spending for housing and education and increased tax breaks for the poor." Furthermore, it has been charged that "Kemp and Heritage have become captive to neoconservative welfare policies," and Heritage, like Kemp—the preferred presidential candidate on its staff in 1988—has a reputation, particularly in the South, for "coddling the black poor."[72]

Despite Heritage's longtime unwillingness to criticize Bush from the Right, Judis notes, the present administration has not often turned to the Heritage staff for advice. Moreover, the foundation's resistance to any idea of protection for national industries—in short, its uncompromising free-trade internationalism—has driven away past benefactors, most disastrously the once generous patron Milliken Foundation of South Carolina.[73]

Judis has exposed only the tip of the iceberg that is overturning the agitated vessel of American conservatism. The concentration of power and money within its neoconservative wing, together with savage reprisals against suspected heretics, has not brought a conservative peace; it may soon turn out that policy foundations will engender increasing costs but diminishing returns to philanthropic organizations. The most respected of the once right-of-center foundations, AEI, is today centrist with decidedly nonconservative fellows like Norman Ornstein, and though Heritage has diligently stayed in the good graces of Washington journalists and has won applause for its civil rights stands from David Broder and other liberals, it cannot shake the image of heavy-handed control and partylining. Isabel Sawhill, senior fellow at the Urban Institute, records her frustration in discussing public issues with Heritage representatives: "As far as they're concerned, there's only one right answer."[74] Another commentator, Roger M. Williams, notes the emptiness of the Heritage claim to be "uncompromisingly principled."[75] The foundation does change its stands, most notably on welfare, while appearing to curry favor steadily among Washington journalists.

The problems of credibility and contagious animosity confronting the Heritage Foundation and similar, less-prominent organizations in greater Washington may be inherent in the foundation's claim to represent the *only* conservative principles or policies. Heritage represents neither, and its attempt to play king of the hill, by punishing dissenters while truckling to both neoconservative donors and liberal journalists, has earned Feulner more ill will than admiration outside the Washington beltway.

Maintaining a sumptuous life-style for its commanders and a few privileged beneficiaries has become essential for those who control conservative funding. Neoconservative academics endowed by the four sisters complain of their suffering at the hands of left-wing faculties, but few humanities scholars on the Left dispose of comparable financial resources. There can be no doubt that the widely published socialist scholar Judith Shklar received less financial support in the late eighties than her neoconservative colleagues in the same political science department at Harvard. Though some conservative scholars have been victims of real discrimination, beneficiaries of the four sisters, many rich beyond the dreams of avarice, are not among them. In a comment on Midge Decter and her by-now-disbanded Committee for the Free World, neoconservative journalist Eric Breindel notes what he considers an unjustified suspicion, that a "collective of enormously wealthy foundations was financing a highly organized ideological struggle led by Midge Decter's Committee and the various little magazines."[76] A survey of their philanthropy, particularly in universities, might lead one to wonder as much about squandered wealth as about the neoconservatives' monopolization of a particular ideological struggle.

Beyond directing a steady flow of funds to scholars of questionable credibility, the staffs of neoconservative foundations themselves have been well-compensated for their management of the wealth made available by benefactors. During fiscal year 1987–88 Michael Joyce, head of the Bradley Foundation, paid himself a salary, including benefits, of $220,000.[77] His assistant, Fradkin, received over $90,000 in the same period. One might compare this compensation paid in relatively inexpensive Milwaukee to the average salary for a president of a nonprofit organization in far-more-expensive Washington.[78] The *Non Profit Times* (October 1989) reports that in 1988–89 this figure came to a mere $137,000. Another recipient of neoconservative largesse, Edwin Feulner, may be, on the basis of figures from *National Journal,* America's most well-paid foundation director. Feulner's Heritage salary in 1990, adjusted for benefits, came to approximately $320,000; to which must be added, for an accurate reckoning, a deferred interest-bearing compensation that by 1991 reached $496,086. This deferred bonus, which increases by $30,000 per year, will belong to Feulner legally if and when he severs his ties to Heritage. Although neoconservative stalwart and AEI director Christopher de Muth collects $250,000 as an annual salary, Feulner has exploited his neoconservative and business connections even more effectively.[79]

It is important not to lose perspective on the impact and extent of conservative funding. The big conservative foundations are dwarfs both in comparison to giants like Ford and Rockefeller and when measured against the vast government sums available to conventional liberals and leftists. Yet the 40-year transformation of a poor but (for the most part) honest set of scholars and journalists has brought about a lucrative but tightly controlled financial empire, with parallels in every nook and cranny of American culture. The strange quality of the conservative success lies in the movement's populist pretensions and its continuing claims to represent the interests of ordinary Americans.[80] One can only speculate on how the small-dollar donors to Washington organizations would react if they knew how their money was actually spent.

Chapter Seven

The Unraveling of the Conservative Movement

Lines of Division

Social and political movements, so long as they are growing and flourishing, rarely have the opportunity for self-conscious reflection upon their histories. Thus the memoirs of movements, like those of ministers, are written in retirement. If the spate of books on conservative phenomena is any indication, the movement was already moribund at the time of George Bush's inauguration as president. In only a few years the conservative movement reached first maturity and then senescence, and hardly a month goes by without a new analysis of its decline. In the early nineties, the main topic of discussion among self-conscious conservatives has been the growing fragmentation on the American political and intellectual Right. R. Emmett Tyrrell, Charles Krauthammer, Ben Wattenberg, and Norman Podhoretz have noted these divisions from the neoconservative side, and *U.S. News and World Report* has added its own opinion that libertarians, evangelicals, isolationists, and internationalists "have never been easily housed in one room." According to Paul Weyrich, "with the weakening of the anticommunist, antiabortion, antitax trinity, the movement is now in greater flux than at any time in the past 25 years."[1]

Although there is widespread recognition of a "conservative crackup," commentators do not always agree on the groups and issues that have brought it about. *The Wall Street Journal* notes sharp disagreement on the Right "over the breathtaking collapse of the enemy."[2] While observing that "anti-Communism has been the glue that held the conservative movement together," the *Journal* exaggerates the rift between the Heritage Foundation, which favors "cutting a deal with the Soviets," and two cold war hardliners, Angelo Codevilla of the Hoover Institution and Jeane Kirkpatrick. Both sides in this putative rift, far from being opponents, still write for the same publications, attend the same conferences, and review the same books.

The same kind of test for who is really fighting whom should be applied to other participants in alleged conservative spats. Washington journalists, for example, offer questionable contrasts between Jeane Kirkpatrick, variously depicted as isolationist and an anticommunist hardliner, and *New Republic* advocates of a democratic internationalist policy.[3] But Kirkpatrick has taken democratic internationalist stands as often as those to whom she is now contrasted.[4] A variation on the same theme is the reported split between Irving Kristol, portrayed as a conservative realist, and Norman Podhoretz and Ben Wattenberg, both now cast as democratic internationalists. Again the evidence does not hold up. Despite his alleged conservative realism, Kristol continues to serve as a patron for such fervent global democratic godchildren as Francis Fukuyama, Gregory Fossedal, and Joshua Muravchik; and his son, William, has become the chief adviser to the main exponent of world democracy in the Bush administration, Vice President Dan Quayle. Even more revealingly, Kristol has never shown any willingness to be reconciled with those paleoconservatives who express the same reservations he does (or claims to) in relation to a global democratic foreign policy. The "real differences" *National Interest* editor Michael Lind has called to my attention in a conversation about the Podhoretz-Kristol rift seem to pale in comparison to other far more meaningful lines of division on the Right. Lind has made the point that most neoconservatives of his acquaintance hold paleoconservative doubts about "Wilsonian democratic crusades." If this is the case, then it seems strange that these doubts can be seen only sporadically in the work of *some* neoconservative commentators. Even these commentators have made no attempt to embrace their paleoconservative counterparts.

Meetings and informal sessions were held among the conservative leadership in 1990 in the face of stormy disagreement. The most widely discussed of such meetings came about through the cooperation of Richard John Neuhaus and William F. Buckley, Jr. At that gathering, which took place at the exclusive Union League Club in New York on 22 January, the troubled leaders of the movement attempted to form a common front, not against their enemies on the Left but against their Old Right critics.[5] In addition to Neuhaus, Buckley, and leading neoconservative allies—Irving Kristol, the Podhoretzes, and Michael Joyce—the "consultation" was also attended by the heads of major Washington organizations, Edwin Feulner and Paul Weyrich. Weyrich explained the absence of paleoconservatives to a *Washington Times* reporter, saying: "I suspect these people weren't there because they have made a career out of attacking so many people who were there."[6] Unfortunately the group was not able to reach any agreement either on Buckley's program, "A Consensus for the 90s" (published later in *National Review*), or on Weyrich's plan for the formation of youth brigades to restore order in the inner city.

While small fissures were developing for some time between the strong and moderate wings of the mainstream internationalist Right, a veritable chasm had opened, separating *National Review* and the neoconservatives from a growing coalition of libertarians, nationalists, and noninterventionists. Members of the new realignment disagreed on many points, such as free trade and America's intervention in the Persian Gulf, but they were all sharply critical of the New York–Washington Right's foreign and domestic policies.[7]

The symbolic event that made the split irreconcilable took place on 5 May 1989. It was then that the Rockford Institute dismissed Richard Neuhaus from his position as director of its Center on Religion and Society. Neuhaus had fought bitterly with the institute's leadership for at least several years, particularly with the editor of *Chronicles,* Thomas Fleming, who had directed repeated barbs against democratic globalism and civil disobedience. A former Lutheran pastor (now a Catholic priest) turned civil rights activist turned neoconservative, Neuhaus believed deeply in the positions that Fleming ridiculed. Neuhaus and the institute were working out terms for a peaceful separation, under which he would receive all the assets and copyrights of the center, when suddenly he made a public attack on *Chronicles'* editor. This came at a gathering of book publishers assembled by the editors of *National Review* and was in direct violation of an agreement that Neuhaus had signed in preparation for his departure from the Institute.[8] Later admitting his error but still upset by Rockford's political positions, Neuhaus subsequently took other actions, detrimental to his employers' interests, that pertained to a grant of $280,000 for fiscal year 1988–89 that the Bradley Foundation had promised the Rockford Institute. On the basis of its expectation of this grant, the Institute had allocated an increase of funds to the New York center. When it transpired, however, that Bradley had decided against the award, after its president Michael Joyce had consulted with Neuhaus, institute president Allan Carlson instructed his New York director to cancel or postpone activities that would involve significant expenditures. The executive committee of the institute's board of directors then fired Neuhaus when he refused to comply.

During the negotiations concerning his release, the already irate Neuhaus had threatened to accuse the institute's leadership of bigotry unless his demands were met. After his dismissal, he kept that promise. In an article on Will Herberg in the 14 July 1989, *National Review,* he laid down the general line of attack: "It is not only totalitarians who cannot stand Jews and Judaism. In this country we are familiar with a brand of conservatism that is marked by nativist and chauvinist sentiment. It advocates a form of cultural coherence that requires a clear line between 'us' and 'them.' In the language of that conservatism, which fortunately is itself now marginal, the Jew is obtrusively marginal."[9] That Neuhaus was speaking of the *Chronicles* circle—which included, ironically, Jewish intellectuals—was clear. He pointed to the use by this group of at least traces of the "classical language of anti-Semitism" that made "deracinated, rootless, and cosmopolitan" into "code words for Jews and Jewishness."

It was on specifics, however, that the brief broke down. *Chronicles,* the complaint went, had opposed unrestricted immigration, but so did many labor unions and civil rights spokesmen. Neuhaus also charged that *Chronicles* had published an essay that treated novelist Gore Vidal as a disgruntled old Republican and an intellectual heir to Henry Adams. Vidal, a compulsive controversialist, had quarreled with both William Buckley and the Podhoretzes, accusing the latter, perhaps unfairly, of belonging to "a small number of American Jews, who . . . have made common cause with every sort of reactionary and anti-Semitic group in the United States" for the sake of defending Israel.[10] His targets then turned around and tarred Vidal with the same anti-Semitic brush. This, as the editors of *Chronicles* insisted, was intended as a blanket charge, to convict Vidal—and anyone who enjoyed his novels—of anti-Semitism. Both Normal Podhoretz and Neuhaus gave that impression by the sweeping nature of their tirades.

Deprived of major sources of funding and excoriated in the conservative press, particularly by *National Review,* the Rockford Institute's leaders began to look for allies who shared their concern about bureaucratic government and dislike for the Eastern establishment. This was the beginning of the "paleorealignment," described by its detractors as a matching up of previously rejected and already graying partners. Yet it turned out to be far more durable than anyone could have imagined.

At least three major groups were involved in this realignment: Old Right traditionalists, libertarians, and neomercantilist nationalists. The members of these groups tended to be clustered around three organizations: the Rockford Institute, the Ludwig von Mises Institute, and the U.S. Business Industrial Council. Signs of a growing consensus were not hard to detect. Old Right journalist Joseph Sobran began writing for libertarian newsletters and journals directed by Llewelyn Rockwell of the Mises Institute. Rockwell, a longtime activist and Rothbard disciple, became a frequent guest on Patrick J. Buchanan's CNN program *Crossfire,* while Fleming and Buchanan both received the American Values Award from the USBIC.

An exploratory meeting of libertarians and traditionalists was held in Rockford, Illinois, in November 1989 as a joint project of the Rockford and Mises institutes. To their considerable surprise, the two groups discovered they had few points of substantive disagreement—free trade being the principal exception. Rothbard later characterized the meeting as a "love-fest," which moved quickly toward planning a strategy for reuniting the scattered conservative remnants still committed to "old-fashioned republican government." As one of the traditionalists explained to the libertarians, they agreed that the size and scope of government had to be radically reduced; only after they had succeeded in cutting it down to the size of the 1920s would they then quibble over details that might divide the two groups.[11]

This burgeoning alliance, so goes the proud boast, took place among excommunicants. Having driven Rothbard from *his* conservative movement in the 1960s, in May 1989 William F. Buckley placed a similar interdict on the Rockford Institute. In an act of pontifical pomp, Buckley came out for Neuhaus and, by implication, the neoconservatives and against Neuhaus's enemies.[12]

From the beginning, the traditionalists had insisted on including nationalists and other groups who favored local and limited government and a foreign policy based on American national interest. The most important of these groups was the USBIC. Some wondered whether a "coalition" was being formed, with Rothbard and Rockwell, both free-trade libertarians, on one side and Anthony Harrigan (former president of the USBIC), a staunch advocate of protectionist measures, on the other. A gentlemanly debate between Rothbard and Harrigan was held at the 1990 Philadelphia Society meeting in Chicago under the auspices of the Rockford Institute's Main Street Committee. Although nothing was settled, the two parties proved that they could engage in a civil discussion.

The next move toward a formal alliance was the establishment of the John Randolph Club, which had its first meeting in Dallas in the fall of 1990. The sessions followed a debate format, pitting traditionalists against libertarians on several key topics: foreign policy (Samuel Francis and Murray Rothbard), immigration (Chilton Williamson and Lew Rockwell), and censorship (E. Christian Kopff and Ronald Hamowy). The meetings were generally friendly, and the expected battle between Francis and Rothbard on defining state sovereignty never materialized. At several points, however, the atmosphere of harmony was jarred by more doctrinaire members of both parties. Nonetheless, significant progress was made toward a consensus on major issues.

Both sides agreed that foreign policy should serve the national interest rather than the democratic values being promoted by neoconservative journalists. While there was some dissension over the definition of national interest—the traditionalists stressing both hemispheric defense and strategic alliances with Europe and the libertarians emphasizing the defense of America's borders—both groups inveighed against defending imperialism—economic as well as military—largely on practical grounds. On domestic policy, both sides opposed most of the provisions of the welfare state—the libertarians out of principle and the traditionalists out of fear of bureaucratic centralization and egalitarian doctrines. After some open debate, the leading participants concluded that the language and arguments concerning civil rights were fundamentally dangerous to local and corporate liberties, no matter how well such language might work in the court of public opinion. On drug policies and censorship, libertarians and traditionalists both opposed national regulation but differed on the propriety of local laws. On immigration and trade policy, the two groups have united behind the principle that no policy should be adopted unless conducive to political liberty in the United States; a widely accepted corollary held that liberty could only be restored in a society that had the moral foundations to exercise it.

Save for a few leftist libertarians among the audience, most of the gathered guests embraced explicitly or implicitly the position long represented in *Chronicles,* and recently expressed by Patrick J. Buchanan, which holds that self-governing societies must have cultural limits. Derisive references were repeatedly made to Ben Wattenberg's view of America as a "universal nation" that enhances its freedoms while becoming increasingly multicultural, and almost all the paleoconservatives inclined toward the opposite view, that liberty and self-government can only prevail in the context of some preexisting community.

The achievement of a provisional consensus on immigration between the two sides may have been the most significant indication of a durable alliance. At the second John Randolph Club meeting 14 months later, all the papers dealing with immigration took an unfailingly restrictionist position. Paleolibertarians accepted this position because of the likelihood of immigrants using and expanding the already existing welfare network. While paleoconservatives agreed, they also raised the issue of American cultural cohesion being further weakened by floods of Third World (particularly Latin American) immigrants.

Both sides seem to have stayed clear of certain potentially disruptive views associated with some of their past allies. Despite their formal support of free immigration as well as free trade, paleolibertarians have at least provisionally accepted the restrictionist immigration position, to the consternation of the neoconservatives and libertarian Left. This is not entirely surprising, given the traditionalist attitudes and nationalist sentiments of Rothbard and Rockwell. The paleolibertarians may also have the better part of the argument with leftist libertarians, such as *Wall Street Journal* editor David Frum. Frum and other leftist libertarians maintain that the welfare state will grow weaker if it is not allowed to dictate immigration policy.[13] Paleolibertarians argue that the record for Latin American immigrants since the sixties overwhelmingly proves the opposite: that welfare state services have increased at least partly in response to immigration. Meanwhile, paleoconservatives, in alliance with paleolibertarians, have had to keep *their* distance from those they might otherwise be tempted to join, particularly "right-wing greens," extreme environmentalists who, because they are also anti-immigrationists and cultural traditionalists, might in other circumstances be the paleoconservatives' natural allies. But *Chronicles* has usually opposed both immigrationists and champions of government bureaucracy, unlike the *Social Contract,* a periodical that has brought together environmentalists and anti-immigrationists and features among its contributors former Governor Richard Lamm of Colorado.

Even by stretching the limits of the realignment, the so-called paleo-alliance would be capable of mustering very limited resources. Nonetheless, the very prominence of some of its members and allies was sufficient to rattle mainstream leadership. Russell Kirk, though staying out of the discussions that lead to the alliance, had nonetheless become embroiled with Midge Decter for making fun of neoconservative Zionism.[14] The newest major adversary of the New York–Washington conservatives, however, would soon become Patrick J. Buchanan. As fate would have it, Buchanan's positions on trade, immigration, and foreign policy were coming to coincide with those of the Randolph Club, which he joined in 1991.

Meanwhile in *Commentary,* in January 1991, veteran neoconservative author Joshua Muravchik scolded Buchanan as an anti-Semitic Teutonophile.[15] Citing presumably interrelated tendencies in Buchanan's writing—being against "crusades for democracy" and against anti-Christian statements by Jewish organizations, defending accused Nazi war criminals, and reproaching the Israelis for mistreating Palestinians—Muravchik traced Buchanan's isolationist stand on the Persian Gulf crisis back to an inveterate contempt for both Jews and Western democracy. Muravchik linked Buchanan's right-wing prejudices to his German ancestry—to the indisputable fact that his maternal family had been German—and to his unwillingness to face up to his own past.

Similar charges came out in a *New York Times* editorial by William F. Buckley's close friend A. M. Rosenthal, and in two scathing essays, one by Jacob Weisberg, in the *New Republic.*[16] Throughout the fall of 1990, moreover, *Time, Newsweek,* and other mass-circulation publications featured stories on Buchanan's war with centrist conservatives and with Abe Foxman, director of the Anti-Defamation League.[17] Most offensive to his critics was Buchanan's assertion on the television program "The McLaughlin Group" that, "there are only two groups that are beating the drum right now for war in the Middle East, and that is the Israeli Defense Ministry and its amen corner in the U.S." Rosenthal retorted that Buchanan had committed "blood libel" by suggesting that "Jews have alien loyalties for which they are willing to sacrifice the lives of Americans." And even before *Commentary* took out its big guns, an editorial in the neoconservative *New York Post* announced that "when it comes to Jews in a group, Buchanan betrays an all too familiar hostility."[18]

What this fray revealed were the already well-defined lines of division between the neoconservatives and their promoters, and the part of the Right that did not identify itself with the neoconservatives. While liberal journalist Jack Germond and, at least initially, even *New Republic* editor Morton Kondracke vigorously defended Buchanan against the accusation of anti-Semitism, William Buckley and his *National Review* judged Buchanan to be "insensitive" to Jewish concerns.[19] At *National Review*'s thirty-fifth anniversary dinner, Buckley saw to it that Rosenthal and other neoconservatives sat on the dais; shortly thereafter, Joseph Sobran, a friend of Buchanan's whom the neoconservative Midge Decter had accused of being a Christian anti-Semite, was demoted from the rank of senior editor to "critic-at-large."[20] Even America's most preeminent scholar of Judaica, Jacob Neusner, long identified as a paleoconservative, began having his commissioned book reviews returned by *National Review* in the wake of the Buchanan incident. Moreover, longtime Buchanan acquaintance, but by then a committed neoconservative, *New Republic* editor Fred Barnes explained that his erstwhile friend had indeed turned anti-Semite, if one takes into account the broad definition of the term as lack of concern for Jewish feelings.[21]

Whereas Buchanan's expanding war with American Zionist organizations evoked savage attacks from neoconservatives, the Old Right cheered him on. Jewish authors Allan Brownfeld and Murray Rothbard agreed with Buchanan's response to Rosenthal, that the accusation of anti-Semitism was a "branding iron wielded by a tiny clique, to burn horribly heretics from their political orthodoxy."[22] Brownfeld, himself a critic of American Israeli lobbyists, maintained that Buchanan had been punished for having gone from being a Zionist enthusiast to a nonsupporter of the Israeli occupation of the West Bank: "Rosenthal's attack was part of a carefully crafted plan to silence free and open debate of U.S. Middle East policy."[23] Rothbard noted that the charge of anti-Semitism came from journalists at the *New Republic* and *New York Times* who were pursuing their discrete ideological aims.

Buchanan, in accepting the USBIC's American Values Award as a "champion of a new nationalism," seized the occasion to outline the doctrine of the dissident Right. Addressing a council luncheon packed with congressmen and other dignitaries on 28 November 1990, at the National Press Club, Buchanan stressed "the deep and fundamental differences we of the Old Right have always had with the interventionists, globalists, and One Worlders." With the collapse of the Soviet Union, he continued, those differences have resurfaced, as the president, advised by democratic globalists, has turned the Persian Gulf crisis into "the test of the New World Order." Alluding to a remark by the paleoconservative Samuel T. Francis, Buchanan joked that "whenever some of us hear phrases like New World Order, we instinctively release the safety catch on our revolvers."[24]

Buchanan's broadsides against the war party in America was the opening shot in the conservative civil war over U.S. involvement in the Persian Gulf, while Iraq's invasion of Kuwait was the first opportunity for the two sides to apply their principles to an expanding national crisis.

Predictably, the mainstream Right joined the war party, but both the traditionalists and the libertarians in the new alliance took a dim view of the aims and conduct of the war. In general, the traditionalists insisted they were not opposed to wars that were both just and demonstrably in the American interest, while the libertarians applied their fixed principle of nonintervention. Patrick Buchanan's response was symptomatic of the Old Right's ambiguous attitude: Highly critical of President Bush's calls for a "New World Order," Buchanan refused to attack the conduct of the war, while American troops were involved.

Until recently Buchanan's allies on the Right, however, had remained a marginal force, due partly to a comparative lack of resources and partly to the compatibility of the neoconservatives (a term that now covers the *New Republic,* most of the contents of *National Review,* and the Heritage Foundation) and the liberal mainstream. As a result, the neoconservative positions on democratic capitalism, free trade, and the conversion of the non-Western world to the current American model of democracy today enjoy support from major newspapers and journals. While *National Review* publishes articles in support of the cold war liberalism it was founded to combat, leading liberal journalists—A. M. Rosenthal, Flora Lewis, Jim Hoagland, Michael Kinsley, and Richard Cohen, for example—often sound like neoconservatives.[25] Moreover, neoconservatives Charles Krauthammer, George Will, Jeane Kirkpatrick, Bruce Bawer, Morton Kondracke, and Ben Wattenberg write for the major newspapers and political magazines in the New York–Washington corridor. Among publications in this venue with more than 20,000 readers, the *Village Voice* and the *Nation,* both situated on the far Left, may be the only ones lacking what Samuel Francis calls "the usual assortment of hard and soft neocons," declared and undeclared neoconservatives advocating secular democracies with modified capitalist economies, freely moving labor forces, and international free trade.[26] The editor of *Telos* magazine, Paul Piccone, ascribes the rapid spread of this vision to the "collapse of Right and Left," the breakdown of critical social thought on both ends of the political spectrum.[27] Christopher Lasch traces the same development to the now prevalent historical view of an all-determining material progress. Lasch considers this vision as the common denominator of American electoral politics and political discourse.[28]

Indistinguishability vs. Marginalization

For all these animadversions it is hard to overlook the mainstream respectability that the neoconservatives have acquired. It is all the more surprising therefore that political observers, including the hostile Daniel Lazare, believe that "despite their backward-looking ideas, the traditionalists have all the vigor of youth, while the neocons, after eight years of Reaganism and less than a year of George Bush, are beginning to show their age."[29] Like Lazare, Sara Diamond and John Judis point to an advancing paleoconservative specter with awe and trepidation. Though these Jewish and leftist commentators sympathize more with the cosmopolitan and pro-Israeli neoconservatives than their "anti-Semitic" opponents, they also speak of the paleoconservatives as beneficiaries of a "profound realignment process" and the "high-risk capitalists" set loose during the Reagan era. Unfortunately for this analysis, no proof is available of paleoconservative anti-Semitism, as opposed to skepticism about "democracy as an all-inclusive ideology" and wariness of foreign entanglements.[30] Nor is there evidence that the neoconservatives believe more in the free market, as their leftist commentators insist, than the paleoconservatives. Even advocacy of free trade and generous immigration policies is not tantamount to a call for a free-market economy. And despite their philosophical objections to internationalism and the "ideology of free trade," the libertarian Murray Rothbard is correct to observe that paleoconservatives are for the free market, as an alternative to the welfare state.[31]

Lazare, Diamond, and Judis are correct, however, in their observation that neoconservatives are anxious about being overwhelmed from the Right. Weyrich, Feulner, and Decter have all expressed fear about right-wing thunder and their alarm may be well-founded after all. Neoconservatives have run out of steam and originality. Moreover, they have lost their fighting edge under the burden of opulence and in the absence of unvanquished enemies to fight on their homefront. Their support elsewhere remains scattered and thin, and none of their electoral outings— with Jack Kemp as a Republican primary contender in 1988, with Linda Chavez and Alan Keyes as Republican senatorial candidates in Maryland, or with John Silber's gubernatorial bid in Massachusetts in 1990—has yielded a single victory.[32]

Even more ominously, neoconservatives have become indistinguishable from the journalists they once criticized—and in some cases have converted to their views. For instance, during the Gulf crisis, which helped enhance neoconservative fortunes, many of the editorials that appeared in the *New York Times* or *Washington Post* could have been written by Norman Podhoretz. The establishment Right has collapsed into neoconservative hands, but the same might be said about liberal columnists who have joined the anticommunist side and have put democratic-capitalist labels on their social democratic prescriptions.[33] Leftists have appropriately wondered aloud what movement conservatives will do without the Soviet and communist threats. For the neoconservatives an even more pressing dilemma concerns how they can distinguish their voice any longer from its echoes. This may be one reason they have recently put money and energy into educational outreach. By fighting for democratic civilization on campuses against black nationalists and radical feminists, neoconservatives can stand out again from those on their Left. They can also recapture their own militant past, when Podhoretz was still "breaking ranks," by confronting as an old-fashioned cold war liberal the sixties New Left. Several "Second Thoughts" conferences already have been called by neoconservative journalists, courtesy of Olin and Bradley, to celebrate the conversion of old time radicals David Horowitz, Peter Collier, Jeffrey Herf, and Ronald Radosh, to global democratic doctrines.[34] These appeals to ancient battles seem strangely out of place in a movement that has coopted, incorporated, or marginalized much of its old opposition.

Unlike the neoconservatives, the paleoconservatives have no trouble distinguishing themselves from everyone else. They are the noncooptable members of the American Right, who pride themselves on their adversarial relationship to the liberal-neoconservative monolith. Though they do respect the postwar Old Right and have discovered roots in Jeffersonian Democracy, Southern Agrarianism, and the prewar anti–New Dealers, Sara Diamond is correct to regard paleoconservatives as a recently formed faction.[35] Unlike the predominantly Catholic or High Church postwar Right, paleoconservatives are mostly Protestant, with a sprinkling of Central European Jews. They have been heavily marked by modernist disciplines, despite their familiarity with classical learning and prefer to cite sociobiologists or political theorists like Machiavelli, Thomas Hobbes, Antonio Gramsci, and James Burnham to the Catholic scholastics so congenial to the postwar Right.[36] Unlike that Right, they are largely indifferent to the siren call of anticommunism and are stridently contemptuous of leftist anti-Communists like Sidney Hook. Indeed, they consider anticommunism, as much as antifascism, a vehicle for an egalitarian bureaucratic state. Unlike the Fascists to whom their opponents compare them, paleoconservatives mock the "welfare-warfare state"; behind this mockery, however, is contempt for the state not as an energizing force but as a leveling and homogenizing instrument. Further, paleoconservatives do not dislike political authority; nor are they categorically opposed to democracy as local and organic self-government. It is democratic pluralism and the welfare state they are against, for destroying already integrated communities.

All paleoconservatives think in terms of process; whence their attraction to leftist critics of corporate liberalism like C. Wright Mills and their bridge-building to revisionist Marxists Eugene Genovese, Elizabeth Fox-Genovese, and Christopher Lasch and to the Frankfurt-School critical theorists grouped around *Telos*.[37] The paleoconservatives point to social and cultural crisis where the neoconservatives and neoliberals find human progress. They perceive an evolving interplay of economic, political, and cultural factors that is bringing about a social breakdown. Like the Italian Marxist Gramsci, paleoconservative Samuel Francis treats culture as the creation of the dominant class; in America that class is seen no longer as the owners of the means of production but as the managers of state and society, masking their political aspirations in egalitarian doctrine.

Obvious ties exist between paleoconservative attacks on global bureaucratic government and those of the European New Right. Like American paleoconservatives, European New Rightists, Alain de Benoist, Marco Tarchi, and Günter Maschke, lament both a politics of faceless bureaucrats and the annihilation of communal identities. Both groups of conservatives exalt the Europeans or Eurocentric character of inherited identities while contrasting abstract human rights to a historically situated personhood.[38] *Chronicles* has published articles by Thomas Molnar and Tomislav Sunic presenting the thought of Benoist and of other European New Rightists. What separates the two conservative sides, however, are the ferocious anti-Americanism and corporate-socialist tendencies of the European New Right. Its publications have featured repeated attacks on "the West" as an invention of American capitalist imperialists; and during the cold war Benoist and his associates tilted conspicuously toward the Soviets—and more recently, toward Iraq's Saddam Hussein.[39]

In view of their defiantly American character and at least residual free-market sentiments, the paleoconservatives are limited in their choice of alliances. They admire the Italian localists who have organized the Lega Lombarda and write occasionally for Benoist's *Nouvelle Ecole* and *Salisbury Review,* whose editor, Roger Scruton, is an English historical conservative. Because the paleoconservatives' energies have been far more fixed on American issues, however, they have looked for friends and well-wishers at home. This venue seems all the more understandable given the posture they have assumed as critics of democratic globalism, with protectionist and neonationalist interests.

The paleoconservatives may nonetheless be in an ideal situation to prosecute their war in the short run. Without real hope of replacing the neoconservatives as the political and cultural spokesmen for the New York–Washington corridor, they still exercise a critical function on the American Right. Above all they raise issues that the neoconservatives and the Left would both seek to keep closed, for instance, questions about the desirability of political and social equality, the functionality of human rights thinking, and the genetic basis of intelligence. In all these assaults on liberal and neoconservative pieties, paleoconservatives reveal an iconoclastic exuberance rarely found on the postwar intellectual Right. Their spirit is far more Nietzschean than neo-Thomistic, and like Nietzsche they go after democratic idols, driven by disdain for what they believe dehumanizes.

The paleoconservatives may in fact be doing a public service by representing what Clinton Rossiter called, in looking at the postwar Right, "the thankless persuasion." They do, after all, carry on their work in the face of growing obstacles. Nonetheless, it is doubtful that others will rush to take their places on the ramparts when this generation of paleoconservatives passes from the scene. Without some prospect for victory or at least for redressing the disparity in power between the two sides, the struggle already begins to seem pointless.

Many Old Right scholars have expressed eagerness to return to universities, where identification with the neoconservative Right has been a considerable liability. Others have intimated that they are less offended by the intelligent Left than by the self-promoting Right and would like nothing better than to explore the possibilities—not all alliances but of cooperative associations. For some time now, scholars in Southern studies (history, sociology, and literature) on the Right and Left have been working together to improve the standards of their disciplines, and similar developments may be expected in other fields. A surprising number of paleoconservatives read the *Progressive,* the *Nation,* and the *Utne Reader,* and find these journals no more alien or irritating than *National Review.* Leftists, paleoconservatives are told, have the courage of their convictions, no matter how bizarre those convictions might seem; the same cannot be said for conservatives. Many on the Old Right have gone so far as to repudiate the conservative label altogether and prefer to call themselves reactionaries or nationalists or libertarians, anything to avoid a term that they see as tainted with cowardice and opportunism.[40]

In the fall of 1991 the neoconservatives suffered noticeable reversals of fortune. During October of last year Elliot Abrams, former assistant

secretary of state and one of the most vocally ideological neoconservatives in the Reagan administration, pleaded guilty in a federal court to
having deceived Congress about aid to Contra rebels in Nicaragua.
Abrams had been open and even vehement about seeking to commit the
United States to the global democratic agenda, and his downfall left his
paleoconservative as well as leftist critics at least quietly satisfied.[41] The
continued endorsement of Abrams and his doctrinal goals in the *Wall
Street Journal* revealed a certain desperation combined with neoconservative militancy.[42] Also in October, in the wake of worsening financial
problems at *National Review* leading to the removal of its publisher, it
was learned that the magazine's editor, John O'Sullivan, had turned down
a commissioned review by the paleoconservative warhorse M. E. Bradford. The canceled piece contained unkind comments about Abraham
Lincoln, and O'Sullivan was clearly concerned about offending his neoconservative editors and sponsors. Attacks against O'Sullivan subsequently surfaced in the usually neoconservative *Washington Times,*
where columnist Samuel T. Francis was given a free hand. Inconsisten-
cies were found to be present in the accounts that *National Review* was
then circulating about why its editors had bumped Bradford's reviews;
letters, also published in the *Washington Times,* detailed the cancellation
of other essays commissioned by *National Review* editors that failed to
take the neoconservative line.[43]

   The ascent of David Duke as a Southern politician may also be seen
as assisting the paleoconservatives. Unlike the neoconservatives and the
movement-conservative Washington foundations, paleoconservatives
have warned against fawning on the civil rights establishment. John
O'Sullivan was correct in the pointed observation he made, in his letter
of 17 October 1991, to the *Washington Times,* that the paleoconservatives blend "old theories" with a "newer and less conservative stress on
recruiting the discontented and alienated in American society against institutions which are now seen as irredeemably corrupt."[44] And while the
Heritage Foundation boasts of its bridge-building to black, Hispanic, and
feminist spokespersons and the neoconservative Dinesh D'Souza calls
for more government aid to lower-class students, the paleoconservatives
continue to preach war against the managerial welfare state. Like the
French Communists of the years between the wars, the paleoconservatives advocate a *politique du pire* intended to shake loose the Washington
power structure and its handpicked conservative opposition. To whatever extent Duke represents a populist indignation that the neoconservative and Washington conservative powerbrokers cannot satisfy while

enjoying the good will of the Washington media, the Louisiana politician is serving paleoconservatives ends. As Evans and Novak point out about Duke's constituency, "these citizens are not Klansmen or Nazis. They do not resemble the hate-filled crowds George Wallace attracted twenty years ago. They are alienated from the political system that has given them David Duke as the only means to redress their grievances."[45] Paleoconservatives recognize this fact and hope to exploit it, however much they also try to dissociate themselves from Duke's past unsavory associations or from his defeat in Louisiana in November 1991. But the rebirth in the South of right-wing populism—in a less dramatic form in Mississippi's gubernatorial race than in neighboring Louisiana—has not, at least thus far, put wind back into the paleoconservatives' sails. No substantial amount of funding has been rechanneled from the neoconservative philanthropic empire, and the major media continue to deal with the neoconservatives as the only respectable opposition.

Another issue that paleoconservatives have tried to exploit in their war with neoconservatives and the Washington conservative establishment is the abandonment of the electoral Right in pursuit of nonexistent constituencies. For example, the close identification of the Paul Weyrich and Edwin Feulner operations with the Zionist Right has not resulted in substantial Jewish movement into the conservative camp. And those who have criticized the establishment Right's unswerving identification with Israeli hawks have often been labeled anti-Semites even by other conservatives. Even less productive to date has been the work of Heritage Foundation's New Majority Project, which aims at bringing primarily blacks into the conservative mainstream. Aside from endorsing black capitalism and enterprise zones, both to be advanced through government fiscal policies, Heritage also stood firmly behind Clarence Thomas during his congressional hearings in the fall of 1991. Despite stated reservations on the Right about Thomas's own judicial activist views and his reduction of natural law to an ill-defined belief in equality, Washington movement conservatives went to his aid as soon as he was nominated to the Supreme Court.[46] One reason for this support was that Thomas's presence on the Supreme Court as a "black conservative," it was hoped would spur the growth of a black conservative electorate. This obviously has not occurred despite the widespread support for Thomas among blacks polled during his confirmation hearings before the Senate. One Harris poll conducted in October and November 1991 nonetheless concludes that movement conservative efforts to drive a wedge between black voters and their left-liberal civil rights leadership have utterly failed:

"Black support for the NAACP stands at 13-1 positive, for the Leadership Conference on Civil Rights at 11-1, for Jesse Jackson at 9-1 and for the Black Congressional Caucus at 8-1." All these ratios are almost precisely the same as they were in the 1970s and in the 1960s. Echoing a theme framed by the paleoconservatives, Earl Graves, publisher of *Black Enterprise* magazine, notes that "black conservatives are the new phantom army."[47] Paleoconservatives were among the early critics of this unsuccessful opening from the Right to black electorates. Yet they have been in no position to alter this strategy, having neither the foundations nor the money nor the media access to effect strategic changes in Republican electoral politics.

Paleoconservatives have, however, been prominent in organizing the America First Committee, which prepared the way for the announcement in December 1991 of a presidential bid by Patrick J. Buchanan.[48] Two problems were inherent in this candidacy neither of which seemed to bode well for the paleoconservatives. One, Buchanan had already suffered devastating assaults from both the neoconservatives and likeminded liberals for the views he had expressed on the American Zionist lobby. While the charges against him were certainly not proved beyond doubt, even the suspicion of anti-Semitism, taken as insensitivity to Jewish concerns, can be politically destructive. Buchanan entered the race after trading dangerous insults with the Zionist lobby, which were likely to hurt his presidential ambitions. His challenge to an incumbent Republican president, moreover, were destined to damage his standing among Republican loyalists, to whom he hitherto had appealed as one of them. While in the past Buchanan and his paleoconservatives allies were identified, for the most part, as loyal Republicans, by the spring of 1992 they were depicted as ideologically driven spoilers. In all Northern states with primaries, Bush enjoyed an approval rating among registered Republicans five times that of Buchanan.

If Buchanan is ever to wage a successful presidential bid, he must first gain the support of Washington–New York conservatives and of such neoconservative publications as the *Wall Street Journal*. At the very least he will need to neutralize this powerful opposition, which in the 1992 campaign combined with his political enemies further on the Left to depict him as a neo-Nazi. This can only happen if Buchanan accepts new and unwelcome counsel; namely, if he abandons the media-weak paleoconservatives for their rivals, who have access to newspapers and TV. Outside of the "respectable" conservative camp, controlled by the neoconservatives and the Washington foundations, Buchanan will have insurmountable trouble attempting to win the Republican presidential nomination even in 1996. In that camp, however, he will lose his freedom of action and be pushed into adopting views similar to those of Jack Kemp and William Bennett, both heroes to liberal journalist David Broder. As a neoconservative vassal, Buchanan would phase into a familiar political type, the socially compassionate and minority-conscious progrowth conservative who enjoys media approval without a solid national electoral base. He would become indistinguishable from neoconservatives who have closer ties to their sponsors and who are less offensive to AIPAC, including Vice President Quayle. [49]

It was unlikely that the populist strategy framed by Buchanan and his advisers, Rockwell and Rothbard, would produce in 1992 the party support and popular votes needed to carry a paleoconservative political critic into the presidency. The "respectable" Right as well as the Left pulled out all stops to prevent this from occurring. Nor did it seem likely that there could ever be a brokered deal between Buchanan and the neoconservatives, a prospect that *National Review* was hoping to arrange in February 1992, given the deep animosities between Buchanan and his neoconservative accusers. Buchanan knew full well the price that such a deal would exact—or so he told me—and would refuse to reconstruct himself in the required manner, even for the sake of the Republican nomination.

The Resurgent Populism

Paleoconservatives and paleolibertarians are correct to insist that they alone have a genealogical claim to be on the American Right. What should be asked is whether the future will contain a Right at all, apart from celebrants of a global age or lobbyists to whom the term right wing has been applied in accordance with changing journalistic criteria.

Right and Left are designations that came into use in the modern West in response to particular upheavals. They may already be destined to pass, like so much else in a specifically Western society. The historical specificity that the paleoconservatives cherish can no longer be reconciled with the globalist ideals of the intellectual and business elites. The triumph of the globalist ideal of political and cultural homogeneity based on democratic equality has become the shared task of all "responsible" intellectuals and journalists. For example, on the front page of the *Washington Post Book World* of 12 January 1992 is a celebratory essay by the onetime critic of feminism and current defender of global democracy George Gilder, a recently appointed fellow of the heavily endowed neoconservative Hudson Institute. The essay reviews *The End of History and the Last Man,* written by another neoconservative and a zealous Straussian, Francis Fukuyama, who presents the case for both the historical inevitability of, and moral necessity for, global reconstruction on the basis of the current American democratic model. Though Gilder cavils with Fukuyama's fascination with heroic, aristocratic ideals, he treats his book, for the most part, as a statement of truth and moral guidance.

His own essay is full of historically problematic generalizations; for example, he states "the U.S. constitutional order of limited democracy and economic system of entrepreneurial capitalism defines the end part of human history" and that "over the last 200 years no liberal democratic state has attacked another."[50] Certainly constitutional, representative regimes have fought each other in the past, as in the First World War and during the American Revolution, though it is impossible to recognize even a liberal democracy, by Gilder's standards, that existed 200 years ago, let alone two such regimes. And does Gilder's identification of the U.S. economic system as "entrepreneurial capitalism" describe accurately our mixed economy or the corporate control of much of our national wealth? Other points in the essay appeal to historical inevitabilities, but rely again on inaccurate generalization or even shrill moralizing: for example, Gilder's denial that "non-democratic regimes have sovereign rights" and his revulsion for "authoritarian capitalist" governments that foster prosperity but "block the no less imperious expression of political thymos and direct it into the economic sphere."[51]

The views expressed by the "conservatives" Gilder and Fukuyama are by now indistinguishable from those that appear with regularity on the *Washington Post*'s editorial page or that are presented by its columnists. Those views center on America's duty to spread the democratic way of life everywhere and to overthrow those who represent the dead hand of the authoritarian past. On these duties, if not on the use of resources to fulfil them, the journalistic and political Right and Left, with the unsettling exception of Buchanan and the paleoconservatives, are in total agreement.

An end of ideology is in fact occurring in at least one area, the widespread acceptance in all Western industrial democracies of extensive welfare states, which the official Right and even much of the Left now designate as "democratic capitalism" because of the retention of a large private sector. The Left and most of the Right see America as a nation that has made admirable progress in fighting antidemocratic discrimination. Both accept a vast bureaucratic structure as the price of preserving that putative progress, though they continue to differ on where the emphasis should be placed on civil rights enforcement.

Most importantly, both Right and Left believe in the necessity of an American crusade on behalf of its improved model of government. For the first time it is now the group with the conservative label that is calling most passionately for the overthrow of "authoritarian capitalist regimes." For though such regimes often uphold property rights far more faithfully than democratic ones, they are plainly nonegalitarian and therefore anathema to the crusading egalitarian American Right.

These observations are made to drive home a dominant argument in this book, that traditional political labels are becoming increasingly irrelevant. The most critical consequence of this development is the substantive disappearance of the Right, even more than the Left, for the principles now represented by American establishment conservatism are a particularly militant form of social democracy, with both Menshevik and Trotskyist residues. Significantly, such internationalist doctrines appeal to corporate elites, particularly as packaged by neoconservative foundation heads. Thus one might question the reliability but certainly not eloquent sincerity of Murray N. Rothbard who in his presidential address at the second annual meeting of the John Randolph Club on 18 January 1992, closed with this hopeful peroration:

With the inspiration of the death of the Soviet Union before us, we know that it *can* be done. With Pat Buchanan as our leader, we shall break the clock of social democracy. We shall break the clock of the Great Society. We shall break the clock of the welfare state. We shall break the clock of the New Deal. We shall break the clock of Woodrow Wilson's New Freedoms and perpetual war. We *shall* repeal the twentieth century.[52]

The response of William McGurn, on behalf of the *National Review* establishment two weeks later made light of the paleoconservatives' pretensions to vast electoral power. Without Buchanan, McGurn maintained, they and their society were nothing; and despite recent, apparently respectful references to *Chronicles* in the *New Republic,* it was foolish to treat any paleoconservative magazine as being politically significant.[53] Though the ridicule was intended to downplay earnest, conspicuous opposition from the Right, McGurn may have been telling the truth without knowing it. The powers in league against the paleoconservative, drawn from the Left and Center, continue to grow, even as they themselves become more visible.

At the same time, paleoconservatives can take heart from a secular tendency that is now asserting itself with increasing force. With the waning of the Religious Right and the New Right, populist reactions against liberal social and cultural elites have moved again outside the New York–Washington conservative movement. In a probing commentary on the 1992 New Hampshire presidential primaries, Kevin Phillips notes that "more than half of the Buchanan backers said that they might or would switch to the Democrats in November's general election." The Republican challenger benefited from "frustration with the nation's power elite"; "economic anger, cultural animosity, and a sense of political betrayal, it seems, do not fit on neat ideological scales."[54] Throughout his campaign Buchanan referred to himself, in a phrase borrowed from Samuel Francis, as "a Middle American revolutionary," and thus the attempt by conservative columnist Tom Bethell, writing in *National Review,* to recast Buchanan as a committed Reaganite misses an obvious point.[55] The Buchanan campaign was informed by the belief that Reagan had failed as a Middle American revolutionary (or counterrevolutionary). He had stopped trying to get bureaucracy off the backs of Americans, and he had handed over his administration to global democrats and Eastern Republicans like the one who succeeded him.

The McCarthy analogy may not be flattering to Buchanan, but his friend and adviser Murray Rothbard brought it up as too obvious to ignore.[56] Like McCarthy, Buchanan has learned that each time he thumbs his nose from the Right at the power establishment and its politics, throngs of blue-collar workers follow him. The initial popularity enjoyed by the Buchanan campaign led the editors of *National Review* into expressing "tactical" support for a figure both Buckley and O'Sullivan had just recently accused of being grossly insensitive to American Jews.[57] Although *National Review* only extended to Buchanan temporary, conditional support, until he had wounded Bush in New Hampshire, this act left the neoconservatives feeling betrayed and indignant. Podhoretz in particular lashed out at Buckley for being only a wavering friend of the American Jewish community.[58] *National Review* began to move tentatively toward Buchanan, after treating him quite critically in December 1991, when his populist future began to look promising. At the same time, in editorial notes, it kept urging him to apologize to those he had offended, hoping to patch things up between Buchanan and his neoconservative critics. Such maneuvering was not intended to show that Buckley and O'Sullivan were breaking away from the *Commentary* circle. Most of their contributors, including senior editor William Bennett, remain neoconservatives; and neither Buckley nor O'Sullivan will respond to letters from rightwing critics of that group or from anyone who, like this author, is perceived as unfriendly to neoconservatives. But both are also realistic enough to keep more than one poker in the fire. For example, *National Review* went far enough toward a reconciliation with Buchanan to appear less hostile to him than other neoconservative-influenced journals. On 22 June 1992 it took another small step away from neoconservative orthodoxy, by publishing a feature article by *Forbes* editor Peter Brimelow entitled "Time to Rethink Immigration." In what could only be described as a paleoconservative brief against the concept of America as a "universal nation," Brimelow aimed his shafts at such neoconservative "authorities" on immigration as Julian Simon and Ben Wattenberg. Significantly, the positions taken by him were also those of presidential candidate Patrick Buchanan. Looking beyond the often tendentious comparison of Buchanan to Joseph McCarthy, a more instructive one can be drawn between Buchanan and the late populist Democrat-turned-Republican Frank Rizzo. The Philadelphia police commissioner, whose biography is now being prepared by Sal Paolantonio of the *Philadelphia Inquirer,* managed to distance himself from all political establishments even after becoming mayor. Building on a Catholic working-class base, he turned the law-and-order issue into a rallying point for families and neighborhoods against the outsiders, social workers, journalists, and underclass criminals whom the establishment was accused of coddling. A black liberal Democrat, Wilson Goode, defeated him in a close election after the revelation of financial improprieties, but in 1991 the 71-year-old Rizzo was favored to win back the mayoralty when he died of a heart attack. By then his populist base had expanded from blue-collar Catholics to include "law and order" black voters. In the Pennsylvania Republican primary, the Buchanan organization drew heavily from Rizzo stalwarts such as George Routter and Jim Finnigan. [59] People bound by personal and Middle American loyalties with a profound contempt for "politicians" and "the two party system" found a political home with both Rizzo and Buchanan. Despite the antielitist message of both populist leaders, their popularity was tied to the feudal and familial loyalties they aroused among their staff and workers. The Latin and Celtic Catholic backgrounds of most right-wing populists parallel those of the urban party bosses earlier in the century, and so does their grassroots support.

What must be considered in summing up is whether such populist organizers can create for themselves a majority constituency in the United States, in defiance of the print and media industries. And can they do this while raising a dangerous challenge to much of the public sector, which they wish to replace or simply close down? At the federal level this seems doubtful. Though it is possible to base Republican party campaigns on paleoconservative and other right-wing populist issues, it does not seem probable that the creators of those issues will succeed in taking over a major party or in electing a conservative president. Not only neo-conservatives but the Republican party flourishes with the expansion of the welfare state. No one is likely to "break the clock of the Great Society" without first having to take on the "respectable" conservative movement and the Republican party. Both now provide steady patronage through bureaucracies either created or expanded by Lyndon Johnson, Jimmy Carter, and Ronald Reagan.[60]

The question should be raised whether the short-lived presidential candidacy of Texas businessman Ross Perot, which took off in the spring of 1992, was tied to the right-wing populism that had infused the campaign of Patrick Buchanan. From the articles in the *New York Times* and *Newsweek* to interviews with former Heritage vice-president Burton Yale Pines, it seemed that Perot had come to represent an essentially conservative reaction against Washington-based politics, summed up by the attitude, as expressed by Pines, that "it's America against Washington."[61] Critical journalists, particularly in the *New Republic,* turned against Perot some of the charges that had been directed against Buchanan, after Perot had said that he would keep adulterers and homosexuals out of his cabinet.[62] From polls we learned that more of Perot's supporters identify themselves as conservative than liberal, though the margin of difference between the two groups is no more than 5%.

Despite these presumed associations with the populist Right, it is difficult to see what exactly Perot did to justify them. In an unguarded moment, New Right activist Gary L. Bauer of the Family Research Council noted that while his colleagues did endorse Perot, "it's not issue-specific. At the moment, many conservatives who support Perot don't care what he stands for."[63] In point of fact, most of Perot's specific comments on social issues seemed designed to placate liberal journalists: for example, taking a prochoice position on abortion and condemning the exoneration of the police officers tried for beating Rodney King.[64] Perot also revived a major theme from the presidential campaign of Jimmy Carter in 1976, with the claim that he would make bureaucracy work more efficiently. Though some may choose to read into this a subterranean conservative message, there is no compelling reason to do so. An efficiently run administration could be rather threatening to the Right, particularly one that pursues a leftist agenda. The last successful presidential candidate who stressed administrative efficiency, Jimmy Carter, left behind a federal bureaucracy which conservatives found appalling. Gary Bauer may be right when he observes that it was not his positive appeal but the chance he provided disgruntled conservatives to play "finger-in-the-eye politics" with Bush which accounted for Perot's right-wing backing.

As this book goes to press in September 1992, a newsworthy development has occurred having relevance for our study: leading neoconservatives have begun to flood into the ranks of campaigners for Democratic presidential nominee Gov. William Clinton. In the 3 August 1992 issue of *New Republic*, Fred Barnes writes about this and emphasizes both the global democratic and pro-Zionist appeals of Clinton's foreign policy.[65] Barnes also points to the residual social democratic sentiments of Joshua Muravchik, Ben Wattenberg, and other Democratic-leaning members of the *Commentary* circle. On 17 August a statement of support for Clinton bearing the names of such familiar neoconservatives as Muravchik, Samuel Huntington, Aaron Wildavsky, Martin Peretz, Penn Kemble, Paul Nitze, and Edward Luttwak was placed prominently in the *New York Times*.[66] In a *Washington Post* syndicated column on 28 August, Stephen S. Rosenfeld noted with apparent jubilation the "return of the neocons," who were now "putting their political weight" behind Bill Clinton.[67] Though it is difficult to understand what Rosenfeld means by the neocons' returning (from where? certainly not from journalistic obscurity!), he is correct in ascribing to his subjects "an influence out of proportion to their numbers."

There is, in any case, nothing unusual or harmful to their individual or collective interests in the decision reached by numerous neoconservatives to move back to the Democrats. In the seventies future neoconservatives deliberately divided their forces between the two major parties; as Daniel Bell explained to me in a letter of 2 November 1983, Irving Kristol had advised his friends to maintain a presence in both camps during the 1972 presidential race. Even more important, it is highly unlikely that "movement conservatives" will abandon the neoconservatives because of the defection of some of them to Bill Clinton. Other neoconservatives, most significantly the Kristol family, have close ties to the Bush administration, and it is certainly conceivable that the Clinton neoconservatives, given their popularity with the mainstream liberal press, would be courted by George Bush if he survives the November election. Furthermore, by now it is silly to treat the New York–Washington conservative movement as a force independent of neoconservative control. Money, organization, and the need for favorable news coverage have all become links attaching conservative activists to the neoconservative empire. These imperial drones will not turn against neoconservatives who have abandoned the Republican Party. They will more likely focus on the defects of that party, which it will be argued have driven away principled foreign policy conservatives. Given the media access and lucrative connections that neoconservative luminaries bring and the general timidity of their movement conservative beneficiaries, certain reactions to the rallying of neoconservatives to Clinton do not seem at all probable. For example, one should not imagine that Republican dependents of the neoconservatives will treat Muravchik, Huntington, Wattenberg, or Luttwak in the same way that William Bennett went after Buchanan and the Old Right. It is also unlikely that the Republican employees of AEI will attack the Clinton neoconservatives, who are supremely well-connected to funding sources and the the New York–Washington press. Power does have its privileges, including in this case the right to move leftward without fear of attack by official conservatives. Or, as a medieval Polish proverb puts it even more succinctly, "What the lord of the manor may do routinely is forbidden to his peasants."

In the end, however, there is one virtue shared by all authentic men of the Right, the combination of short-term pessimism with long-term optimism. No social order can endure for much longer than a few centuries, and the rise and fall of civilizations cannot be halted by propaganda, no matter how generously funded by foundation grants. America will one day be "one with Nineveh and Tyre," and all the particularities that conservatives have striven to maintain will disappear. Only the more general principles for which they struggled, if they are (as conservatives believe) an enduring part of a natural order ordained in Heaven, will reappear, when circumstances favorable to civilization return, like desert flowers after rain.

Notes and References

Preface

1. "Symposium: How Has the United States Met Its Major Challenges Since 1945?" *Commentary* 80 (November 1985):37.

2. Ibid., 30.

3. See Robert Nisbet, *Conservatism* (Minneapolis: University of Minnesota Press, 1986), 25.

4. Aristotle, *Politica* I, 1260a, 20–24.

5. Although some of Aristotle's interpreters—for example, George Sabine and, more recently, Henry Jaffa—present him as a forerunner of modern democratic thinking, their work has usually included a highly selective reading of the *Politics,* particularly the middle books. Classical philologists and historians are less likely to pursue such a line of interpretation. See, for example, Sir David Ross, *Aristotle,* 4th ed. (London: Methuen, 1949). For a recent attempt to relate Aristotle's hierarchical view of the household and society to his understanding of nature, see Stephen R. L. Clark's essay in *Aristotle's Man* (Oxford: Oxford University Press, 1983), 99–113, and Wolfgang Kulman, "Equality in Aristotle's Political Thought," in *Equality and Inequality of Man in Ancient Thought,* ed. Iiro Kajanto (Helsinki, 1984), 372.

6. Alain de Benoist, *Vu de Droite* (Paris: Copernic, 1979), 18–26.

7. James Burnham, in *National Review,* 12 May 1972, 514.

8. See William F. Buckley, *American Conservative Thought in the Twentieth Century* (Indianapolis: Bobbs-Merrill, 1970), xv–xi; and the information about the J.B.S.'s precarious state in the *Baltimore Sun,* 15 September 1983.

9. Eric von Kuehnelt-Leddihn, in *Washington Times,* 18 November 1986, 3D.

10. James Burnham, in *National Review,* 12 May 1972, 516.

11. John Lukacs, *Outgrowing Democracy: A History of the United States in the Twentieth Century* (New York: Doubleday, 1984), 329.

12. Ibid., 330–41.

Chapter One

1. The best account of the isolationists is Wayne S. Cole's *Roosevelt and the Isolationists, 1932–45* (Lincoln, Nebraska: University of Nebraska Press, 1983). For the America First Committee, see Cole's *America First: The Battle against Intervention, 1940–41* (Madison: The University of Wisconsin Press, 1953); Justus Doenecke, *In Danger Undaunted: The Anti-Interventionist Movement of 1940–41 as Revealed in the Papers of the America First Committee* (Stanford: Hoover Institution Press, 1990); for Robert Taft, see Ronald Radosh, *Prophets on the Right: Conservative Critics of American Globalism* (New York: Simon & Schuster, 1975) and James T. Patterson, *Mr. Republican: A Biography of Robert A. Taft* (Boston: Houghton Mifflin, 1972); for John T. Flynn, see Radosh, pp. 197–273, and Michele Flynn Stenehjem, *An American First: John T. Flynn and the America First Committee* (New Rochelle, N.Y.: Arlington House, 1976.). For Harry Elmer Barnes, see Clyde R. Miller, "Harry Elmer Barnes' Experience in Journalism," in *Harry Elmer Barnes: Learned Crusader* ed. A. Goddard (Colorado Springs: Ralph Myles, 1968). For the early period of the postwar individualist right, see Murray N. Rothbard, "The Foreign Policy of the Old Right," *Journal of Libertarian Studies,* II, 1 (1978): 85–96. We have also made use of an unpublished Rothbard manuscript on the history of the Old Right. On John T. Flynn, see Radosh *Prophets on the Right,* 197–273; and Flynn's own analysis, *As We Go Marching* (New York: Doubleday-Doran, 1944). The standard history of the postwar Right remains George Nash, *The Conservative Intellectual Movement in America Since 1945* (New York: Basic Books, 1976).

2. Mortimer Smith, "Individualism Talks Back," *Christian Century* 62 (February 14, 1945): 202.

3. Reported in *New York Times,* 2 August 1945, 1, 9.

4. H. S. Hughes, "Capitalism and History," *Commentary* 17 (1 April 1954):407.

5. For assessments of Hayek's significance as a social thinker by his disciples and erstwhile colleagues, see *Essays on Hayek,* ed. Fritz Machlup (New York: New York University Press, 1976). On the same subject, it may also be useful to read Lawrence K. Frank, "The Rising Stock of Dr. Hayek," *Saturday Review* 28 (12 May 1945):4–6; and Paul Gottfried, "The Road to Serfdom Revisited," *American Journal of Jurisprudence* 17 (1972):38–45.

6. William A. Rusher, *The Rise of the Right* (New York: William Morrow & Co., 1984), 33.

7. Quoted in John P. Diggins, *Up from Communism* (New York: Harper & Row, 1975), 344.

8. Rusher, *The Rise of the Right,* 42–44.

9. Whittaker Chambers, *Witness* (New York: Random House, 1952), 9.

10. See *The Gallup Poll,* vol. 2 (New York: Random House), 1220.

11. For a critical, impressionistic study of the effects of the cold war on

American society and of the struggle itself, see John Lukacs, *A New History of the Cold War* (Garden City, N.Y.: Doubleday, 1966).

12. W. F. Buckley, Jr., and L. Brent Bozell, *McCarthy and His Enemies* (Chicago: Henry Regnery Co., 1954), 323.

13. James Burnham, in *National Review,* 1 June 1957, 518.

14. Frank Chodorov, *Out of Step: The Autobiography of an Individualist* (New York: Devin Adair, 1962). For Buckley's eulogy of Chodorov, see W. F. Buckley, Jr., *The Jeweler's Eye* (New York: Putnam, 1968), 343–49.

15. See Diggins, *Up From Communism,* 326–29, for a study of Burnham's break with the Democratic Left, anticommunist American Committee for Cultural Freedom.

16. See, for example, Willmoore Kendall, "The Bill of Rights and American Freedom," in *What Is Conservatism?,* ed. Frank S. Meyer (New York: Holt, Rinehart, & Winston, 1964), 41–64.

17. As illustrations of Kendall's attempt to demonstrate the nonhistorical utopian character of the open society, see the posthumous anthology of his essays, *Willmoore Kendall Contra Mundum,* ed. Nellie D. Kendall (New Rochelle, N.Y.: Arlington House, 1971).

18. See especially Buckley, *McCarthy and His Enemies,* 308–40.

19. See *Protracted Conflict,* ed. Stefan Possony and Robert Strausz-Hupe (New York: Harper Colophon, 1963), and Stefan Possony, *A Century of Conflict: Communist Techniques of World Revolution* (Chicago: Henry Regnery Co., 1953).

20. For a study of the European, particularly Hegelian, aspect of American conservative theory, see Paul Gottfried, *The Search for Historical Meaning: Hegel and the Postwar American Right* (DeKalb: Northern Illinois University Press, 1986).

21. Herbert J. Gans, *Popular Culture and High Culture* (New York: Basic Books, 1974), 54.

22. William F. Buckley, Jr., in *National Review,* 16 January 1962, 21.

23. Will Herberg, ibid., 10 April 1962, 250.

24. Editors, ibid., 24 August 1957, 149.

25. Jeffrey Hart, ibid., 18 June 1968, 604.

26. Frank Meyer, ibid., 4 October 1966, 998.

27. James Burnham, *Suicide of the West: An Essay on the Meaning and Destiny of Liberalism* (New Rochelle, N.Y.: Arlington House, 1964), 197–98.

28. See Richard Weaver, *Ideas Have Consequences* (Chicago: University of Chicago Press, 1948), particularly the introduction, and Bruce M. White, "Richard M. Weaver: Dialectic Rhetorician," *Modern Age* 26 (Summer–Fall 1982):256–59.

29. Rusher, *The Rise of the Right,* 28.

30. Two short appreciations of Kirk's work as a conservative theorist are Henry Regnery, "Russell Kirk and the Making of the Conservative Mind," *Mod-*

ern Age 21 (Fall 1977):338–53, and E. C. Kopff, "Russell Kirk: A Bohemian Tory," *Southern Partisan* 1 (Spring–Summer 1981): 11–13.

31. Russell Kirk, *The Conservative Mind* (Chicago: Henry Regnery Co., 1953), 8.

32. Rusher, *The Rise of the Right,* 28–29.

33. See Russell Kirk's foreword to Peter J. Stanlis, *Edmund Burke and the Natural Law* (Ann Arbor: University of Michigan Press, 1958).

34. Two essays dealing with this shift of emphasis in Kirk's thinking are Donald Atwell Zoll, "The Social Thought of Russell Kirk," *Political Science Reviewer* 2 (Fall 1972):112–29, and W. Wesley McDonald, "Reason, Natural Law, and Moral Imagination in the Thought of Russell Kirk," *Modern Age* 27 (Winter 1983):15–24.

35. Kirk and Nisbet are both quoted on their intellectual debt to Nock in Nash, *The Conservative Intellectual Movement in America Since 1945,* 15.

36. Burke's modern critics as well as defenders have tried to find connections between his support of a market economy and his social traditionalism. See, for example, Michael Freeman, *Edmund Burke and the Critique of Political Radicalism* (Chicago: University of Chicago Press, 1980).

37. Meyer, "Freedom, Tradition, Conservatism," in *What Is Conservatism?,* 14.

38. Meyer's views on modern judicial activism are stated in a book by a close colleague that he helped inspire. See L. Brent Bozell, *The Warren Revolution: Reflections on the Consensus Society* (New Rochelle, N.Y.: Arlington House, 1966).

39. M. Morton Auerbach, in *National Review,* 30 January 1962, 57.

40. Quoted in Russell Kirk, *T. S. Eliot and His Age,* 2nd ed. (LaSalle, Ill.: Sherwood Sugden & Co., 1984), 385.

41. Ibid.

42. Frank S. Meyer, "The Ballot in the Hand," *National Review,* 6 December 1958, 1986.

43. Frank S. Meyer, in *National Review,* 16 May 1967, 527.

44. Ibid., 21 August 1968, 859.

45. Weaver, *Ideas Have Consequences,* vi.

46. Donald Davidson, *Still Rebels, Still Yankees* (Baton Rouge: Louisiana State University Press, 1957), 4–5.

Chapter Two

1. *U.S. News & World Report,* 20 July 1964, 41.

2. Ibid., 83.

3. S. M. Lipset and P. G. Altbach, "Student Politics and Higher Education in the United States," in *Student Politics,* ed., S. M. Lipset (New York: Basic Books, 1967), 219–20, and Richard G. Braungart, "SDS and YAF: Backgrounds

of Student Political Activists" (mimeograph, Pennsylvania State University, Department of Sociology, 1966), 9–11.

4. W. F. Buckley, Jr., *God and Man at Yale* (Chicago: Henry Regnery Co., 1951), and Nash, *The Conservative Intellectual Movement in America Since 1945*, 376.

5. Taken from an interview with Larry Uzzell in Washington, D.C., October 1984.

6. Richard W. Flacks, "The Liberated Generation: An Exploration of the Roots of Student Protest," *Journal of Social Issues,* July 1967, 52–75; and Lawrence F. Schiff, "The Obedient Rebels: A Study of College Conversions to Conservatism," *Journal of Social Issues* 20 (October 1964):91, and "Conservatives on the Campus," *Newsweek,* 10 April 1961, 35.

7. See Samuel Lubell, "The People Speak" (news releases on student activism at Berkeley, 1966), 1–2, and S. Robert Lienters and Stanley Rothman's *Roots of Radicalism: Jews, Christians, and the New Left* (New York: Oxford University Press, 1982).

8. Braungart, "SDS and YAF," 38; see also Richard G. Braungart and David L. Westby, "Class and Politics in the Family Background of Student Political Activists," *American Sociological Review* 31 (1966):690–92.

9. M. Stanton Evans, *Revolt on the Campus* (Chicago: Henry Regnery Co., 1961), 68–70.

10. Lipset and Altbach, "Student Politics," 207.

11. *The Gallup Poll,* vol. 3 (1959–71), 129–93, 1479–80, 1912–13.

12. Ibid., vol. 2 (1949–58), 1201–2, 1220–21.

13. Ibid., vol. 3: 1784.

14. For the Declaration of Principles, see the appendix to J. Daniel Mahoney's *Actions Speak Louder: The History of the New York Conservative Party* (New Rochelle, N.Y.: Arlington House, 1968), 376–81.

15. *The Gallup Poll,* 3: 1772, 1785; and Andrew Greeley and Peter Rossi, *The Education of Catholic Americans* (Chicago, 1966).

16. For a provocative interpretation of these data, see Kevin P. Phillips, *The Emerging Republican Majority* (New Rochelle, N.Y.: Arlington House, 1969), 168.

17. William A. Rusher, "Crossroads for the GOP," *National Review,* 12 February 1963, 109–12. A short incisive critique of Rusher's underlying assumptions is available in Nelson Polsby and Aaron Wildavsky, *Presidential Elections,* 4th ed. (New York: Scribners, 1984), 161.

18. See Phillips, *The Emerging Republican Majority,* especially 458–60.

19. F. Clifton White, *Suite 3505: The Story of the Draft Goldwater Movement* (New Rochelle, N.Y.: Arlington House, 1967), especially the epilogue; and Rusher, *The Rise of the Right,* 159.

20. White, *Suite 3505,* 409.

21. Ibid., 413.

22. Craig Schiller, *The (Guilty) Conscience of a Conservative* (New Ro-

chelle, N.Y.: Arlington House, 1978), 122–125. For a more conventional—that is, left-of-center—critique of the Goldwater campaign, see Richard Rovere, "The Conservative Mindlessness," *Commentary* 39 (March 1965):38.

23. Phillips, *The Emerging Republican Majority,* 166.

24. *The Gallup Poll,* 3:1917–18.

25. See Rusher, *The Rise of the Right,* 291–321, and M. Stanton Evans, *The Future of Conservatism: From Taft to Reagan and Beyond* (New York: Holt, Rinehart, & Winston, 1968). Although Evans's attempt to plot the upward course of postwar conservatism ends in 1968, he presents Reagan as presidential timber—and as the authentic heir of the political philosophy of Robert Taft and Barry Goldwater. Evans's work can be interpreted as a plea addressed to conservatives and Republicans to rally around Reagan as a presidential candidate—in preference to Goldwater's candidate, Richard Nixon.

26. Barry Goldwater, *The Conscience of a Conservative* (Shepherdsville, Ky.: Victor Publishing Co., 1960), 10–11.

27. William Rusher, in *The Rise of the Right,* 155, describes "Goldwater shying away from the very insight [conservatism] that made his candidacy different from any other. At heart Goldwater was, and remains, a perfectly orthodox, budget-balancing, main-line Republican, whose heart beats in near accord with Jerry Ford's." In view of Rusher's formative role in promoting Goldwater as a "conservative" presidential candidate, this judgment is truly damning.

28. See James Burnham, "Must Conservatives Be Republicans," *National Review,* 1 December 1964, 652.

29. For the 1964 Republican Presidential Platform, see *U.S. News & World Report,* 20 July 1964, 35.

30. This platform is given in Meyer's essay in *Left, Right, and Center,* ed. R. A. Goldwin (Chicago: Rand-McNally, 1965), 9–10.

31. Carl Oglesby and Richard Shaull, *Containment and Change* (New York: Macmillan, 1967), 166ff.

32. *It Usually Begins with Ayn Rand* (New York: Stein and Day), 101ff.

33. For the Randian movement, see Murray N. Rothbard, *The Sociology of the Ayn Rand Cult* (Burlingame, Calif.: Center for Libertarian Studies, 1990); Jerome Tuccille, op cit., as well as the self-serving accounts of Barbara Branden in *The Passion of Ayn Rand* (Garden City, N.Y.: Doubleday, 1986) and of Nathaniel Branden in *Judgment Day: My Years with Ayn Rand* (Boston: Houghton Mifflin, 1989). I have also drawn on interviews held with various former Randians.

34. The evidence is presented in a 1992 *Chronicles* article by Justin Raimondo.

35. Nathaniel Branden, e.g., repeats Rand's claim that Isabel Paterson relied on Rand for the chapter "The Humanitarian with the Guillotine" in *The God of the Machine, Judgment Day,* 123.

36. Nathaniel Branden, *Judgment Day,* 132, however, claims credit for converting Greenspan to free-market economics.

37. See Barry Goldwater's plea to conservatives to support Nixon over Wallace in the *National Review,* 22 October 1968, 1060–62.

38. Patrick Buchanan, *Conservative Votes, Liberal Victories* (New York: Quadrangle, 1975).

39. Rusher, *The Rise of the Right,* 263–90.

40. Meyer comments on the NYCP in the *National Review,* 3 July 1962, 486.

41. See the concluding chapter of Mahoney, *Actions Speak Louder.*

42. A point that Phillips disregards, but that Liberal Catholic Andrew Greeley stresses, is that Catholics usually gave nonconservative responses to social and economic questions in answering polls in the 1960s. (Abortion, birth control, and aid to parochial schools were consistent exceptions.) In October 1968 only 12 percent of Catholics expressed support for George Wallace. The same Gallup Poll had Wallace's Protestant support at 25 percent. See *The Gallup Poll,* 2:2166. Although many Catholics may have voted for Wallace without admitting it, it was obviously not something they were proud of. It expressed resentment far more than moral conviction. Nor was this hidden Catholic support for Wallace related to a publicly professed worldview, as it was among many Southern traditionalists.

43. See, for example, Jack Kemp, "Democratic Equality: A Conservative Idea?," *Intercollegiate Review* 20 (Spring–Summer 1985):51–56.

Chapter Three

1. Seymour Martin Lipset and David Riesman, *Education and Politics at Harvard* (New York: McGraw-Hill, 1975), 203.

2. Evans, *Revolt on Campus.*

3. Allan C. Carlson, "Luce, Life, and 'The American Way,'" *This World,* Winter 1986, 56–74.

4. Everett Carll Ladd, Jr., and Seymour Martin Lipset, *Academics, Politics, and the 1972 Election* (Washington, D.C.: AEI Domestic Affairs Studies, 1973), 2, 5ff.

5. Michael Lerner, "Respectable Bigotry," *American Scholar,* Autumn 1965, 606–17.

6. Lipset and Riesman, *Education,* 230.

7. *Freedom and Order in the University,* ed. Samuel Gorovitz (Cleveland: Press of Western Reserve University, 1967), 89ff.

8. George F. Kennan, *Democracy and the Student Left* (Boston: Little Brown, 1968).

9. Russell Kirk, *Decadence and Renewal in the Higher Learning* (South Bend, Ind.: Gateway, 1978), 23–24.

10. Jacques Barzun, *The House of Intellect* (1959; reprint, New York: Harper Torchback, 1961), 100.

11. Quoted in Albert Jay Nock, *The Theory of Education in the United States* (1932; reprint, New York: Arno Press, 1969).

12. Kirk, *Decadence,* 113.

13. *Against Mediocrity: The Humanities in America's High Schools,* ed. Chester E. Finn, Jr., Diane Ravitch, and Robert T. Fancher (New York: Holmes & Meier, 1984), 241ff.

14. Adam B. Ulam, "Where Do We Go From Here?" *Daedalus,* Fall 1974, 80–84.

15. Clark Kerr, *The Uses of the University* (Cambridge, Mass.: Harvard University Press, 1963).

16. Edward Gross and Paul V. Grambsh, *University Goals and Academic Power* (Washington, D.C.: American Council on Education, 1968).

17. Derek Bok, "On the Purpose of Undergraduate Education," *Daedalus,* Fall 1974, 159–72.

18. Jerry Farber, *The Student as Nigger* (New York: Contact Books, 1969).

19. Carl R. Rogers, "The Person of Tomorrow," 1969 commencement address at Sonoma State College.

20. Gerald F. Else, "Some Ill-Tempered Reflections on the Present State of Higher Education in the United States," *Daedalus,* Fall 1974, 138–42.

21. John A. Howard and Bruce Franklin, *Who Should Run the Universities?* (Washington, D.C.: American Enterprise Institute), 4ff.

22. Wayne C. Booth, *Now Don't Try to Reason with Me: Essays and Ironies for a Credulous Age* (Chicago: University of Chicago Press, 1970), 173.

23. Robert H. Bork, Howard C. Krane, and George D. Krane, *Political Activities of Colleges and Universities: Some Policy and Legal Implications* (Washington, D.C.: American Enterprise Institute, 1970).

24. Robert Wood, "Academe Sings the Blues," *Daedalus,* Winter 1975, 45–55.

25. For a survey, see Howard Gardner, *The Mind's New Science: A History of the Cognitive Revolution* (New York: Basic Books, 1985); see also Owen J. Flanagan, Jr., *The Science of the Mind* (Cambridge, Mass.: MIT Press, 1984).

26. Noam Chomsky, in *Language* 35 (1959):26–58.

27. See the discussion in Flanagan, *The Science of Mind,* 138ff, and Jerry Fodor, *The Language of Thought* (Cambridge, Mass.: Harvard University Press, 1979).

28. Brent Berlin and Paul Kay, *Basic Color Terms: Their Universality and Evolution* (Berkeley: University of California Press, 1969).

29. See Daniel G. Friedman, *Human Infancy: An Evolutionary Perspective* (Hillsdale, N.J.: Halsted Press, 1974), and Peter C. Reynolds, *On the Evolution of Human Behavior: The Argument from Animals to Man* (Berkeley, Calif.: University of California Press, 1981).

30. See especially Charles J. Lumsden and Edward O. Wilson, *Promethean Fire: Reflections on the Origin of Mind* (Cambridge, Mass.: Harvard University Press, 1983).

31. Edward O. Wilson, *Sociobiology: The New Synthesis* (Cambridge, Mass.: Harvard University Press, 1975), and *On Human Nature* (Cambridge, Mass.: Harvard University Press, 1978).

32. See, for example, E. E. Maccoby and C. N. Jacklin, *The Psychology of Sex Differences* (Stanford, Calif.: Stanford University Press, 1974); Camilla P. Benbow and Julian C. Stanley, "Sex Differences in Mathematical Ability: Factor or Artifact?," *Science* 210 (1980):1261–64; and Melvin Konner, *The Tangled Wing: Biological Constraints on the Human Spirit* (New York: Holt, Rinehart, & Winston, 1982).

33. See the classic work of G. P. Murdock, *Social Structure* (New York: Macmillan, 1949); William N. Stephens, *The Family in Cross-Cultural Perspective* (New York: Holt, Rinehart, & Winston, 1963); and B. B. Whiting, *Six Cultures: Studies and Child Rearing* (New York: Wiley, 1963).

34. Sherry B. Ortner, "Is Female to Male as Nature Is to Culture?," in *Women, Culture, and Society,* ed. M. Z. Rosaldo and L. Lamphere (Stanford, Calif.: Stanford University Press, 1974), 67–68.

35. See especially Carol Gilligan, *In a Different Voice: Psychological Theory of Women's Development* (Cambridge, Mass.: Harvard University Press, 1982).

36. Leah Fritz, *Dreamers and Dealers: An Intimate Appraisal of the Women's Movement* (Boston: Beacon Press, 1979).

37. Lenore Weitzman, *The Divorce Revolution: The Unexpected Social and Economic Consequences for Women and Children in America* (New York: Free Press, 1986).

38. Martin Daly and Margo Wilson, "Child Abuse and Other Risks of Not Living with Both Parents," *Journal of Ethology Sociobiology* 6 (1985):197–210.

39. Steven Goldberg, *The Inevitablity of Patriarchy* (New York: William Morrow, 1973), 233–34.

40. George Gilder, *Sexual Suicide* (New York: Quadrangle/New York Times Book Co., 1973).

41. R. C. Lewontin, Steven Rose, and Leon J. Kamin, *Not in Our Genes: Biology, Ideology, and Human Nature* (New York: Pantheon Books, 1984), 273 n.

42. Thomas Molnar, "Ethology and Environmentalism: Man as Animal and Mechanism," *Intercollegiate Review,* Fall 1977, 25–43.

43. Paul Johnson, *Modern Times: The World from the Twenties to the Eighties* (New York: Harper & Row, 1983), 734.

44. George Homans, *Coming to My Senses* (New Brunswick, N.J.: Transaction Books, 1984).

45. See especially Talcott Parsons and Edward E. Bales, *Family Socialization and Interaction Process* (New York: Free Press, 1955).

46. Steven Stack, "The Effect of Religious Commitment on Suicide: A Cross-National Analysis," *Journal of Health and Social Behavior* 24 (1983):362–74.

47. Edward C. Banfield, *The Unheavenly City: The Nature and the Foundation of Our Urban Crisis* (Boston: Little Brown, 1968), 16–17.

48. Milton Friedman, *Capitalism and Freedom* (Chicago: University of Chicago Press, 1967).

49. Milton Friedman, *A Monetary History of the United States 1867–1960* (Princeton: Princeton University Press, 1963).

50. See Stigler's papers collected in *The Intellectual and the Marketplace* (Cambridge, Mass.: Harvard University Press, 1964); and *The Economist as Preacher and Other Essays* (Chicago: University of Chicago Press, 1984).

51. *Chronicles,* September 1985, 32–33.

52. See my portrait of Jacob Neusner in *Chronicles* (May 1990):31–34.

53. William F. Buckley, Jr., *God and Men at Yale* (South Bend: Gateway Edications, 1986), especially 157–62. Though Buckley in an asterisked gloss (page 159) on the original text published in 1951 denies that he wishes to impose democratic "Truth" as was done in postwar Germany and Japan by the victorious Americans, it is not at all clear in what way he opposes this imposition. The Truth that he intends to have universities teach seems to lie at the vector point at which democracy, private enterprise, and Christianity all happily meet.

54. See *Willmoore Kendall Contra Mundum* (New Rochelle: Arlington House, 1971), 619–21. Kendall's criticisms, although made gently, are all the more remarkable in view of his close association with the evolution of the book. See Buckley's introduction to the 1986 edition, vi–vii; and John Judis, *William F. Buckley, Jr.: Patron Saint of the Conservatives* (New York: Simon and Schuster, 1988), 87.

55. See Joel Schwartz, "Rousseau Revisited," *National Review,* 25 February 1991, 47 and 48, and the responses by Claes G. Ryn (letters section) *National Review,* 15 April 1991, and Scott P. Richert, "Rousseau: Conservative or Totalitarian Democrat," *Humanitas,* 5.3 (Summer 1991):1–7. An even more devastating attack was launched on *National Review* for its choice of the socialist Conor Cruise O'Brien as a commentator on Edmund Burke by the eighteenth-century studies scholar Peter J. Stanlis. Stanlis placed his remarks in *Chronicles* (May 1991):51–54, after *National Review* had declined to publish them in the letters section.

56. See *Political Theory* 18.1 (February 1990):159.

57. *American Political Science Review* 83 (September 1989):100S.

58. The author holds a photocopy of William Bennett's dissertation on ethics written under the directorship of John Silber at the University of Texas. A repetitious and ungrammatical text, it illustrates most of the conceptual and aesthetic flaws that Bennett attributes to his academic critics. Fortunately for editors, Bennett has never tried to publish it.

Edwin Feulner received a doctorate from Edinburgh (cf. *Who's Who in America,* 14th ed. [1990–91], 1024) for a self-congratulatory work on the current American conservatism, which his staff later turned into *Conservatives Stalk the House* (Ottawa, Ill.: Green Hill, 1983).

Since 1987 Michael Joyce has been describing himself in *Who's Who in America* as the 1974 recipient of a doctorate from Walden University. A school which advertises in the *New York Times,* Walden claims to provide degrees for "business executives in a hurry." In view of the already long-confirmed absence of a dissertation for Joyce in the Library of Congress, it seems that Walden did accommodate his tight schedule. See the entry for Joyce in *Who's Who in America* (1990–91), 1698.

59. Revealed to the author in conversation with M. E. Bradford, 10 September 1991.

60. The NAS publishes a statement of purpose "for reasoned scholarship in a free society" inside the back cover of each issue of *Academic Questions* (brought out by Transaction Periodicals Consortium).

61. See *Washington Times,* 7 June 1991, F1.

62. Dinesh D'Souza, *Illiberal Education* (New York: Free Press, 1991). For a particularly telling criticism of D'Souza as an educational egalitarian by an avowed Marxist reviewer, see Eugene Genovese's comments on "Illiberal Education," *New Republic,* 15 April 1991, 30–35. For less probing reviews, see *Time,* 6 May 1991, 71; and *New York Times Book Review,* 31 March, 1991, 12.

63. In the case of the first of the recent neoconservative *livres de succès,* the Straussian Werner J. Dannhauser, in *American Spectator* (October 1988):17–20, notes the initial "chorus of acclaim" that greeted Bloom's work in conventionally liberal publications, e.g., *New York Times, New York Times Book Review,* and the *Washington Post Book World.* Not surprisingly neoconservatives Roger Kimball and S. Frederick Starr were commissioned as reviewers by the last two. The *New York Times* ran several laudatory pieces on Bloom's accomplishment, including Richard Bernstein's "A 'Minute of Hatred' in Chapel Hill," *New York Times,* 25 September 1988, 26, and Christopher Lehmann-Haupt's "Book Review: *The Closing of the American Mind,"* ibid., 23 March 1987, 13. See also my review "A Half-Open Mind," *Chronicles,* 11.9 (September 1987):30–33.

64. See Paul Gottfried, "On Teaching Democratic Values," *Essays on Political Economy,* 12 (October 1991), for remarks concerning "A 50-Hour Core Curriculum for College Students," "The Humanities in America," and other publications written by Cheney and her staff. The argument in my essay is that the defense of Western Civilization courses offered by Cheney is strongly tailored for the multiculturalist opposition—and could not be as offensive to that audience as it would be to cultural traditionalists.

Chapter Four

1. The two autobiographical works that treat these Bildungsjahre are Norman Podhoretz's *Making It* (New York: Harper Row, 1967), and *Breaking Ranks* (New York: Harper Row, 1979).

2. See "Counter Culture and Its Apologists," *Commentary* 50 (December 1970): 40–59.

3. See, for example, E. Raab, "Black Revolution and the Jewish Question," *Commentary* 47 (April 1969):6, and N. Glazer, "Blacks, Jews, and the Intellectuals," *Commentary* 47 (April 1969):33–39.

4. See Isidore Silver, "What Flows from Neoconservatism," *Nation,* 9 July 1977, 49, and Alexander Bloom, *Prodigal Sons* (New York: Oxford University Press, 1986).

5. For a perceptive but partisan interpretation of these data, see Arthur Hertzberg, "Reagan and the Jews," *New York Review of Books,* 31 January 1985, 11–14.

6. A discussion of American Jewish political and moral attitudes can be found in a symposium, "Jews and American Politics," in *This World* 10 (Winter 1985):4–38.

7. See John B. Judis, "The Conservative Wars," *New Republic,* 11 August 1986, 15–18; and George Archibald's report on the same topic on the front page of the *Washington Times,* 9, 16 June 1986.

8. For a clarification of Bradford's beliefs, see his *Remembering Who We Are: Observations of a Southern Conservative* (Athens: University of Georgia Press, 1985); and Paul Gottfried's investigation of that book and its critics, "Looking Back," *The World and I* 8 (August 1986):460–64.

9. See Sidney Blumenthal, *The Rise of the Counterestablishment: From Conservative Ideology to Political Power* (New York: Times Books, 1986), especially 122–66.

10. Christopher Hitchens, "A Modern Medieval Family," *Mother Jones,* July 1986, 52–56; August 1986, 74–76.

11. See Jeane Kirkpatrick, "Dictatorships and Double Standards," *Commentary* 68 (November 1979):34–45; and Alexander Bloom, *Prodigal Sons,* 370–71.

12. This Bicentennial issue of *Public Interest* was subsequently published as *The American Commonwealth,* ed. Nathaniel Glazer and Irving Kristol (New York, 1976).

13. For Glazer's critical comments about the evolution of the civil rights movement, see Nathan Glazer, "Blacks, Jews, and the Intellectuals," *Commentary* 47 (April 1969):35; and "The Limits of Social Policy," *Commentary* 52 (September 1971):51–58; "Is Busing Necessary?," *Commentary* 52 (March 1972):39–52. See also Banfield, *The Unheavenly City.*

14. See Edward Shapiro, "Conservatism and Its Discontents," *The World and I* 9 (September 1986):565–72.

15. See Irving Kristol, *Reflections of a Neoconservative: Looking Back, Looking Ahead* (New York: Basic Books, 1983), xii; and "The David I Knew," *Wall Street Journal,* 9 May 1986, 26.

16. See George Will, *Statecraft as Soulcraft: What Government Does* (New York: Simon & Schuster, 1983), 93–94.

17. See Allan Carlson's *Persuasion at Work,* 9 (August–September 1986); and Peter L. Berger's remarks in *Commentary* 80 (November 1985):30–31.

18. See Brigitte Berger and Peter L. Berger, *The War over the Family: Capturing the Middle Ground* (New York, 1983), for a telling critique of modern welfare state "family policy."

19. See George F. Gilder, "Still Different," *National Review,* 30 November 1984, 48–50.

20. See for example, Michael Ledeen, "How to Support the Democratic Revolution," *Commentary* 76 (March 1985):43–46; and Carnes Lord, "In Defense of Public Diplomacy," *Commentary* 77 (April 1984):42–50.

21. Podhoretz, *Breaking Ranks,* 356–58.

22. Diane Ravitch, "The Precarious State of History," *American Educator,* Spring 1985, 10–17.

23. See Suzanne Garment's column in the *Wall Street Journal,* 11 October 1985, 26.

24. In *The Rise of the Counterestablishment,* 151–54, Sidney Blumenthal takes seriously the assertions made in *Reflections of a Neoconservative* and elsewhere about Kristol's Straussian attachments. Blumenthal goes so far as to interpret Kristol's political theory on the basis of them.

25. For a representative tribute to Lionel Trilling by a moderately conservative Jewish follower, see Steven Marcus, "Lionel Trilling 1905–1975," *New York Times Book Review,* 8 February 1976, 32–34. See also Podhoretz, *Breaking Ranks,* 296–300; and Mark Krupnick, *Lionel Trilling and Cultural Criticism in America* (Evanston: Northwestern University Press, 1986).

26. Bloom, *Prodigal Sons,* 37–39.

27. The view that the individual is morally and emotionally dependent upon community identity and firmly established tradition is an *idée maîtresse* in the writings of Robert Nisbet. His most recent book, *Conservatism* (Minneapolis: University of Minnesota, 1986), is a summing-up of his entire conservative social theory.

28. See *Intercollegiate Review* 21 (Spring 1986):66.

29. Two interesting accounts of the heated exchanges that occurred at the Philadelphia Society, one sympathetic to the neoconservatives and the other written from a moderate leftist perspective, are Jeffrey Hart, "Conservative Warfare in Chicago," *National Review,* 6 June 1986, 32–34, and John B. Judis, "The Conservative Mental Breakdown," *New Republic,* 1 August 1986, 15–18. On the same subject, see also Paul Gottfried, "Editorial Notes," *Continuity* 10 (Spring 1985):i–iii.

30. See Gillian Peele, *Revival and Reaction: The Right in Contemporary America* (Oxford: Clarendon Press, 1984), 1–51, and Gregory Wolfe, *Right Mind: A Source Book of American Conservative Thought* (Chicago: Regnery/Gateway, 1986), for a survey of conservative and neoconservative think tanks and celebrities. For a demonological but comprehensive view of the same sub-

ject, see John S. Saloma III, *Ominous Politics: The New Conservative Labyrinth* (New York: Hill & Wang, 1983), 7–37.

31. Representative of the neoconservative view of McCarthy and Mc-Carthyism is Joseph Bishop, "The End of Senator Joe McCarthy," in the neoconservative *American Spectator* 16 (December 1983):16–20. The same issue features a drawing of Senator McCarthy sitting in a garbage can covered with litter.

32. See the information on AEI in *Insight,* 7 April 1986, 26–27 and 21 July 1986, 21; and "A Thinktank at the Brink," *Newsweek,* 7 July 1986, 67.

33. In conversation with one of the authors on 28 July 1986.

34. *Intercollegiate Review,* 21 (Spring 1986):24.

35. For representative neoconservative polemics against those perceived as unfriendly to Israel or Jews, see Daniel Pipes, "PLO, Inc.," *American Spectator* (February 1991):27–28; by the same author, see "The Muslims Are Coming! The Muslims Are Coming!" *National Review,* 19 November 1990, 28–31; and David Frum, "The Conservative Bully Boy," *American Spectator* (July 1991):12–14.

Chapter Five

1. Peele, *Revival,* 52.

2. James C. Roberts, *The Conservative Decade: Emerging Leaders of the 1980's* (Westport, Conn.: Arlington House, 1980), 7.

3. Richard A. Viguerie, *The New Right: We're Ready to Lead* (Falls Church, Va.: Viguerie Co., 1980), 54–55.

4. Alan Crawford, *Thunder on the Right: The "New Right" and the Politics of Resentment* (New York: Pantheon, 1980).

5. John S. Saloma III, *Ominous Politics: The New Conservative Labyrinth* (New York: Hill & Wang, 1984), 46ff.

6. Peele, *Revival,* 67–68.

7. Dinesh D'Souza, *Falwell Before the Millenium: A Critical Biography* (Chicago: Regnery/Gateway, 1984), 97.

8. Ibid., 151.

9. Stuart Rothenberg and Frank Newport, *The Evangelical Voter: Religion and Politics in America* (Washington, D.C.: Free Congress Research & Education Foundation, 1984), 133.

10. Kenneth Wald, *Religion and Politics in the United States* (New York: St. Martin's Press, 1987), 205.

11. Linda Metcalf and Kenneth Dolbeare, *Neopolitics: American Political Ideas in the 1980's* (Philadelphia: Temple University Press, 1985), 165.

12. For varied observations on the declining Religious Right, see *Economist,* 6 June 1987, 26; Sean Wilentz, "The Trial of Televangelism," *Dissent* 37

(Winter, 1990):42–48; and André J. M. Prévos, "Television as Religion," *Journal of Popular Culture,* 25 (Winter 1990):113–30.

13. *Whose Values?: The Battle for Morality in Pluralistic America,* ed. Carl Horn (Ann Arbor, Mich.: Servant Books, 1985), 183.

14. George Gilder, "Sexual Politics," *Chronicles,* June 1986, 10.

15. See *Phyllis Schlafly Report* 13, no. 1 (1979).

16. Joseph Sobran, *Single Issues* (New York: Human Life Press, 1983), 16.

17. See Joseph Scheidler, *Closed: 99 Ways to Stop Abortion* (Westchester, Ill.: Crossway Books, 1985).

18. See, for example, *Persuasion at Work,* January, August, September, November 1985.

19. Mary Pride, *The Child Abuse Industry: Outrageous Facts and Everyday Rebellions Against a System That Threatens Every North American Family* (Westchester, Ill.: Crossway Books, 1986).

20. John Whitehead, *Parents' Rights* (Westchester, Ill.: Crossway Books, 1985).

21. Phyllis Schlafly, ed., *Child Abuse in the Classroom* (Alton, Ill.: Pere Marquette Press, 1984).

22. Paul Vitz, *Censorship: Evidence of Lies in Our Children's Textbooks* (Ann Arbor, Mich.: Servant Books, 1986), 60.

23. Ibid., 75.

24. Viguerie, *New Right,* 77–78.

25. See *Grass Roots: The Leadership Quarterly of the Conservative Caucus,* December 1985–January 1986.

26. *The New Right Papers,* ed. Robert W. Whitaker (New York: St. Martin's Press, 1982).

27. Ibid., 106–27.

28. Ibid., 180–200.

29. Ibid., 123–24.

30. Ibid., 200.

31. Ibid., 64–83.

32. Ibid., 80.

33. "Louder Thunder on the Right," *Fortune* 23 (January 1984):36–37.

34. Richard Viguerie, in *National Review,* 19 October 1984.

35. See David Brooks, "Please, Mr. Postman: The Travails of Richard Viguerie," *National Review,* 20 June 1986, 28–32.

36. William S. Lind, "What Is Cultural Conservatism," *Essays on Our Times,* March 1986.

37. Chester Finn, "Giving Shape to Cultural Conservatism," *American Spectator,* November 1986, 14–16.

38. For balanced examinations of the abortion controversy, particularly since the Supreme Court's ruling in *Webster* v. *Reproduction Health Services* in 1989, see in *Christianity Today,* "One by One, States Continue Tackling the

Abortion Issue," 19 March 1990, 56; and "Abortion's New Battlefield," 22 October 1990, 44–46; and M. Good, "A Moral Choice," *Atlantic Monthly,* April 1990, 78.

39. On the NEH and its controversial expenditures, see *Newsweek,* 9 April 1990, 72–74; B. W. Bloch, "Wasteful Images," *New Leader,* 22 January 1990, 22–23; and William F. Buckley, "Understanding Mapplethorpe," *National Review,* 11 June 1990, 63.

Chapter Six

1. Michael W. Miles, *the Odyssey of the American Right* (New York and Oxford: Oxford University Press, 1980), 32.

2. *Ibid.,* 30–31.

3. George H. Nash, *The Conservative Intellectual Movement Since 1945* (New York: Basic Books, 1976), 22–35; and Murray N. Rothbard *Ludwig von Mises: Scholar, Creator, Hero* (Auburn: Ludwig von Mises Institute, 1988), 61–62.

4. Lawrence Soley, "Right Think," *The Boston Phoenix,* 14 December 1990, 20.

5. On H. Smith Richardson and his family's political connections, see Wayne S. Cole, *Roosevelt and the Isolationists* (Lincoln: University of Nebraska Press, 1983), 30–33; and James Allen Smith, *The Idea Brokers: Think Tanks and the Rise of the New Policy Elite* (New York: The Free Press, 1991), 17.

6. Jerome L. Himmelstein, *To the Right: The Transformation of American Conservatism* (Berkeley and Los Angeles: University of California Press, 1990), 147–49. See Thomas Fleming's review of Himmelstein in *Political Science Quarterly* (Summer 1991):370–71.

7. For movement-conservative denunciations of the Old Right for its stand against American involvement in the Persian Gulf War, see "Come Home America?" in *National Review,* 20 August 1990, 12–14; see also J. Cramer, "Look What's Anti-War Now," *Time,* 10 September 1990, 27–28.

8. See James Weinstein, *The Corporate Ideal in the Liberal State 1900–1918* (Boston: Beacon, 1968); and Weinstein's article coauthored with Martin J. Sklar, "Socialism and the New Left," 200-02 in *For a New America: Essays in History and Politics,* ed. James Weinstein and David W. Eakins (New York: Random House, 1970), 317–26. Though both trace the turning from entrepreneurial to corporate capitalism and the accompanying cultural changes in twentieth-century America, Weinstein pushes the event back into an earlier period than Miles in his book cited above.

9. *Time,* 3 December 1990, 114.

10. All funding allocation figures have been taken from the 990 forms filed with the IRS by the foundations under discussion. The author obtained copies of these forms from either the Foundation Center in Washington, D.C., or the Phil-

adelphia Service Center of the IRS. See Sarah Scaife Foundation, 990-PF, 1989, 10–11; John M. Olin Foundation, 990-PF, 1986–89, 10–11; and Harry and Lynde Bradley Foundation, 990-PF, 1986, 1987, 1988–89, 10–11.

11. Bradley 1988–89, 10; *1988 Annual Report of the John M. Olin Foundation, Inc.,* 6; Bradley 990-PF, 1986, 10–11.

12. Illustrative of Paul Weyrich's activist approach to culture is his essay "Conservatives Can Turn the Tide," *Conservative Digest* 15 (May/June 1987):77–80; see also J. M. Wall, "Right-Wing Activists Take Aim at Bush," in *The Christian Century,* 106, 15 February 1989, 163–64.

13. See Bradley 990-PF, 1986, 1987, 1988–89, 10; *1988 Smith-Richardson Foundation Annual Report,* 16; and Scaife 990-PF, 1989, 10; and *Chronicle of Higher Education,* 12 September 1987, A72–A75.

14. Bradley, 990-PF, 1988–89, 10. For a detailed account of Bennett's ties to Bradley and the center, see the *Milwaukee Sentinel,* 2 March 1989, 6.

15. See Roger M. Williams, "Capital Clout," *Foundation News,* 30.4 (July/August 1989):16–19; and the Heritage Foundation's *1989 Annual Report,* 6.

16. *1989 Annual Report,* 31.

17. See Michael Massing, "Trotsky's Orphans," *New Republic,* 22 January 1987, 18–20. In an almost naive overture to the Old Right, Ernest van den Haag, John M. Olin Professor of Jurisprudence at Fordham, proposed that the belief in world democracy could serve as a bridge between the neoconservatives and their Old Right critics. See van den Haag's "The War Between Paleos and Neos," *National Review,* 24 February 1989, 21–23; and the subsequent exchange between van den Haag and S. T. Francis, *National Review,* 7 April 1989, 43–45. For representative neoconservative statements on the democratic faith, see Carl Gershman, "Democracy as the Wave of the Future," *Current* 312, (May 1989):18–25; Ben Wattenberg, "Back to Our Prime Mission," syndicated in *Washington Times,* 9 March 1989; and Gregory Fossedal's *Exporting the Democratic Revolution* (New York: Basic Books, 1989), a work setting forth the neoconservative geopolitical and historical mission funded by the Olin Foundation and endorsed by Irving Kristol, Allan Bloom, and Jeane Kirkpatrick. For a biting riposte to this mission statement, see Claes G. Ryn, "The Democracy Boosters," *National Review,* March 24, 1989, 31–32.

18. For a useful critique from the Left of neoconservative cultural determinism, see Jürgen Habermas, *The New Conservatism: Cultural Criticism and the Historians,* trans. Shierry W. Nicholson, (Cambridge: MIT Press, 1990).

19. *1988 Annual Report of the John M. Olin Foundation,* 16; Bradley 990-PF, 1988–89, 10; and Scaife 990-PF, 1989, 10.

20. Learned in discussion with former members of the center's staff, including Dr. Lefever.

21. R. J. Neuhaus, "Democratic Conservatism," *First Things* 1 (March 1990):65–67.

22. Syndicated column in *Washington Times,* 24 December 1987, D1; see the belated response by Patrick Buchanan, *ibid.,* 9 January 1991, G1 and G4.

23. See the report on the Philanthropic Roundtable in *Chronicle of Higher Education*, 12 September 1987, A75. Two useful biographies of Joyce are "The $390,000,000 Man" by Lois Blankhorn, *Wisconsin*, 3 May 1987, 10–17, and "The Right Stuff" by Bruce Murphy, *Milwaukee* (December 1988):52–65.

24. On the National Endowment for Democracy, see Cort Kirkwood's remarks in *Chronicles* (March 1990):22–25. The same author is writing a monograph on the N.E.D.'s politics and funding sources.

25. *1988 Annual Report of the John M. Olin Foundation*, 6. For Kristol's candid admission of his own financial success in the 1980s, see the *Wall Street Journal*, 11 September 1991, AB.

26. *1988 Annual Report*, 13; Bradley 990-PF, 1986, 1987, 1988–89, 10–11.

27. *Chronicle of Higher Education*, 2 September 1987, A74.

28. *1988 Annual Report of the John M. Olin Foundation*, 14, 25; Jon Wiener "Dollars for Neocon Scholars," in *Nation*, 1 January 1989, 12–14. Newsworthy Olin grants in 1988 that Wiener does not investigate are those totaling $270,000 for the constitutional studies of neoconservative-Straussian Harvey C. Mansfield. Strictly speaking, Mansfield is neither a constitutional scholar nor an Americanist. See the *1988 Annual Report*, 13–14.

29. *Ibid.*, 8. This information was learned during interviews with the former chairman of the politics department at Catholic University of America, on 12 January 1991.

30. For Podhoretz's admission to being in on the attack, see Robert Moynihan, "U.S.A.: War Between Conservatives," *30 Days*, (September 1989): 71.

31. See the portraits of Rader by Ray Kenney in *Milwaukee Journal*, 29 September 1988, and in *Wall Street Journal*, 14 May 1985, 1.

32. Bradley 990-PF, viii. See also *Milwaukee Journal* editorial "The Jury Is Still Out," 26 February 1987.

33. *1986 Lynde and Harry Bradley Foundation Annual Report*, 1.

34. *1988 Smith-Richardson Annual Report*, list of governors, 1.

35. *1990 Heritage Foundation Report*.

36. Roe Foundation, 990-PF, 1989, 10–11.

37. *Chronicle of Higher Education*, 12 September 1987, A75.

38. Interview with James Taylor on December 29, 1990.

39. *Hudson Institute: Report and Prospectus* (Hudson Institute: Indianapolis, 1990), 4, 5, 16.

40. The author has obtained copies of correspondence between Joseph Baldacchino of the National Humanities Institute and the Olin Foundation about a research grant requested in 1988. After being led to believe that the foundation looked favorably on his proposal, providing that it could be properly structured, Baldacchino then learned that the revised project was "still slightly afield" of Olin's "highest priorities at the present time."

41. Learned in conversation with George Carey and other I.S.I. board members.

42. See the revealing comments on the National Legal Center by Jeane Kirkpatrick in *Washington Post* (8 January 1990), A17.

43. *1988 Annual Report of the John N. Olin Foundation*, 11, 22; Scaife 990-PF, 1989, 10–11; Bradley 990-PF, 1988–89, 10.

44. See the brochure *Social Philosophy and Policy Studies*, issued by Transaction Press.

45. "Finding Our Place in the World Foreign Policy after the Cold War," *Reason* 22.10 (March 1991):25–29.

46. See the report on the Podhoretz-Kristol family connections with the *Washington Times* by Charlotte Hays, a columnist who left the paper, in the *New Republic*, 17 February 1992, 16–18.

47. This point has eluded John Judis, E. Alterman, and other critics of the Unificationists, who dwell on their authoritarian chain of command and entanglement with South Korean business interests. Cf., for example, John Judis's comments in *U.S. News and World Report*, 27 March 1989, 27–29; and E. Alterman, "In Moon's Orbit," *New Republic*, 27 October 1986, 12–14. Little attention thus far has been paid to the overlap between neoconservative and Unificationist themes; e.g., the symbolic importance for both of Martin Luther King, Jr., the simultaneous support of free trade and the welfare state, and a selective revulsion for nationalism. In an otherwise perceptive report, "Moonie Journalism," *Washington Monthly* (October 1987):23–28, T. McNichol failed to emphasize these affinities. While Unificationists have tried to gain influence among other groups of journalists and intellectuals, their support for recognizable neoconservatives has been truly overwhelming. They have given money to this group with only one condition known to me, desisting from savage attacks on the South Korean government.

48. *1988 Annual Report of the John M. Olin Foundation*, 13; Smith-Richardson, 990-PF, 1989, 11.

49. See the newsletter of the Acton Institute, *Religion and Liberty* (January/February 1991):6.

50. Scaife, 990-PF, 1989, 11.

51. The author holds a photocopy of William Simon's correspondence with Ed Crane on the subject of Olin's decision to drop the Cato Institute as a grant recipient. Particularly informative is Simon's letter to Crane dated 8 April 1991.

52. See the interview with Ed Crane in *Liberty* 42 (November 1990):54–64.

53. See, e.g., Walter Berns, *The First Amendment and the Future of Democracy* (New York: Basic Books, 1976); and *In Defense of Liberal Democracy* (Chicago: Regnery, 1984).

54. Sarah Scaife, 990-PF, 1990, 11.

55. David H. Koch Foundation, 990-PF, 1989, 10–11.

56. Claude R. Lambe Foundation, 990-PF, 1990, 10–11.

57. Charles G. Koch Foundation, 990-PF, 1990, 10–11.

58. *Responsive Philanthropy* (Winter 1990):7–10. Philip Marcus's detailed and still unpublished study of the differences in funding preferences between right-wing and left-wing foundations shows that Scaife is not alone in its predilection for cold war activists.

59. For information on the Koch family, see *Forbes,* 1 October 1984, 101.

60. *New York Times,* 30 November 1990, A22.

61. *Liberty* 42 (November 1990), 64. These fulminations were partly in response to Llewellyn H. Rockwell's "The Case for Paleo-Libertarians," *Liberty,* (January 1990):34–38.

62. This new direction is obvious from Crane's letter to William Simon (April 15, 1991) on the Cato Institute's efforts to cultivate liberal journalists; see the institute's *1989 Annual Report,* 27; and Crane's Colorado Springs address on 5 January 1991, *Vital Speeches,* 1 June 1991, 497.

63. Quoted in Ralph Z. Hallow's "Conservative War Over Dinner," *The Washington Times,* 5 February 1990, A6.

64. Learned in discussion with staff members of *Human Events* who had seen a copy of Feulner's letter to Novak.

65. Revealed to the author by the Rockford Institute president, Dr. Allan Carlson in August 1990.

66. Roger M. Williams, "Capital Clout," *Foundation News,* 30.4 (July/August 1989), 40. Though Heritage claims to receive contributions from 140,000 different donors, it remains heavily dependent on about a dozen philanthropic foundations, among them the four sisters. See also George Archibald's report on Heritage in *Washington Times,* 2 December 1991, A7.

67. Drawn from a conversation (28 June 1991) with a longtime Aequus board member. The author holds detailed correspondence with the same board member and copies of an exchange of letters between that member and Edwin Feulner on related matters. According to the material in my possession, "the takeover of the [Aequus] board was effected at an illegal meeting—one for which improper notification was made, and of which Mansfield was kept ignorant. The same was true for the subsequent seizure of the corporation's documents, seal, bank account, etc." Also the same letter implicates in these questionable activities Larry Arnn, the executive director of Aequus and the Straussian chairman of the Claremont Institute: "While in the employ of Mansfield, Arnn was the gopher who organized the secret meeting of the Feulner group. He then personally stole the records and corporate seal. Armed with the materials provided by Arnn, the Feulner group presented themselves at Mansfield's brokerage firm, claiming to be the legal board, taking title of the accounts, and freezing Mansfield out."

68. *Heritage Today* (September/October 1990).

69. Dick Kirchten, "Come In! Come Out!" *National Journal,* 19 May 1990, 1208–09.

70. See the *1990 Annual Report of Credit International Bank,* 1–2.

71. John B. Judis, "The Conservative Crackup," *American Prospect* 3 (Fall, 1990):30. R. Emmett Tyrrell has also entered the conversation about the passing of the Right by publishing his opinions on this subject in *The Conservative Crack-Up* (New York: Summit Books, 1992). Despite Tyrrell's making sport of William F. Buckley as a political accommodationist, and his justifiably unkind remarks about conservative activists in Washington, his own work does not show conspicuously independent judgment. All of Tyrrell's neoconservatives are presumed to be searching after abstract truth, without regard to the political consequences; whereas the paleoconservatives are presented as fuddy-duddies or uncomplicated bigots. In looking for the causes of the breakup he claims to be investigating, Tyrrell never rises to any kind of analytical rigor. The passing of the Reagan presidency, the disintegration of the Soviet Empire, and the unwillingness of the ignorant to accept distilled neoconservative truths are all cited in passing as reasons for the descent of the conservative movement into warring factions. Presumably one might have avoided this disaster, had Ronald Reagan remained the American president, someone else Soviet dictator, and the neoconservatives unchallenged in their truth claims. The worst feature of this defective analysis, aside from its aspect of wishful thinking, is Tyrrell's inability to take the neoconservatives seriously as ideologically motivated pursuers of power. The neoconservative accomplishment was an exercise not in Platonic meditation, but in the accumulation of power through the use of money and intimidation. At any point, had they wished, they could have made overtures to the incipient opposition on the Right, and have accepted the kind of compromise which characterizes European conservative movements that have anti-Communist social democrats, conservative anti-immigrationists, and classical liberals coexisting politically and journalistically. The neoconservatives rejected such a compromise and proceeded to reconstruct the Right in their own image. That they fell somewhat short of total success seems less interesting than the fact that their project almost succeeded and may still succeed. Tyrrell's neglect of any discussion of this situation is like an attempt to treat the rise and fall of the Spanish Empire without considering the interplay of power and religious orthodoxy.

72. Judis, 39. During 1991 the Heritage Foundation worked desperately to build bridges to foundations on the Left as typified by its cosponsoring of a conference with the Progressive Policy Institute. See *New Republic,* 25 November 1991, 18–19. On Jack Kemp's expensive management of HUD, see Jeffrey A. Tucker, *Chronicles* (February 1992):39–40.

73. Judis, 31; see also Robert Kuttner's "Bleeding Heart Conservative."

74. Quoted in Roger M. Williams, "Capital Clout," *Foundation News,* 30.4 (July/August 1989), 17. A similar charge of Bradley partisanship appeared in an article by Kenneth R. Camke in the *Milwaukee Sentinel,* 6 March 1989.

75. Williams.

76. Eric Breindel, "Mission Accomplished," *New York Post,* 10 January 1991, 31.

77. Bradley 990-PF, 1987–88, VIII.

78. *Ibid.*

79. See Carol Matlack, "Profitable Payday," *National Journal*, 15 December 1990, 3010–22; even more revealing is Archibald's breakdown of Feulner's earnings in *Washington Times*, 2 December 1991, A7.

80. See Jacob Weisberg, "Hunter Gatherers: Neocons vs. Paleocons," *New Republic*, 2 September 1991, 14–15.

A final observation may be in order about the research incorporated into this chapter. Only a small part of my accumulated material about the building and financing of the neoconservative foundation and publications empire has been presented or cited in the preceding pages. Most of this material has been around for some time now. Those who gave it to me had also offered to make it available to leading newspapers and newsmagazines, which had failed to show interest. Though this situation may be attributable to negligence, another, more plausible explanation is that journalists have tried to protect neoconservatives and movement conservatives from what is presumed to be the far Right.

A telling case in point was a series of conversations in August 1991 held between myself and Jacob Weisberg of the *New Republic*. Weisberg, who initiated these contacts, was then planning a feature article on conservative wars. In our conversations Weisberg expressed his deep admiration for the "objectively presented" research conclusions I shared with him, but then treated my report as mere propaganda in his subsequently published essay. From his printed comments it was clear that he had not read more than a few paragraphs of my dense first draft of this chapter, but nonetheless identified me as a "ringleader" of the old right. His real assignment may have been to embarrass someone assumed to be the wrong kind of critic of his magazine's accustomed neoconservative positions. For Weisberg and for other journalists of his leanings, criticizing neoconservatives from the correct standpoint may count for more than the informational value of the revelations I offered. Though my judgments here are necessarily speculative, they coincide with those of my collaborators in doing research on this chapter.

Chapter Seven

1. *U.S. News and World Report*, 5 February 1990, 27.

2. *Wall Street Journal*, 16 November 1989, A-20.

3. Strobe Talbott, "Thunder on the Right," *Time*, 13 May 1991, 38; see also Charles Krauthammer on the state of conservatism, *Washington Post*, 22 September 1989, A27; and Ralph Z. Hallow, "Neoconservatives' 'Peace Dividend' Is Internal Strife," *Washington Times*, 30 April 1990, A1 and A10.

4. Jeane Kirkpatrick, "The American 90s: Disaster or Triumph," *Commentary* 90 (September 1990):14–16; and "Beyond the Cold War," *Foreign Affairs* 60 (Special Issue 1990):1–16.

5. Ralph Z. Hallow, "Conservatives War Over Dinner," *Washington Times,* 5 February 1990, A6.

6. See Ralph Z. Hallow, "Conservative Split into Warring Camps," *Washington Times,* 2 June 1987, A1 and A6.

7. See the affirmation of support for Buchanan and his neoisolationism against attacks against him from predominantly neoconservatives, *New York Times,* 15 October 1990, A24. Almost all the signers were involved in the conservative realignment.

8. Learned in discussion with Rockford Institute President Allan Carlson and Rockford Institute Trustee George D. O'Neill, Jr.

9. See *National Review,* 14 July 1989, 52; *Chronicles* (March 1989):14–16; and Neuhaus's anguished review of the first edition of this book in *Religion and Society Report* (May 1988):4.

10. Gore Vidal, "How to Take Back Our Country," *Nation,* 4 June 1988, 781–82.

11. In "The 'New Fusionism': A Movement for Our Times," *Rothbard-Rockwell Report* 2 (February 1991):1, 3, 8–9, Murray Rothbard correctly notes that despite disagreement on a range of issues, starting with the concept of state sovereignty, paleoconservatives and libertarians both favor the "voluntary action of property holders" and detest social Democrats even more than Communists. See also Thomas Fleming, "The New Fusionism," *Chronicles* 15 (May 1991):10–12; and Llewellyn H. Rockwell, "The Case for Paleolibertarianism: Realignment on the Right," (Burlingame, California: Center for Libertarian Studies, 1990).

12. William F. Buckley, "Unpleasant Business," *National Review,* 16 June 1989, 12.

13. See David Frum's remarks in *Saturday Night,* January/February 1991, 10–11.

14. See Norman Podhoretz, "The Hate That Dares Not Speak Its Name," *Commentary* 82 (November 1986):21–32; "Anti-Semitism, Right and Left," *ibid.* 83 (March 1987):2–3, for the opening salvos in the neoconservative campaign against right-wing anti-Semitism. Also instructive in this regard is J. M. Wall, "Neoconservatives Want to Rewrite the Script," *Christian Century,* 22 October 1986, 907–88; and David Frum, "Cultural Clashes on the Right," *Wall Street Journal,* 2 June 1989, A16.

15. Joshua Muravchik, "Patrick J. Buchanan and the Jews," *Commentary* 91 (January 1989):12–14.

16. Jacob Weisberg, "The Heresies of Patrick Buchanan," *New Republic,* 22 October 1990, 22–27; and Abe Rosenthal's column in the *New York Times,* 14 September 1991, A-33. The same charges are leveled by John Leo, "Pat Buchanan's Loyal Apologists," *U.S. News and World Report,* 24 February 1992, 25.

17. See, e.g., *Newsweek,* 24 September 1990, 28; *ibid.,* 1 October 1990, 33.

18. *New York Post,* editorial page, 19 September 1990.

19. See William F. Buckley's comment in "Rosenthal vs. Buchanan," *National Review,* 15 October 1990, 22–23.

20. Midge Decter as quoted in Howard Kurtz's front-page commentary in the *Washington Post*'s style section, 20 September 1990.

21. See Murray N. Rothbard's "Pat Buchanan—Accused of Anti-Semitism!" in *Conservative Review* 1.7 (November 1990):10–14.

22. Cf. Allan Brownfield, "False Anti-Semitism Charges Inhibits Free Discussion," *Washington Inquirer,* 12 October 1990, 5; and Len T. Hadar, "The 'Neocons': From the Cold War to the 'Global Intifada,'" *Washington Report on Middle East Affairs* (April 1991):27–28.

23. In a provocative piece published in *Tikkun* 63 (May/June 1991):12, John Judis details the neoconservative connection to the hawkish Committee for Peace and Security in the Gulf. The group received money from Zionist organizations but—even more significantly—also received $200,000 from Michael Joyce of Bradley for "research."

24. Cited in the U.S. Business and Industrial Council *Bulletin* (January 1991):3.

25. See Morton Kondracke's essay on the convergence of the respectable Right and the respectable Left, "The Democracy Gang," *New Republic,* 6 November 1989, 30; Flora Lewis, "Postcommunist Blues," *New York Times,* 22 September 1990; David Ignatius on the global democratic revolution in *Washington Post,* 26 August 1990, C2; David Broder on defending the democratic idea, *Washington Post,* 3 January 1990, A15; by the same author on democratic capitalism in the Soviet Union, see *ibid.,* 11 February 1990, C7; Jim Hoagland on the need for capitalism in the Soviet Union, *ibid.,* 2 July 1989 H1; on the new economic order in Eastern Europe, *ibid.,* 15 June 1990, A25; on Nelson Mandela and global democracy, *ibid.,* 19 April 1990, A12.

26. Samuel T. Francis, "Beautiful Losers: The Failure of American Conservatism," *Chronicles* 15 (May 1990):14–17.

27. Cf. Paul Piccone's incisive comments on New Class political domination in "The Crisis of American Conservatism," *Telos* 74 (Winter 1987–88):3–29.

28. Christopher Lasch, "The Obsolescence of Left and Right," *New Oxford Review* 56 (April 1989):6–15.

29. Daniel Lazare, "Thunder on the Right," *Present Tense* (December 1989), 30.

30. See the caustic, penetrating response to Lazare by Murray Rothbard in the letter section of *Present Tense* (February 1990).

31. In "'The New Fusionism': A Movement for our Times," *Rothbard-Rockwell Report* 2 (February 1991):1, 3, 8–9, Murray Rothbard correctly notes that despite disagreement on a range of issues, starting with the concept of state sovereignty, paleoconservatives and libertarians both favor the "voluntary action of property holders" and detest social democrats even more than Communists.

32. Despite his own bias, Sidney Blumenthal in "Hi, Yo Silber," *New Republic,* 22 October 1990, 12–14, is correct to view Silber's gubernatorial bid in Massachusetts as the electoral last hurrah of Reaganite "neoliberalism," a.k.a. neoconservatism.

33. In *The New Jacobinism* (Washington: National Humanities Institute, 1991), 77–91, Claes G. Ryn maintains that the sudden appeal to capitalism by egalitarian Democrats is both provisional and tactical, aimed at subverting traditional cultures through restricted capitalist techniques. Ryn's idea seems borne out by C. S. Becker's essay "Democracy is the Soil where Capitalism Flourishes Best" in *Business Week,* 28 January 1990, 18.

34. See S. Churcher, "Radical Transformations," *New York Times Magazine,* 6 July 1989, 30–31.

35. Sara Diamond, "Rumble on the Right," *Z Magazine* (December 1990), 24–25.

36. See Paul Gottfried's portraits of second-generation paleoconservatives in "Toward a New Fusionism," *Policy Review* 42 (Fall 1987):64–71.

37. See Elizabeth Fox-Genovese's generally favorable comments on Thomas Fleming in *Feminism Without Illusion: A Critique of Individualism* (Chapel Hill: University of North Carolina Press, 1991), 47–50, 103, and 146. A conference on "Populism and the New Class" took place at Elizabethtown College, Pennsylvania, from April 5–7, 1991, featuring participants Christopher Lasch, Samuel T. Francis, Claes G. Ryn, Paul Gottfried, Paul Piccone, and other editors of *Telos.*

38. See Samuel T. Francis, "Our European Cousins," *Chronicles* (April 1991):31–33; and Tomislav Sunic, "The Gulf Crisis in Europe," *Chronicles* (May 1991):49–50.

39. Alain de Benoist, "L'Occident tel qu'il est en lui-même," *Le Monde,* 6 December 1990, 2.

40. Alarmed by the alliance of disaligned rightists with former Marxists, Danny Postel warns that socialism may be abandoned as the price of this regrouping in *In These Times,* 24–30 April 1991, 18–19. Samuel T. Francis explicitly advocates the abandonment of the term "conservative" by the real Right in his syndicated column in the *Washington Times,* 3 December 1991, F1.

41. *Washington Post,* 8 October 1991, A1 and A5.

42. *Wall Street Journal,* 9 October 1991, A14.

43. *Washington Times,* 4 October 1991, commentary section, 29 October 1991, F2; and 3 November 1991, B2. The author holds a copy of the letter sent by Bradford to O'Sullivan on 8 September 1991, ending Bradford's "association of almost twenty-five years" with *National Review.*

44. *Washington Times,* 17 October 1991, G2.

45. See Evans and Novak syndicated column in *Washington Post,* 13 November 1991, A19.

46. For overlapping critical comments on Judge Thomas from a neoconser-

vative and a paleoconservative who rarely ever agree, see Bruce Fein, *American Bar Association Journal* (October 1991), and Samuel T. Francis, *Chronicles,* October 1991:10–12. William McGurn provides an establishment-conservative defense in "Targeting Thomas," *National Review,* 9 September 1991, 21–22.

47. Reported in the *Chicago Tribune,* 15 November 1991, 1A; for a more upbeat account of the same situation, see the interview with Edwin Feulner in *Policy Review* 58 (Fall, 1991):5–16.

48. In October 1991 invitations to join the America First Committee were sent out to a number of paleoconservative and paleolibertarian spokesmen over the signatures of Patrick J. Buchanan and Samuel T. Francis. The two accompanying essays by Buchanan, "America First—and Second, and Third" and "Now That Red Is Dead, Come Home, America," summed up the case against global democracy made repeatedly by the invitees.

49. On Bush's strategy of linking Buchanan to David Duke and the aberrant Right, see Paul Bedard in *Washington Times,* 19 November 1991, A1 and A9. A. M. Rosenthal, who picks up on the same theme, directs more emotion at Buchanan than Duke, in his *New York Times* syndicated column of 20 November 1991, "The Lessons of Louisiana." Illustrative of the neoconservative Quayle hype is "Travels with My Veep" by Thomas Mallon, *American Spectator* 24 (September 1991):16–20.

50. *Washington Post Book World,* 12 January 1992, 1–4, and Francis Fukuyama, *The End of History and the Last Man* (New York and Toronto: Free Press, 1992).

51. For my responses to the new global democratic enthusiasts, see "At Sea with the Global Democrats," *Wall Street Journal,* 19 January 1989, and "Therapeutic Democracy," *The World and I* (April 1992):326–31.

52. Cited from the original manuscript of "A Strategy for the Right."

53. See *National Review,* 17 February 1992, 41–42.

54. See *Washington Post,* 23 February 1992, C1 and C2.

55. *National Review,* 2 March 1992, 34.

56. Murray N. Rothbard, "Right Wing Populism," *Rothbard-Rockwell Report* 3 (January 1992):5–7.

57. See the editorial note, "Four More Years?" in *National Review,* 17 February 1992, 12, and W. F. Buckley's statements in "Score One for Buchanan," *ibid.,* 16 March 1992, 55.

58. See Norman Podhoretz's charges in "Buchanan and the Conservative Crackup," *Commentary* 93 (May 1992), 30–35.

59. Interview with Routter, who helped organize campaigns in Northeast Philadelphia for Rizzo and Buchanan. See also the portrait of Rizzo by J. Lombardi in *Esquire* (August 1989):114–17; and Rizzo's obituary in *Time,* 29 July 1991, 152. For a critical view of the political tendencies discussed above from an old-fashioned constitutionalist standpoint, see M. P. Federici, *The Challenge of Populism: The Rise of Right-Wing Democratism in Post-War America* (Westport, Conn.: Greenwood Press, 1991).

60. A provocative work on the Reagan years that has been surprisingly (or perhaps unsurprisingly) ignored is Larry M. Schwab's *The Illusion of the Conservative Reagan Revolution* (New Brunswick: Transaction, 1991). Schwab argues, on the basis of exhaustive research, that Reagan was even more of a "big-spending liberal" presiding over tax hikes than the ill-fated Democrat Jimmy Carter, whom Reagan ousted from office. Schwab also cites evidence that in public debates in 1980 and 1984 Reagan successfully blurred ideological distinctions between himself and his Democratic opponents. In conversation, Schwab seems genuinely puzzled that neither liberals nor establishment conservatives have displayed much interest in his findings.

61. In Knight-Ridder News Service article by Walter V. Robinson, syndicated in *Lancaster New Era,* 26 June 1992, "Commentary," 2.

62. See, for example, the editorial "The Present Danger of Ross Perot," *New Republic,* 29 June 1992, 27–29, and Sidney Blumenthal's "The Paranoid Journey of Ross Perot!," *ibid.,* 15 June 1992, 23–29.

63. Bauer is quoted in Robinson column cited above. See also "The Plutocratic Populist," in *Time,* 6 April 1992, 19; and Janice Castro's "Don't Underestimate Perot!," *ibid.,* 20 April 1992, 21.

64. See the comments on liberal pollster Patrick H. Caddell, then still wavering in his loyalties between "Brown or Perot?" in *New York Times,* 16 April 1992, A10–A16.

65. Fred Barnes, in *New Republic,* 3 August 1992, 12–13.

66. *New York Times,* 17 August 1992, A15.

67. Stephen S. Rosenfeld, in *Washington Post,* 28 August 1992, A23.

Bibliographic Essay

Among the general surveys on postwar American conservatism, the most comprehensive and best known is George H. Nash, *The Conservative Intellectual Movement Since 1945* (New York: Basic Books, 1976). Other less detailed and certainly more subjective accounts of the conservative movement are Clinton Rossiter, *Conservatism in America: The Thankless Persuasion* (New York: Viking, 1962); *National Review* editor Jeffrey Hart, *The American Dissent* (New York: Doubleday, 1966); John P. Diggins, *Up from Communism* (New York: Harper & Row, 1975); Gillian Peele, *Revival and Reaction: The Right in Contemporary America* (Oxford: Clarendon Press, 1984)—a valuable perspective by an English liberal; William A. Rusher, *The Rise of the Right* (New York: William Morrow & Co., 1984)—a personal account by one of the key figures; and Sidney Blumenthal, *The Rise of Counterestablishment: From Conservative Ideology to Political Power* (New York: Times Books, 1986)—an inaccurate, biased but sometimes insightful essay by a then *Washington Post* political reporter.

More recent books dealing with an evolving or collapsing American conservatism are J. L. Himmelstein, *To the Right: The Transformation of American Conservatism* (University of California Press, 1989), a detailed study marked by an ideologically determined insistence on conservative-movement continuity since the thirties; J. David Hoeveler, Jr., *Watch on the Right: Conservative Intellectuals in the Reagan Era* (Madison: University of Wisconsin Press, 1991) for the same thesis with a neoconservative spin; E. J. Dionne, Jr., *The War against Public Life: Why Americans Hate Politics* (New York: Simon and Schuster, 1991); M. P. Federici, *The Challenge of Populism: The Rise of Right-Wing Populism in Post-War America* (Westport, Conn.: Greenwood Press, 1991); Larry M. Schwab, *The Illusion of a Conservative Reagan Revolution* (New Brunswick: Transaction Books, 1991); and Shadia B. Drury, *The Political Ideas of Leo Strauss* (New York: St. Martin's, 1988).

Books that represent particular streams of American conservatism are Russell Kirk, *The Conservative Mind: From Burke to Eliot,* 7th ed. (Chicago: Regnery Books, 1986)—arguably the most influential conservative book written after

194

World War II; Irving Kristol, *Two Cheers for Capitalism* (New York: Basic Books, 1978)—a classic work of neoconservative analysis; and Robert A. Nisbet, *Conservatism* (Minneapolis: University of Minnesota Press, 1986). For works that continue to exemplify the southern agrarian spirit, see Clyde N. Wilson, ed., *Why the South Will Survive* (Athens: University of Georgia Press, 1981), and Melvin E. Bradford, *Remembering Who We Are* (Athens: University of Georgia Press, 1985). As examples of Old Right intellectual analysis, see Claes G. Ryn, *Democracy and the Ethical Life* (Baton Rouge: Louisiana State University Press, 1978), and Paul Gottfried, *The Search for Historical Meaning: Hegel and the Postwar American Right* (DeKalb: Northern Illinois University Press, 1986). The best conservative interpretation of the Constitution is given by Forrest McDonald, *Novus Ordo Seclorum: The Intellectual Origins of the Constitution* (Lawrence: University Press of Kansas: 1985). For a popular exercise in pure capitalism, see Milton and Rose Friedman, *The Tyranny of the Status Quo* (New York: Harcourt Brace Jovanovich, 1984); Murray N. Rothbard, *Man, Economy, and State* (New York: Van Nostrand, 1962); Charles Murray, *Losing Ground: American Social Policy, 1950–1980* (New York: Basic Books, 1984); George Gilder, *The Spirit of Enterprise* (New York: Simon & Schuster, 1984); Michael Novak, *The Spirit of Democratic Capitalism* (New York: Simon & Schuster, 1982); and Robert Bork, *The Antitrust Paradox: A Policy at War with Itself* (New York: Basic Books, 1980). Finally the populist strain is exemplified in Robert W. Whitaker, ed., *The New Right Papers* (New York: St. Martin's Press, 1982), and Kevin P. Phillips, *Post-Conservative America: People, Politics and Ideology in a Time of Crisis* (New York: Random House, 1982).

Other works representative of particular conservative currents are Charles J. Sykes, *Profscam: Professors and the Demise of Higher Education* (Washington: Regnery Gateway, 1988); Allan Bloom, *The Closing of the American Mind* (New York: Simon and Schuster, 1988); Michael Levin, *Feminism and Freedom* (New Brunswick: Transaction Books, 1987); T. G. Carpenter, *Collective Defense or Strategic Independence* (Washington: Cato-Lexington Books, 1989); Joshua Muravchik, *Exporting Democracy: Fulfilling America's Destiny* (Washington: American Enterprise, 1991); Dinesh D'Souza, *Illiberal Education: The Politics of Race and Sex on Campus* (New York: Free Press, 1991); Ben J. Wattenberg, *The First Universal Nation: Leading Indicators and Ideas about the Surge of America in the 1990s* (New York: Free Press, 1991); Francis Fukuyama, *The End of History and the Last Man* (New York: Free Press, 1991); M. E. Bradford, *Against the Barbarians* (Jefferson City: University of Missouri Press, 1992); J. L. Simon, *Population and Development in Poor Countries* (Princeton, N.J.: Princeton University Press, 1992); Claes G. Ryn, *The New Jacobinism: Can Democracy Survive?* (Washington: National Humanities Institute, 1991).

Works written since 1945 that have profoundly affected American conservative thought are Friedrich Hayek, *The Road to Serfdom*, 17th ed. (Chicago: Phoenix Books, 1963); Whittaker Chambers, *Witness* (New York: Random House, 1952); Robert A. Nisbet, *The Quest for Community* (Oxford: Oxford University Press,

1953); Richard M. Weaver, *Ideas Have Consequences* (Chicago: Phoenix Books, 1948); Eric Voegelin, *The New Science of Politics* (Chicago: Phoenix Books, 1952); Leo Strauss, *Natural Right and History* (Chicago: Phoenix Books, 1965); L. Brent Bozell and William Buckley, *McCarthy and His Enemies* (Chicago: Regnery, 1954); Willmoore Kendall, *The Conservative Affirmation* (Chicago: Regnery, 1962); Thomas Molnar, *The Decline of the Intellectual* (New York: Meridian Books, 1962); Frank S. Meyer, *In Defense of Freedom* (Chicago: Regnery, 1962); James Burnham, *Suicide of the West: An Essay on the Meaning and Destiny of Liberalism* (New York: John Day, 1964); Edward C. Banfield, *The Unheavenly City: The Nature and the Foundation of Our Urban Crisis* (Boston: Little, Brown & Co., 1970); Norman Podhoretz, *Breaking Ranks* (New York: Harper & Row, 1979); Alasdair MacIntyre, *After Virtue: A Study in Moral Theory* (Notre Dame, Indiana: University of Notre Dame Press, 1984); Patrick J. Buchanan, *Right from the Beginning* (New York: Little, Brown & Co., 1988); Christopher Lasch, *The True and Only Heaven: Progress and Its Critics* (New York: Norton, 1990); and John Lukacs, *Outgrowing Democracy: A History of the United States in the Twentieth Century* (Garden City, New York: Doubleday, 1984).

More paleo- than neoconservative books have been placed in this last category for reasons that should be apparent to readers of this book. Though neoconservative works usually come out with more prestigious publishing houses and are assured more critical notice, they do not influence the already fixed ideological character of the movement with which they are associated. Neoconservatives commission, publish, and publicize works that spread their largely unchanging doctrines. Paleoconservatives, by contrast, have allowed themselves to be swayed by books they read and write, which may be one of their weaknesses as well as strengths.

Index

The Author

Paul Gottfried is professor of humanities at Elizabethtown College and editor-in-chief of *This World*. He has also served as senior editor of *The World & I* and has been a Guggenheim recipient. Gottfried has written over eighty articles for various journals and is the author of four books, including *Conservative Millenarians, The Search for Historical Meanings,* and *Carl Schmitt: Politics and Theory.*